Rock Hudson

▲

Fish

Head

Soup

and

Other

Plays

comforter = cold

loss / sheets = colors (warm)

jeans = cold

· colors

Clerk 414 /116, 1110, 8

Fish

Head

Soup

and

Other

Plays

Philip Kan Gotanda

Introduction by Michael Omi

University of Washington Press

Seattle and London

▲

Design: Christine Taylor
Composition: Wilsted & Taylor Publishing Services

LIBRARY OF CONGRESS CATALOGING-IN-PUBLICATION DATA
Gotanda, Philip Kan.
    Fish head soup and other plays / Philip Kan Gotanda ;
introduction by Michael Omi.
        p.   cm.
        ISBN 0-295-97417-6 (cloth : alk. paper). — ISBN 0-295-97433-8
(paper : alk. paper)
        1. Japanese Americans—Drama.   I. Title.
    PS3557.07934F57   1995
    812'.54—dc20   95-18878
                                                         CIP

The paper used in this publication meets the minimum requirements of
American National Standard for Information Sciences—Permanence
of Paper for Printed Library Materials, ANSI Z39.48-1984.

For

Diane

Contents

I want to express my gratitude to the Asian American theaters around the country, in particular the Asian American Theatre Company, East West Players, Northwest Asian American Theater, and Pan Asian Repertory. Without them I would not have had a career in theater. I would also like to thank the Mark Taper Forum, Berkeley Repertory Theatre, and the Manhattan Theatre Club for their continued support and their willingness to commit to Asian American works.

Finally, I would like to acknowledge the following friends and associates, for they made my life in theater possible: Eric Hayashi, Mako, Nobu McCarthy, Gordon Davidson, Oskar Eustis, Sharon Ott, Anne Cattaneo, David Hwang, Rick Shiomi, Lynne Meadow, Jean Erdman, Andre Bishop, Sab Shimono, Tisa Chang, Jim Lewis, Dan Kuramoto, Lydia Tanji, and Helen Merrill. And all the others, too numerous to mention.

Philip Kan Gotanda
San Francisco
September 1994

Introduction

Michael Omi

Philip Kan Gotanda possesses precisely the "imagination" that C. Wright Mills said was necessary to understand that "neither the life of an individual nor the history of a society can be understood without understanding both."[1] The plays in this volume reveal a deep appreciation for both history and biography, and for the complex and intimate connection between the two. They illuminate how individuals, shaped by historical circumstances, in turn help to define and to create the realm of possibility.

Gotanda helps us to understand that the Asian American experience is an important American story, one in which racism, in its various incarnations, has affected the manner in which we both live and are conscious of our lives. Such a perspective has been drawn and distilled from his personal history and from his reflections on his experiences.

Gotanda is a Sansei, a third-generation Japanese American. His father, Wilfred Itsuta Gotanda, originally from Kauai, came to the mainland to attend medical school at the University of Arkansas and subsequently settled and opened a practice in Stockton, California. With the outbreak of the war with Japan and President Roosevelt's decision to remove Japanese Americans from the West Coast, Wilfred Gotanda ironically found himself back in Arkansas, this time as a result of relocation and confinement to a concentration camp in Rohwer. Upon his release, he returned to Stockton to prac-

[1]C. Wright Mills, *The Sociological Imagination* (New York: Oxford University Press, 1959), p. 3.

tice medicine, where he met and married a schoolteacher, Catherine Matsumoto. Philip Kan Gotanda is the youngest of their three sons.

Growing up in Stockton, Gotanda remembers the easy commingling of various cultural influences. The Japanese festivals, samurai movies, and the athletic leagues of the Buddhist church were enjoyed and appreciated alongside episodes of "The Twilight Zone" and "Star Trek" and his brothers' recordings of Bob Dylan and Miles Davis. Theater, however, was something he was not much exposed to as he was growing up. What few plays he did see held little interest for him.

From early childhood to early adulthood, Gotanda was conscious of two competing sides to his character—an "artistic, creative" side and a "serious professional" one. Growing up, he felt an uneasy tension between the two, often oscillating from one position to the other. His first creative passion was music. Beginning at age thirteen, he took up the guitar, composed songs, and played in bands. His interest in music continued, but he entered the University of California at Santa Cruz in 1969 with the goal of eventually becoming a psychiatrist.

At the university, he conducted field work at the Agnew State Hospital in San Jose and was drawn to the radical therapies of R. D. Laing. On campus, he participated to a limited extent in the then newly formed Asian American Political Alliance. These were heady political times, with the organization involved in the broader antiwar movement and in challenging forms of institutional racism on the campus and within surrounding Asian American communities.

In 1970, in the midst of escalating political conflicts in the United States, Gotanda went to Japan, ostensibly to study ceramics. He was, in fact, going to Japan to carve out a space in which he could rethink his interests:

*I didn't go to Japan, I left America. Here, I felt that I just
couldn't find my niche. In Japan, I had a somewhat mystical
experience. For the first time in my life, I experienced a sense
of racial anonymity. I was living without the burden of
racism, I didn't have to work at constantly deflecting it.
The mantle of racism lifted off my shoulders and drifted
away. What an extraordinary feeling.*[2]

Issues of American minority status and identity, however,
receded only to be replaced by another sense of marginality.
Like many Sansei who visit Japan, Gotanda came to realize
just how much he was not Japanese; a trip to the ancestral
homeland only underscored his "Americanness."

Gotanda returned to the United States with a "renewed
sense of clarity and vision." He enrolled at the University of
California at Santa Barbara, and became drawn to the "cultural" dimensions of the emergent Asian American movement. His interests were spurred on by the cultural possibilities presented by the poetry of Lawson Inada and Jessica
Hagedorn, the music of Charlie Chin, Nobuko Miyamoto,
Chris Iijima, and Hiroshima; the documentary filmmaking
of Visual Communications; and the cultural radical journal-
ism of the Los Angeles newspaper *Gidra*. What was being
expressed through these mediums was a new sensibility, the
formation and articulation of a uniquely Asian American
identity:

*I realized that I could give voice to an experience that was
my experience—that I could look in the mirror and write
about this particular face. It was a liberating feeling. I was
drawn to a particular vision of what Asian American
creative expression could be.*

After graduating in 1973, Gotanda spent the next two
years as a song writer and singer, performing original music

[2]All quotes from an interview conducted with Philip Kan Gotanda, May 13, 1992.

in various venues. He composed dozens of songs whose themes, quite naturally, dealt with his unfolding Asian American consciousness. This was expressed in titles such as "Ballad of the Issei" and "All-American Asian Punk." A visit to Los Angeles in 1974 to pitch songs to record companies became a disappointing and frustrating adventure. Given the industry's concern with marketing demographics, he failed to get a decent hearing for a collection of folk-rock songs about Asian Americans. Undaunted, Gotanda continued to pursue his interest in music by auditioning as a singer for Hiroshima. He did not join the band, but this marked the beginning of a continuing artistic collaboration with the group's leader, Dan Kuramoto. Gotanda did go on to form a band with playwright David Henry Hwang (on violin), which played in several venues before its members pursued other interests. Gotanda's work with Hwang spilled over to a theatrical context, with Hwang directing several of Gotanda's earlier plays for the Asian American Theatre Company in San Francisco.

Gotanda subsequently satisfied the "professional" side of his nature by pursuing legal studies and eventually graduating from Hastings College of Law in 1978. His artistic interests, however, were still very much alive. While finishing his legal degree and doing community work for the North Beach–Chinatown Legal Aid in San Francisco, he wrote his first play, *The Avocado Kid or Zen in the Art of Guacamole.*

Interestingly, Gotanda's initial foray into play writing came about because of what he perceived as the limitations of the song format. He was never satisfied with the simple rendering of a song:

> *I was never content to have my songs just sung. I always saw staging, costumes, and the use of theatrical gestures to convey what I wanted to say.*

The Avocado Kid is essentially a musical. Thinking that he would start simply, Gotanda took a classic Japanese children's tale, "Momotaro the Peach Boy," and radically recast it. The result is an odyssey of outcasts, who find that by banding together they can collectively transcend the oppressive conditions of their existence. In many respects, *The Avocado Kid* is a distinctively Asian American play—it takes familiar elements drawn from Asian and Asian American culture and subverts them. Its "hip" dialogue and style, combined with aggressive music and dance, celebrate the spirit that playfully captures the ongoing Asian American engagement with popular culture.

It was fortuitous that Gotanda was beginning to explore play writing at the moment when the developing Asian American theater companies, such as East West Players in Los Angeles, the Asian American Theatre Workshop in San Francisco, and Pan-Asian Repertory Theatre in New York, were desperately searching for new material. East West Players initially formed in 1965, and began by dramatizing the works of Asian novelists like Yukio Mishima and by featuring Asian American actors in classic American and European plays. By contrast, with the emergence and growth of a distinctively Asian American consciousness in the 1970s, actors, writers, producers, and directors sought to find, create, and popularize a uniquely Asian American cultural aesthetic.

The distinction was profound and important. As playwright Frank Chin has often noted, Asian Americans are not seen as the producers of a "living art and culture" in the popular imagination, but are simply viewed as custodians of ancient "Oriental" legends and folk arts. Chin argued for artistic work that would capture the uniqueness and irreducibility of Asian American culture, something that could not be reduced to some curious combination of "Oriental" and "Occidental" elements.

Gotanda took this challenge seriously. His first major opportunity came when East West Players asked to stage *The
Avocado Kid*. He graduated from law school and went to Los
Angeles to begin production. He had no idea how a play was
transformed from text to material reality. The experience
with the theater group was both instructive and exhilarating.

In developing his craft, Gotanda began to read more
widely. Of particular importance was his discovery of Sam
Shepard's *Angel City*. Shepard's own roots in music, and his
use of American iconography, contributed to a unique style,
tone, and phrasing, which became, for Gotanda, a source of
inspiration, opening up the possibilities of what a play could
be.

From 1979 to 1985, Gotanda wrote plays for Asian American theater companies on both coasts. His plays during
this period reveal an evolution from "musicals," such as *Bul-
let Headed Birds*, to more straight dramas, including, as in
The Dream Of Kitamura, the incorporation of different
performance-piece devices.

With the success of these plays, more mainstream theatrical venues were interested in staging his work. *A Song For A
Nisei Fisherman* and *The Wash* were featured at the Mark
Taper Forum in Los Angeles, and *Yankee Dawg You Die* at
the Berkeley Repertory Theatre. With these productions,
Gotanda went from speaking to a mainly young, "politically
correct," and hip Asian American audience to a more diverse
one of Asians and non-Asians:

> *Even though my work was being presented at these larger
> venues, I refused to compromise the material or try to make
> it more accessible to a particular audience. The audience
> should come to you. This may seem arrogant, but what it
> amounts to is a leap of faith.*

The result of Gotanda's leap from the "margins" to the
mainstream of the theater world has been a broadening of his

audience without a dramatic shift in subject or tone on his part. In several plays, Japanese American references and vernacular are treated as "natural" elements of the dialogue, with little effort expended to make it accessible or intelligible to non-Japanese American audiences. His cultural specificity, however, is strategically utilized as a way of affording his audience a more expansive look at who and what America really is.

As Gotanda was growing up, his perception of America was mediated by the Japanese American community in Stockton, where he was immersed in a network of family, friends, and organizations. The community's economic and cultural activities—such as the growing and selling of produce, fishing, bazaars and festivals—forged, along with its engagement with the larger society, a distinctive world and outlook. Drawing upon the sensations experienced in the Japanese American community in Stockton, Gotanda recreates a slice of that world and illuminates it for his audience. He depicts the rituals, the relationships, the conversations, and, in essence, the sight, sounds, and smells of Japanese America.

The selection of plays presented in this volume captures this world along with other intriguing aspects of the Asian American historical experience and sensibility. To Gotanda's credit, he presents themes and issues in a manner that is neither heavy-handed nor didactic. His characters are multidimensional, and full of the contradictory motives and feelings that come to represent the human condition. At the same time his characters function, in Weberian terms, as "ideal types." They exemplify specific Asian American traits and values, and are the products and agents of a particular historical experience.

In order to write "beyond himself" and his immediate experiences, Gotanda collected voices. He conducted taped interviews with Nisei men and women to get a sense of their experiences, how they perceived their immediate world and the surrounding environment, and how they expressed themselves—their style, tone, and phrasing. One such voice he collected was his father's. Wilfred Gotanda's experience and Philip's understanding of it became the basis for *A Song For A Nisei Fisherman*.

A Song For A Nisei Fisherman provides a concise history of Nisei (second-generation Japanese Americans) by charting the life course of one man. Itsuta "Ichan" Matsumoto, the Nisei fisherman, encounters the frustrations, dilemmas, and fulfilled and unfulfilled dreams of a generation.

Raised in relative poverty in Kauai, the fisherman battles the odds, including discriminatory barriers, to realize his dream of practicing medicine. The fisherman experiences the terrible upheaval of the internment camps and the agonizing decisions of proving one's loyalty as an American. The period of resettlement after the war gives way to patterns of accommodation and assimilation, and debates with sons Robert and Jeffrey, the third generation, over how they choose to live and define their lives. These themes and issues are nicely woven together and interspersed in a framework of "catching," "cleaning," "cooking," and "eating" fish. One comes away from the play with an understanding of a man and a generation.

A central relationship in *A Song* is the fisherman's relationship to his wife, Michiko. Michiko represents the long-suffering wife who lives not for her dreams, but to help others achieve theirs. Such a perspective emerged from Gotanda's taped interviews with Nisei women:

> *One woman poignantly observed that Nisei women have no dreams of their own. They live their lives in order to help their husbands realize their dreams, and the dreams of their children.*

This same theme is carried over in *The Wash* with dramatically different results. The initial idea for the play drew on two real-life sources. One was a friend whose elderly Nisei mother had left her father and begun a new relationship, something generally unheard of in the Japanese American community. The second source was a writer whose ex-husband still came to mow her lawn even after the divorce. The lawn became the laundry and *The Wash* was born.

In this play, a Nisei woman, Masi Matsumoto, does the unthinkable. She leaves her husband and tries to carve out a new life for herself. This is not accomplished without considerable guilt. She says to her new lover, Sadao:

> *Something's wrong with me, huh. Now you make me feel too happy. I don't like it. It makes me . . . unhappy.*

Her estranged husband, Nobu, is almost a caricature of the stubborn, authoritarian Nisei man. Frustrated in his career as a produce man, he is unable to show affection for his wife, and he refuses to see the grandson who is the product of his daughter's interracial marriage. Despite his aloofness and arrogance, it is Nobu, in the end, who proves to be the dependent one.

The Wash details the relationships within a Nisei family, and how Nobu's and Masi's separation impacts each family member and their significant others. It is a wonderful story of people coming to terms with themselves. For Masi, it is doing things that make her happy after years of denial. For Nobu, it is to tragically confront his own emotional needs and to begin to articulate them when it is already too late.

Gotanda wanted to describe in the play how what appears on the surface to be a stable relationship quickly unravels:

> *Traditions which worked before are subject to the winds of change. I wanted to depict people struggling to live their lives after a serious rupture in the way things are.*

It takes Masi and Nobu some time to step outside of their familiar relationship, and to deal with one another on a different basis. The crafted exchanges between Masi and Nobu not only reveal aspects of their relationship, but show a crucial dimension of Japanese American dialogue as well. "What's not said is as important, if not more important," Gotanda notes, "than what is said."

Given media presentations of the elderly as either helpless or demanding, or as perverse imitators of youth, it is refreshing to see elderly men and women portrayed in a compelling fashion. Gotanda believes that he has always had a strong affinity for the elderly and their lives.

Asian American theater companies are driven by actors and material. The staging of his material has meant that Gotanda has had the opportunity to work with different generations of Asian American actors. *Yankee Dawg You Die* is his sympathetic homage to them, which touches upon the difficulties and agonizing choices they confront in their craft:

> *The older actors would always complain about the younger ones—that they didn't appreciate what their generation went through, and that they were too critical about the industry. I wanted to capture the difficulty of maintaining one's dignity as an actor and as a person, given the world they live in.*

In *Yankee Dawg You Die*, Vincent and Bradley convey the past and contemporary dilemmas that Asian American actors face. While Bradley, a young actor who will not take demeaning or stereotypic roles, can look down on Vincent as a "Chinese Stepinfetchit," Vincent justifies his career as a product of limited historical choice:

> *. . . you don't think I wouldn't have wanted to play a better role than that bucktoothed, groveling waiter? I would have killed for a better role where I could have played an honest-*

to-god human being with real emotions. I would have
killed for it. . . . Back then there was no Asian American
consciousness, no Asian American actor, and no Asian
American theaters. Just a handful of "orientals" who for
some godforsaken reason wanted to perform. . . . You
wouldn't be here if it weren't for all the crap we had to put
up with. We built something. We built the mountain, as
small as it may be, that you stand on so proudly looking
down at me.

In the end, their viewpoints are ironically reversed when
Bradley rationalizes his acceptance of a role in an exploit-
ative film, while Vincent decides to perform in an independent Asian American feature. While they gaze at the North
Star, it is not clear what direction each will follow.

The play is peppered throughout with hilarious references
to Anna Mae Wong, Neil Sedaka, and Godzilla. It serves as
filmography by chronicling movies from *Bad Day at Black
Rock* to *Year of the Dragon*, noting the twists and turns in the
presentation of Asians on the silver screen. The play assumes
added significance given the controversy that exploded over
the casting decisions made by Cameron Mackintosh in his
production *Miss Saigon*. The question of stereotypic roles,
the debate over white actors in "yellowface," and the access
to leading roles for Asian American artists remain highly volatile issues. *Yankee Dawg You Die* does an excellent job of
surveying what Asian American actors have had and continue to go through in order to claim a place in the spotlight.

Fish Head Soup, read alongside *A Song For A Nisei Fisherman* and *The Wash*, is the third part of a family trilogy.
Although such a series was not Gotanda's conscious inten-
tion, the three plays nonetheless represent his attempt to
continue to explore the Japanese American family, to delve
deeper and deeper into it.

Fish Head Soup is an often violent portrayal of the familial and generational conflicts tearing apart a Japanese American family in the San Joaquin Valley. Mat Iwasaki, who had years before faked his suicide, returns home to find his father existing in an illusory world, his mother having an affair with a white man enamored of Orientalism, and his brother still reliving the nightmare of the Vietnam War. While Mat attempts to get the family to mortgage the house to finance his cinematic aspirations, each member confronts the internal manifestations of racism that ironically bind them together.

There is a dramatic and marked difference between this play and the earlier *A Song For A Nisei Fisherman*. The latter was a historical celebration of the Nisei as seen through the somewhat romanticized eye of a Sansei. Gotanda's vision in *Fish Head Soup* is much darker. It explores what lurks below the surface of a Japanese American family.

Fish Head Soup signifies, and responds to, an overall change in the political and cultural climate. Among other things, Gotanda believes that the Japanese American community has matured and evolved over the past twenty years, and is now able to entertain more critical perspectives on its condition:

> *The community can now appreciate works which don't paint such a pretty picture. They don't need plays which are merely self-congratulatory.*

The play treats the manner in which racism is internalized and manifested in our familial relationships, the generational effects of this legacy, and the ugly reality of anti-Asian sentiments and violence. Gotanda raises a disturbing issue for the community to reflect on and actively confront:

> *Japanese Americans are in tremendous denial as to what extent racism has affected how we live our lives. How it forces us to act in all sorts of peculiar ways. This finds expression in forms of self-hate and overcompensation.*

Fish Head Soup is reflective of Gotanda's own personal journey—from an understanding of the external manifestations of racial oppression, to a growing awareness of the internal dynamics of racism and how it manifests itself within the family:

> *Internalized racism is a fact of life. If you live in America, you have been infected by it. By internal I mean how we buy into racism, how we participate in it, and how we engage in a kind of dance of allowing ourselves to be victimized.*

In the play, Mat's father describes "the disease":

> *The moment you leave your mama's stomach it begins to feed on you. Entering your body, your blood, your mind— so that your thoughts, your thinking, it's all filled with the sickness. The sickness that is pushing and moving your life with its silent hands. Cutting its way into your skin with lies, into your body, all inside of me. Eating me up, like a cancer, eating me away . . .*

Mat hopes to avoid the "sickness," but finds he has inherited it as a generational legacy. During an attack by street toughs motivated by anti-Asian sentiments, Mat feels himself succumbing to it:

> *Then I hear this tiny voice. Coming from somewhere deep inside me. I couldn't recognize it before. And I wouldn't put a name to it because I knew if I listened to it I would die. But this time. This time I had to listen to it. And I knew what it was. It was you, Papa, you. And as I listened to you inside me I felt the fear. The intimidation. The sickness. And I began to cower in front of these white men. And as they began to hit me and kick me I still had to listen. To let your voice grow and grow and fill me with its sound . . . I felt you inside of me. But Papa, it wasn't just the sickness. No, no, it was much, much more. It was the ability to see it, give the sickness a name. You didn't know that Papa, did you? To know its face and be able to hurl it back out of one's soul. Shout it out of one's being.*

The ability to give racism a face, give it a name, or simply to acknowledge its existence becomes an empowering experience, one that is in essence a collective response:

> They'll run Papa. They'll have to run because it won't be
> just my voice. . . . It will be our voice—yours and mine,
> Mama's and Victor's, Ojiichan's and Obaachan's, on and
> on. GATHERING LIKE A STORM DEEP DOWN
> INSIDE AND HURLING OUT WITH A FURY OF
> BEATINGS, HOWLS AND SCREAMS! THEY'LL
> HAVE TO RUN—CUT, BOUND, RIPPED TO
> SHREDS BY ITS FORCE!

A window of hope emerges from this exorcism. Despite the debilitating effects of racism, people can rise above it to claim some nobler sense of humanity. It is a theme that links all the plays in this collection. Gotanda captures the incredible resilience of human beings and the human spirit. In the depths of a crisis, individuals—like Nobu, Vincent, and Mat—can in fact change, carve out a sense of worth and purpose, and transcend their perceived situation of powerlessness.

Gotanda recently took a year off to reevaluate what he wanted to accomplish as an artist, and to figure out his own "internal journey." His self-imposed sabbatical allowed him to return to his work with a renewed vision and sense of purpose. He still has stories to tell and things he wants to convey:

> If I could just finally say exactly what it is I want to say,
> get it all out, I could give it all up. Then maybe I would do
> the things I always imagined I'd end up doing—lying on
> some beach in Kauai—getting fat, eating mangoes. But
> everything I say, never quite says it. So I keep going back
> and trying to figure out how to say this thing that just keeps
> eluding my grasp.

After his sabbatical, Gotanda directed plays and decided to do a film. Gotanda has always been interested in film as well as music, but its costs have made the medium generally prohibitive. Influenced by a wave of low-budget films and the possibilities they offered, he began to reconsider film as an increasingly attractive option. Gotanda wrote, produced, and directed *The Kiss*, in which he stars as a nerdish office worker who rises to the occasion to become a "hero." *The Kiss* received critical notice and was screened at the Sundance Film Festival, and the Berlin, Edinburgh, and San Francisco film festivals.

What is striking about the short film is the virtual absence of dialogue. This was intentional. A playwright's strength is dialogue, but Gotanda wanted his foray into film to be a radical departure from what he has brought to the stage. With *The Kiss*, he explored how to create meaning and communicate it through an actor's expression or the framing of a scene.

Gotanda has not abandoned plays, and a number of new projects have emerged. He has completed a new play, *Day Standing On Its Head*, which is jarringly different in theme and style from the creative turf he has previously explored. He has also completed a spoken work piece, *in the dominion of night*, in which he will play the fictitious joe ozu with Dan Kuramoto of Hiroshima as his musical collaborator.

While he continues to be well received in more mainstream theatrical venues, Gotanda retains an unwavering commitment to Asian American theater companies:

> *I see the Asian American theater world as family. Asian American theater may not have all the bells and whistles, the production values of more mainstream venues, but it's the one place you can truly define what this thing called an Asian American theatrical aesthetic is. It's the place where you can develop it in its purest form.*

That said, Gotanda also believes we must have an expanded vision of what Asian America is, a vision that must continually evolve to embrace ever more apparent diversity and complexity:

Some people think that Asian American theater is a static art form. People think it's about dealing with Angel Island, the railroads, the camps, etc. But our culture is a live beast.

The rise of anti-Asian violence, the devastation caused by the Los Angeles riot, and the smuggling of human cargo from Asia add troubling dimensions to the Asian American experience, ones which add a certain urgency to Gotanda's ongoing work:

Asian America is under siege at this point. Artistically this makes for a volatile but creative situation. The sweeping sense of anti-Asian sentiment means that a lot of new young voices have a need to say something, a reason to say something, a fire to say something. I see all kinds of energy coming from Southeast Asians, second-generation Korean Americans, "mixed race" Asians, and gay and lesbian Asian Americans. They are finding their voice. And it all bodes well for a new resurgent Asian American cultural voice. We have to tell the stories that allow the world to see us on our own terms, not defined by others. We have to force ourselves to be heard, to be seen. Whether it's a poem, a play, or a defiant shout.

Gotanda's work compellingly conveys the hopes, fears, shattered dreams, and triumphs that collectively make up the Asian American experience. It is the telling of an American story in an America that is continually being re-formed:

This can truly be an exciting time. We are all participating in the reinvention of America, from the ground up. As an artist and a citizen of the world, what a grand time to be alive.

Berkeley, California
September 1994

▲

Fish

Head

Soup

Fish Head Soup
First production at the Berkeley Repertory Theatre, 1991

DIRECTOR. Oskar Eustis
SCENIC AND LIGHTING DESIGN. Kent Dorsey
COSTUMES. Lydia Tanji
SOUND DESIGN. James LeBrecht
ORIGINAL COMPOSITION. Dan Kuramoto
STAGE MANAGER. Meryl Lind Shaw
FIGHT DIRECTOR. Michael Cawelti

Cast

PAPA IWASAKI. Alberto Isaac
DOROTHY IWASAKI. Dian Kobayashi
MAT IWASAKI. Stan Egi
VICTOR IWASAKI. Kelvin Han Yee

Fish Head Soup received a workshop as part of the Mark Taper
Forum's New Work Festival in 1989. Gordon Davidson was the
artistic director. It was also included in workshops at the Sundance
Institute, Bay Area Playwrights Festival, and Berkeley Repertory
Theatre.

Second production of *Fish Head Soup*
East West Players in association with the Mark Taper Forum,
January 1993

DIRECTOR. Oskar Eustis
PRODUCER. Nelson Handel
SCENIC DESIGN. David Hoffman
LIGHTING DESIGN. Richard Hoyes
MUSIC COMPOSITION. Dan Kuramoto
SOUND DESIGN. Gino Chang
COSTUMES. Christine Souza
PROPS. Ken Takemoto
STAGE MANAGER. Yuki Nakamura
FIGHT DIRECTOR. Randy Kovitz

Cast
PAPA IWASAKI. Sab Shimono
DOROTHY IWASAKI. Nobu McCarthy*
VICTOR IWASAKI. Nelson Mashita
MAT IWASAKI. Stan Egi
*Dian Kobayashi took over the role during run.

Author's thanks to Sharon Ott, Peter Brosius, Nobu McCarthy,
Rick Shiomi, Anthony Taccone, Robert Egan, and David Kranes.

Very special thanks to my friend Oskar Eustis, who shepherded this
along from beginning to end.

Characters

TOGO IWASAKI, "PAPA," Japanese American, mid-sixties in age,
seemingly mentally ill
DOROTHY IWASAKI, his wife, in her middle fifties but still attractive,
waitress in a Japanese restaurant
VICTOR IWASAKI, their older son, in his mid to late thirties, tour-bus
driver for a Japanese hotel, Vietnam veteran
MAT IWASAKI, their younger son, late twenties to early thirties
Voices of THREE YOUTHS
VIET CONG SOLDIER
The voice of a DRILL SERGEANT

Time
Late fall, into winter, 1989.

Place
Town in the San Joaquin Valley, California.

Settings

ACT ONE. The Iwasaki house, Friday evening to Saturday morning.
ACT TWO. The Iwasaki house and various locales around the town,
Saturday evening.
ACT THREE. The Iwasaki house and various locales around the town,
Sunday.

Lights up on VICTOR *and* PAPA. *It's very wet and foggy outside. They've just returned from a church memorial service.* VICTOR *is helping* PAPA *into his overstuffed chair.* VICTOR *has a pager in his belt.* PAPA *starts to jerk his hands up and down in front of him, mouthing "Mat."* VICTOR *notices and gently grabs his hands, stopping him. He lets go and* PAPA *starts again.* VICTOR *stops him.* VICTOR *and* PAPA *look at each other.* VICTOR *slowly releases his hands. He watches.* PAPA *doesn't move his hands.*

DOROTHY enters through the front door with a dripping umbrella and crosses to the upstage bathroom.

DOROTHY: How is he? Is he all right now?

VICTOR (*nodding*): Un-huh.

DOROTHY: I can't believe he acted like that . . . (*She goes into the bathroom and puts the umbrella into the shower stall.*)

DOROTHY (*calling from inside*): The toilet seems fine, Victor, it's not running, I don't see why you're making such a fuss about it . . .

(VICTOR *helps* PAPA *out of his wet coat.* DOROTHY *reenters.*)

DOROTHY (*taking off coat*): And in front of all those people—Mat's baseball coach, what's his name, big tall fellow . . .

VICTOR: Mr. Guilfoyle.

(DOROTHY *moves to the corner table with a small* obutsudan *[Buddhist shrine] sitting on top of it.*)

DOROTHY: . . . Yes, yes, he was there, and Mr. Sanders the principal, Mrs. Thompson his debate teacher—they all came up and talked to me so nicely you know, before the

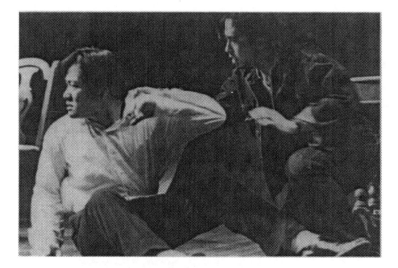

Kelvin Han Yee as Victor and Stan Egi as Mat in the world premiere of Fish Head Soup, *Berkeley Repertory Theatre, February 1991*
Photo by Ken Friedman, courtesy Berkeley Repertory Theatre

Stan Egi (Mat) and Kelvin Han Yee (Victor)
in Fish Head Soup
Photo by Ken Friedman,
courtesy Berkeley Repertory Theatre

Fish

Head

Soup

memorial service began. After all this time they still remember . . . *(Fingering* MAT's *photo)* and then he jumps up and starts screaming and yelling . . .

VICTOR: I was watching him, okay, Mama.

*(*VICTOR *begins wiping* PAPA's *face.)*

DOROTHY: I was so embarrassed, all those folks there, wanting to show how much they loved and respected Mat and he gets up and starts to do that. I think he does it on purpose. Did you do it on purpose, Papa? Huh? To embarrass me in front of all those people . . .

VICTOR: He didn't, Mama.

DOROTHY: How do you know? Who knows what goes on inside of there? Besides, you said you'd keep an eye on him.

VICTOR: I was, I said I was watching . . .

DOROTHY: It's bad enough they have to sit there in a Buddhist church, incense smelling up the place, all that mumbo jumbo sutra chanting. I mean, it's okay for us Japanese, we're used to it. But they have to sit there breathing in that stuff and then they have to go up there in front of everyone and gassho . . . *(Starts to laugh)* Did you see Mr.—what did you say his coach's name was . . .

VICTOR: Guilfoyle.

DOROTHY: Right, right, he's so tall he nearly bumped his head on that lantern near the shrine and then he didn't know what to do with the incense . . . *(Stops laughing, looking at* PAPA. VICTOR *is combing* PAPA's *hair.)* And then he starts doing that thing with his hands. *(Upset)*

DOROTHY: You have to go in today?

VICTOR *(shaking head)*: Un-uh. I called in.

*(*DOROTHY *watches* PAPA *for a beat.)*

DOROTHY: Victor, the toilet's fine. Okay, Victor? Victor?

VICTOR *(nodding)*: Un-huh.

DOROTHY: I have to get dressed.

*(*DOROTHY *turns and exits into the back hallway.)*

*(*VICTOR *stands there for a moment, then pulls out a large*

wrench from his back pocket. Grips it, staring down at
PAPA. *Then turns and disappears into the upstage*
bathroom door. We begin to hear the banging of pipes
coming from within.)
(Lights fade to black. VICTOR's *banging changes into a*
watery, echoing din. We hear a droning sound. PAPA *lit in*
a pool of light standing on top of his chair. Staring out, he
begins to jerk his hands up and down wildly as if
snagging with an imaginary fishing pole.)

PAPA *(calling in a raspy voice)*: Mat. Mat. Mat . . .
(Upstage, the silhouette of a man is brought up in a bluish
watery shaft of light. Drowning in very slow motion—
grasping upwards, mouth and eyes gaping.)

DOROTHY *(off)*: Victor!
(Lights immediately up on the house. Sound cuts
away. PAPA *stands, disoriented, on his chair, perched*
precariously. VICTOR *is emerging from the bathroom*
carrying a toilet in his arms, struggling to make his way
carefully to the hallway. PAPA *starts to fall.)*

DOROTHY *(off)*: Victor! Victor!
*(*VICTOR *notices* PAPA *falling, hurriedly puts down the*
toilet. Starts to move towards PAPA *when his pager goes*
off. Unable to make up his mind—should he phone in
or catch his father? The pager continues to beep and his
father continues to totter. He rushes over and catches
PAPA *just before he falls.* DOROTHY *speaks the following*
during the above described action.)

DOROTHY *(off)*: Know what I hate most about going to
work this time of year? Know what? The fog. Know what
I hate second most? Driving in this fog. It's so scary, can't
see more than a few feet in front of you. And you can't slow
down 'cause those damn semis will run you right off the
road. So what do you do? You can't go forward 'cause you
can't see but you have to keep going forward or you'll get
run over—so what do you do, huh? What do you do?
*(*VICTOR *puts* PAPA *back in his chair, then hurries to the*
phone, checking the phone number on the beeper.)

Fish

Head

Soup

VICTOR *(phoning)*: Hello, Mr. Toyama? Mr. Toyama-san?
Fish   . . . Yes, moshi-moshi, yes it's . . . Yes, moshi-moshi, Vic-
         tor desu . . . Hai, hai . . . I'm, uh, uh . . . boku wa very
Head   busy desu . . . Not suppose to be on call today, desu, call
         the office desu . . . Yes, yes, sayonara desu . . .
Soup   *(*VICTOR *hangs up and goes back to his toilet moving.)*
DOROTHY *(off)*: Victor!
         *(*VICTOR, *struggling with the toilet, ignores her calls.*
         PAPA *is climbing back up on his chair, teetering.)*
DOROTHY *(off)*: Victor! Victor!
         *(*VICTOR *sees* PAPA *starting to fall again. His pager starts*
         beeping. Momentary confusion, then rushes over just as
         PAPA *begins to slip off the chair. They tumble to the*
         ground in a heap this time. Dorothy, dressed in a kimono,
         enters from the back hallway, awkwardly walking in
         ministeps owing to the constraints of the kimono.)
DOROTHY: Victor, you have to keep an eye on him, you just
         can't . . . there's no telling what he'll do . . .
VICTOR *(helping Papa up)*: Yeah, but I'm trying to . . . *(Con-*
         tinues.)
DOROTHY *(overlapping)*: What's that sound?
VICTOR: . . . fix the toilet and then I'm supposed to be
         watching Papa . . .
DOROTHY *(interrupts)*: It's not broken, Victor . . . *(Spots the*
         ripped-out toilet sitting on the floor)
VICTOR *(shutting off beeper)*: And my clients are calling
         me . . .
DOROTHY *(staring)*: What the hell did you do . . . Victor,
         didn't I tell you . . .
         *(*DOROTHY *turns back to* VICTOR *and sees* PAPA *moving*
         his hands again in an agitated fashion.)
DOROTHY *(unnerved)*: Victor, he's doing it again. He's doing
         it again, Victor . . .
         *(*VICTOR *hurriedly stops* PAPA. DOROTHY *tries to*
         compose herself.)
DOROTHY: I have to go to work. *(Turns to leave)*

VICTOR: You coming home late again?

DOROTHY: Look, we just need the money, okay? I can't help
it. Ice cream executives. A special party or something.

PAPA: Mama. I want Mama. I want Mama. Mama?
(DOROTHY *looks at* PAPA *for a beat. Something in her*
softens. Crosses to him, smiling.)

DOROTHY *(reaching in to stroke his cheek)*: Here I am, silly,
Mama's right . . .

PAPA *(knocks her hand away)*: I want Mama. I want Mama.
(They stare at each other for a beat. She starts to adjust
his clothing. He resists and tries to push her hands away,
but she overpowers him, forcing him to sit still while
she adjusts his clothing. She speaks during the above
struggle.)

DOROTHY: He started walking when he was just eight
months old. I mean, really walking. Everyone was amazed.
And when I took him to swimming lessons, like a minnow,
just like a little minnow. Everyone right away started talking about the Olympics. And they were always trying to
skip him—second grade, fifth grade—but Daddy wouldn't
let them. Just wouldn't let them. Said it was showing
off, "What would other people think, putting our kid
ahead like that?" *(Finishes. Beat. Catching her breath.)* Mat
would've been something very important by now. Something high up, like one of those international business bro-
kers between Japan and America . . .
(DOROTHY *hikes up her kimono between her legs and*
turns to leave.)

DOROTHY *(muttering to herself as she exits awkwardly)*: Why
do they make them like this, you can barely move. Damn
thing . . .
(VICTOR *watches her leave, then turns back to* PAPA.
Notices he's upset.)

PAPA: Mat's not my son, Mat's not my son . . .

VICTOR *(comforting him)*: Papa? We were climbing this tree.

You know, Mat and me? And Mat kept going higher and higher. "Stop, Mat, you crazy? Come back down." I was scared 'cause we were way up there you know, and if anything happened to him, Mama always blamed me, always. I kept telling Mat, "Come back, come back down," but you know Mat, he just kept going up and up. And then I fell. I broke my arm. Mat came down and looked at me. He started crying. Mama got so mad at me. "What if Mat broke his neck and killed himself?" *(Beat)* Sometimes I dream about him. Mat. He's somewhere far away, Papa. He's happy, too. And he's so high up, the world could never pull him back. Never pull him under . . .

PAPA *(sadly shakes his head back and forth)*: Victor's house, Victor's house . . .

VICTOR: No, no, Papa's house. Papa's house . . .

(Dim to darkness on VICTOR *and* PAPA.*)*

(Night. Iwasaki house. Foggy outside. Shadowy figure enters through the window, flashlight and carry bag in hand. Late 20s to early 30s, dressed like a cross between a Japanese gangster and a sleazy Hollywood producer. Appears as if he's been up for several days, unshaven, hair unkempt. Flashes light around. Begins picking up objects, touching them, inhaling their smells. Picks up a vase, quietly studies it for a beat, then playfully tosses it from one hand to the other hand. Crosses to PAPA's *chair. Notices* PAPA's *hat sitting on the seat. Picks it up, examining it, and then puts it on. He sits in the chair. Lights come up abruptly.* VICTOR *is standing by the light.)*

MAT: Hi, Victor.

(Silence. VICTOR *stares, wide-eyed.)*

MAT: It's me.

(More silence. VICTOR *continues to stare.)*

MAT *(moving towards* VICTOR*)*: It really is, Victor, it's . . .

VICTOR *(raising wrench threateningly)*: Stay back . . .

*(*MAT *stops.)*

MAT: I know this is a bit of a shock—I mean, after all this
time and everything. But it's me.   Fish
   *(VICTOR, desperately confused, begins to make high-
   pitched whimpering sounds.)*   Head
MAT *(worried)*: No, no, don't do that, Victor, don't do that
   . . . you're all right, you're all right, you're going to be just Soup
   fine . . .
   *(VICTOR starts to move around the house with MAT
   following him.)*
VICTOR: See, see, I'm fixing the house, I am 'cause it's all
   broken down and rotting and Mat can't see up, 'cause
   he's so high up and it's all beneath the surface, inside the
   walls under the floors and I'm ripping it out, ripping . . .
   (Continues.)
MAT *(overlapping)*: Calm down, calm down. It looks great,
   you're doing a great job, you are . . .
VICTOR: . . . it out, the pipes all leaky, all the wiring, making
   it better, making it better. See, see inside, inside here . . .
   (Continues.)
MAT *(overlapping, moving closer)*: It is me, Victor. It's me,
   Mat. I'm back, Mat's back . . .
VICTOR: . . . all copper pipes, all copper pipes, all copper
   . . . NO!
   (VICTOR swings his wrench wildly at MAT.)
MAT *(ducking)*: Victor, what the hell you . . .
   (PAPA enters from the hallway.)
PAPA: Mat? Mat, is that you?
   (MAT notices PAPA's strange appearance.)
MAT: Yeah, it's me, Papa . . .
   (PAPA stares at MAT.)
PAPA: You kids better go to bed now. I want to get an early
   start tomorrow. Victor, tell Mama I want fried chicken
   and onigiri.* More salt, too, on the rice—not enough salt
   last time. *(Beat)* Who knows? Maybe we'll get lucky this

*Rice balls.

time and catch him. Yeah. Haul him in kicking and screaming like some big striped bass.

MAT: Papa, it's me. Mat. I'm back.

(PAPA *stares at* MAT.)

PAPA: Mama? Mama! Where the hell is she? It's 1:30 in the morning, where the hell is she, Victor?

VICTOR: She has to work late sometimes.

PAPA: Victor, make sure all the equipment is loaded into the car. And don't forget the chum I got frozen in the icebox. Oh, and pack my old pole, too. (*To* MAT) It's yours now. (PAPA *turns and walks to the hallway. Stops and turns to* MAT.) Aren't you dead?

VICTOR: Namu Amida Butsu, Namu Amida Butsu . . .

(PAPA *turns and exits. Lights begin a slow fade.* VICTOR *withdraws into the shadows, continuing to watch* MAT. MAT *is isolated in a pool of light.* VICTOR *fades to black.*) (MAT *lit alone.*)

MAT: I didn't like myself. I didn't like anything about myself. No. I hated myself. Yes. Hated. I hated my yellow face. My flat nose. The name that no one could ever pronounce correctly. So I got rid of them. Got rid of them and started all over. From the ground up. This time it was going to be my way, my creation.

(*Fade in*) I became Italian. I went on a fruit and water diet, worked out religiously on various contraptions of self-torture. My butt was so taut and my pants so tight you could have skied off the drop. But the rest of me? No curves, no soft lines. Only angles. Sleek angles and sharp edges. And I would purposely walk down the darkest alleys in the most dangerous parts of town knowing not a soul would touch me because I was like a shiny stiletto cutting this way and that way . . . My name was Paolo. I loved saying it. It was like some exotic bird taking flight off my tongue. And when other people said it, "Paolo? Paolo?"— "Yes?" . . . I was a million miles from here.

(*Looks back at* PAPA'*s hat on his chair*)
But then, after a while, it began to sound like my old   *Fish*
name. Feel like my old name. Someone would say,
"Paolo?" and I would hear your voice calling me through   *Head*
it. So I changed it again. I became Joaquim. Joaquim
dressed in black exclusively, drank only espresso, and   *Soup*
spoke with an accent that could have been Peruvian, that
could have been Panamanian, but that could not have
been, nor ever be, mistaken for Japanese . . . (*Moves
towards chair*) But then I started to hear you again. Every
time someone said my new name—"Joaquim?" "Joaquim?"—I could almost feel your voice. Your voice, like a
big hand reaching right out through it and grabbing me by
the scruff of the neck—"Mat, Mat" . . .
  (*Pause.*)
Then one night as I lay in bed, I began to change . . .
(*Lighting change*) My head pushes out forward, grows
long, and my eyes move to the sides of my head. My body
elongates like a shiny torpedo. And the trick to the whole
thing is my tail. And the two fins on the sides of my head.
(*Starts to move around*) I begin to move with a knowing. I
mean, I don't know but I know. My body just seems to be
. . . (*Continues.*)
  (PAPA *and* VICTOR *lit upstage in a shadowy light.* PAPA
  *stands shivering in a wide-rimmed bucket, filled with
  water.* PAPA *is naked.* VICTOR *dips a small container into
  the bucket to get water, then pours it over the body of*
  PAPA. *As it touches his skin he makes a mournful high-
  pitched wailing sound. It intermingles with the sound of
  the water splashing into the bucket.*)
MAT: . . . leading me, taking me somewhere. Turn here, turn
  there, go straight here . . . Piece of cake, I'm on automatic
  pilot, I've been doing this forever—Look, Ma, no hands!
  Wait, wait, what's this? Up ahead, I hear a growing roar.
  Then I see it . . . The rapids . . . The current picks up, I'm

being swept along . . . Suddenly I'm pulled under, tumbling and rolling along the bottom, pebbles like tiny razors scraping at my skin. *(Breaks through surface gasping for air)* Ahhh . . . What's this . . . Rocks! Big, small, jagged—leap out like flying car fenders! Ouch! *(Bangs into furniture, knocking things over)* Ahh! Ahhh! Leap high, high out of the water! Then deep, deep, deep . . . Finally, I surface. Over there, a quiet pool of water beneath a shady tree. *(Pulls himself along floor now)* My left side has a deep gash, my dorsal fin is ripped. But I must keep going . . . Then I see something . . . yes, yes, I know this place . . . There, I recognize that street, it's where I used to play as a kid. And, and that gas station, I used to fill up the air in my bicycle tires there . . . And those maple trees . . . And there, on the corner, I see it . . .

(MAT passes out on the ground. PAPA and VICTOR dim to darkness.)

(DOROTHY enters house in semi-darkness, trying not to make noise. All dressed up, carrying shoes. She stumbles on MAT's sleeping body.)

MAT *(waking up)*: Mom?

(DOROTHY sees him.)

DOROTHY: AAHHH! *(Silence. DOROTHY stares as MAT gets up.)*

MAT: Mom?

(MAT slowly approaches DOROTHY. He reaches out and embraces her. She is rigid with shock. She slowly comprehends the situation.)

DOROTHY *(embracing him)*: Mat, Mat, you're alive. My baby's . . . *(Continues.)*

MAT *(overlapping)*: It's all right, Mama, it's all right. I'm back. Mat's home.

DOROTHY: . . . alive. My baby's come back to me. Mat, Mat, Mat . . .

(DOROTHY stops, suddenly angry. She starts to attack

him, striking at him. MAT *has to grab her flailing arms as*
they whack at him.)

DOROTHY: How could you? Do you know what you put us
through? Do you know? Do you? He just stood by the
river, by the river all night . . . *(Can't take it, breaks down,*
reaching out and embracing him again) Mat, Mat, Mat . . .

(As MAT *stands there being held by* DOROTHY, *lights*
fade to half. PAPA *enters, dressed in his worn robe and*
holding a bowl of mush. He makes his way across the
room towards his chair. His slow movements and blank
expression give his appearance an eerie quality. MAT
watches this strange apparition that is his father move
across the room. A weeping DOROTHY *continues to cling*
to him.)

MAT: Mama? Mama?

*(*DOROTHY *looks up.)*

MAT: It's the middle of the night. Where were you?

(They stare at each other. Fade to black.)

Lights up full on the house. Morning. PAPA *is seated in his*
chair, napkin around his neck, eating. VICTOR *is trying to*
straighten up all the tipped-over furniture. MAT *stands*
drinking coffee, staring at PAPA.

VICTOR *(cleaning up)*: What happened here last night?

*(*MAT *is silent, continues to stare at* PAPA.*)*

VICTOR: Look at this place, it's a mess.

MAT: I had a bad dream.

VICTOR *(continuing to clean, watching* MAT *looking at* PAPA*)*:
I got a job now. At a hotel. I'm a driver. I drive people
around. Japanese. It's a Japanese hotel. They just built
it . . .

MAT: That's all he does? I mean, he just sits there?

(No response.)

MAT: I mean, can he carry on a conversation? Can he do
things?

VICTOR: "Do things"?

Fish   MAT: Yeah, yeah, you know, stuff around the house—take care of bills, sign things . . .

Head   VICTOR: Don't touch him! *(Beat)* It's my job, okay? Okay, Mat?

Soup   (VICTOR *moves to* PAPA's *side, takes the spoon away from him and begins to spoon-feed* PAPA *himself.* DOROTHY *enters from the hallway. Stands by the corridor and watches* MAT.)

MAT: What's going on here, Victor?

VICTOR: I kept telling Mama we'd get a postcard from you. From some far-off land. You'd have a funny hat on and be wearing a grass skirt and it'd say, "Love, Mat." But after a couple of months . . .

MAT: Victor, Victor, listen to me. He's sitting there like a goddamn zombie, you're feeding him like he was a baby or something. I mean, did you take him to a doctor or anything?

VICTOR: Yeah.

MAT: And?

VICTOR: And, what?

MAT: What did they say, Victor? What's wrong with him?

VICTOR: Nothing's wrong with him.

MAT: What do you mean, "Nothing's wrong with him"? Look at him, Victor, look at him!

VICTOR: Don't yell, Mat, don't yell at me.

MAT: I'm not yelling, Victor, I'm not . . . *(Continues.)*

VICTOR *(overlapping)*: That's just the way he is now, that's just the way he is!

MAT: . . . yelling at you. I just want to know what kinds of things he can do . . .

(MAT *and* VICTOR *interrupted as* DOROTHY *walks in. Silence as she moves to stove to get coffee.)*

DOROTHY *(at stove)*: Sometimes he looks right at you and speaks. He says your name and everything. He seems fine,

you know. And then you start to talk to him and you realize
you're not talking to anyone.

(MAT *watches her pouring her coffee.*)

MAT: You sleep okay?

DOROTHY: Un-huh. You?

MAT: Good.

DOROTHY: The couch was okay then?

MAT: No, no, it was fine.

DOROTHY: It's just your room . . . Papa uses it.

MAT: The couch was okay, really.

DOROTHY: Because of the way he is now, Mat.

(*Awkward pause.* MAT *crosses room.*)

MAT (*looking into a door*): Where's the toilet? Who took the
toilet?

VICTOR: Don't touch anything in there.

DOROTHY: I keep telling him it's fine the way it is.

VICTOR: No, it isn't, Mom. The water was running.

MAT (*coming out*): What'd you do with the toilet, Victor?

VICTOR: I'm fixing it, okay?

MAT: Then fix it, don't just leave it—there's nothing in there
now. Just a big hole.

DOROTHY: Just use the bathroom in the back, Mat. The one
in the hallway.

(MAT *stares at* VICTOR *and* DOROTHY *for a beat, then
exits shaking his head.* DOROTHY *moves to table.*)

DOROTHY (*to* VICTOR): I tried to sleep, I couldn't. I'd close
my eyes, nothing would happen. Then I'd think I was
dreaming the whole thing and come out and look at Mat.
I did that all night. Just watching him.

(MAT *returns. He's splashed water on his face and head.
Slicks back his wet hair with his hands.*)

MAT: Ahh, that feels better. More coffee. (*Gulps down rest of
coffee and goes to get another cup*) You know what part of
my body feels the best in the morning? You know what
part? (*Beat*) These. (*Laughing, holds up his bare foot*) I've

been wearing these new Japanese shoes. Got 'em in L.A. They're so pointy, they're like knives. I'm in a dark alley, someone jumps me? *(Kicks)* Hah! Dead. But they're killing my feet.

(MAT laughs at his own joke. Notices DOROTHY and VICTOR are not laughing. Embarrassed silence. DOROTHY upset.)

DOROTHY *(quietly)*: Is that where you've been? In Los Angeles?

(Awkward beat.)

MAT: Most the time, yeah.

(Pause.)

DOROTHY: What have you been doing?

(Slight pause.)

MAT: Things. All kinds of things.

DOROTHY: Well, all this time . . . I mean, what do you do now? You've been gone for almost, what? How many years have you been . . .

MAT: Oh, oh, I'm an actor. You know, like in the movies, TV?

DOROTHY: An actor?

MAT: Un-huh.

(DOROTHY and VICTOR exchange looks.)

VICTOR: I've never seen you.

MAT: Well, it's been a bit slow. I did a couple commercials.

VICTOR: I watch TV all the time. I've never seen you.

MAT: I said it's been a bit slow, Victor, okay?

DOROTHY: An actor? But Mat . . . All this time . . .

(MAT gets up and goes to sink to wash hands.)

MAT: I get to be all these different people, Mom. People I could never be in real life. That's what makes it so much fun. I can play anyone.

(DOROTHY watches MAT vigorously washing hands.)

DOROTHY: Mat? Why? Why'd you do it?

(MAT can't respond. Awkward silence. VICTOR watches.)

DOROTHY: I was telling Victor how during the night? I would come out and watch you. One time—this is kind of silly—I thought you stopped breathing. I did. I got so scared. I bent down real close to you to see if you were still alive. I was listening. Trying to hear your heart. Silly, huh? *(DOROTHY starts to cry.)*

VICTOR: Mama? You okay, Mama? *(Getting up and going to DOROTHY)*: Mama, don't cry. Please don't cry.

DOROTHY *(waving VICTOR away)*: I'm all right, I'm all right. *(Pause.)*

MAT: I just did a movie. Mom? A movie, I did one. Just like in the theaters—big budget, everything. And we shot it in Japan. Tokyo. We shot it on location there. Flew me in there, put me up in a nice hotel. *(MAT takes out snapshots and shows them to DOROTHY.)*

DOROTHY *(composing herself)*: A movie?

MAT: Yeah, yeah—I played the lead. Well, there're two of us actually. A man and a woman—a love story, you know the usual stuff. I kept thinking, wouldn't it be nice if Mom were here. To see me.

DOROTHY *(looking)*: In Japan?

MAT *(nodding)*: Un-huh—see, that's her, the blond girl. Some of the crew, that's the director . . .

DOROTHY *(noticing, excitedly)*: It's you.

MAT: Un-huh, yeah. And you can be a celebrity there over-night. I mean it, really. I walk down the street, people jump all over me there. I'm not exaggerating—tear my clothes off, I'm standing there almost naked, they're taking pictures, shooting video. I'm practically famous in Japan, almost a movie star.

DOROTHY *(holding photos)*: Look, Victor, look. *(Back to MAT)* Japanese are just too smart, huh. Whatever they want to do—cars, TVs, no one can keep up with them. I keep telling Victor, learn to speak Japanese, go work for the Japanese.

VICTOR *(moving back to feed* PAPA*)*: I am, I am, Mama.
(DOROTHY *shrugs, unimpressed. She stares at* MAT *for a beat.)*

MAT: What?
(Dorothy moves to Mat and starts to take his coat off.)

MAT: What are you doing?

DOROTHY: This coat, Mat, really.

MAT: I like it, it cost a lot of—

DOROTHY: Shhh, shhh . . . Remember that favorite sport coat of yours? The one you used to wear to all the awards dinners?

MAT: Yeah? . . .

DOROTHY: Victor, go get it. Victor?

VICTOR: I've been wearing it to work now, Mama . . .

DOROTHY *(impatient)*: Oh, never mind . . . *(Hurries off to get it herself)*

DOROTHY *(exiting)*: Where did we get that jacket? . . . Bravo and McKeegan on Pacific Avenue, that's where I bought it . . .

MAT *(calling after her)*: Really, Mom, if Victor's using it now it's no big . . .
*(*MAT *and* VICTOR *stare at each other uneasily.)*

DOROTHY *(off, excitedly)*: Oh, and here's your old tuxedo, the one you wore to the senior prom with Lucy Snow . . . *(Enters, with coat and tux)* Papa said to rent, but who wants to wear somebody else's clothes? . . . Besides I figured Victor might need it someday, huh Victor? *(*DOROTHY *starts to put it on* MAT.*)*

MAT *(resisting)*: Mom, really I don't want to . . . I— *(Continues.)*

DOROTHY *(overlapping)*: Come on, you'll look so good in—

MAT *(jerking his arm)*: —don't, really I DON'T!
(Silence. DOROTHY *holds arm as if she's been hurt.)*

VICTOR: Mama?

DOROTHY: Last night. When Mat came home . . .

VICTOR: It's all— *(Continues.)*   Fish

DOROTHY *(overlapping)*: Black and blue, yes . . .

VICTOR: —bruised.   Head

MAT: I'm sorry, I didn't know I was that rough.

DOROTHY: It's all right, baby.   Soup

MAT: I'm sorry, Mama, really I'm sorry.

DOROTHY: It's all right, Mat. It's all right? *(Pause)* When I first had you? These spots appeared on you. I thought, "Mat's special, my baby's got a special mark." *(Beat)* The doctors called the police, took us in. They thought we were beating you. *(Beat)* A lot of oriental babies get these spots. Nothing special. Quite ordinary actually.

> *(DOROTHY looks at MAT for a beat, then turns away. Silence. DOROTHY quietly sips coffee. VICTOR motions for MAT to put the coat on. MAT puts it on.)*

VICTOR: How does it look? Mom?

DOROTHY: Hmmm?

MAT: What do you think? How do I look?

DOROTHY: You put on a little weight, huh?

MAT: Yeah, well . . .

DOROTHY: You look kind of fat, huh Victor? *(Beat)* But you still look good. Handsome. Very handsome. Let's see if the tux still fits you. *(DOROTHY starts to lead MAT away. Notices PAPA refusing to eat.)* Victor, he's had enough.

VICTOR: He hasn't eaten enough. He has to eat yet, Mama.

MAT *(moving towards Victor)*: If he doesn't want to eat, don't force him. Victor?

VICTOR *(trying to contain himself)*: I'm not forcing him, he hasn't eaten enough, okay? I can take care of— *(Continues.)*

DOROTHY *(overlapping, leading MAT away)*: Let him alone, let him alone Mat, he knows how to handle him . . .

VICTOR: —Papa now, I know how to take care of him, all right? . . . *(As lights dim, DOROTHY and MAT are in the*

kitchen where they can be heard laughing in half-light. VIC-
TOR *continues to stubbornly feed* PAPA, *gets upset at* PAPA's
refusal to eat, starts to force the food into his mouth.) Eat,
eat. . . *(Catches himself and stops, ashamed. Begins to gently
wipe* PAPA's *mouth with the napkin.)*
        (Dim to darkness.)
        *(*PAPA *lit.)*

PAPA: Remember how I used to take the kids out to Ojiichan's farm and show them around? From over there to
over there, that's all Grandpa's land. Biggest in the whole
San Joaquin Valley. They don't care, they just want to pick
up the potatoes and throw them at each other. I have to
bawl them out. See this? This isn't a potato, this is your college education, and this one here is your son's college education. They don't understand. They think Papa's crazy.
They say, "No, no, Daddy, it's just a potato." I should take
them out there, huh. Let them look at Grandpa's farm . . .
        (Dining room table lit.)

DRILL SERGEANT'S VOICE: Private Iwasaki? Get your ass
up here! We need you again!
        *(*VICTOR *runs into light holding a hammer.)*

DRILL SERGEANT'S VOICE: Atten-hut! *(Pause, thinking)*
No, no . . . Get up on this chair. Yeah, stand on this chair
so they can all see you. Come on, come on, chop, chop,
chop.
        *(*VICTOR *gets up on the table and stands at attention.)*

DRILL SERGEANT'S VOICE: Atten-hut! Boys, pay close
attention. This is the gook enemy. Black hair, yellow skin,
slanty eyes . . . Atten-hut!
        *(*DOROTHY *enters, putting on her kimono.* PAPA *sits in
        his chair in the shadows.* DOROTHY *sees* VICTOR.)*

DOROTHY: What are you doing up there?
        *(*VICTOR *notices where he is. Confused for a beat, then
        steps down.)*

DOROTHY *(cautious)*: Victor?
        (Pause.)

VICTOR: You say, "Japanese is good"?

DOROTHY: Well, yeah . . . *(Pause.* DOROTHY *concerned.)* **Fish** Victor? *(No response.* MAT *lit upstage in half-light looking at the house.)* It's good to have him back, huh? *(*VICTOR *stares* **Head** *at* MAT *for a beat, then turns away.)* Well, I think it's wonderful. The best thing for this family. **Soup**

VICTOR: He doesn't have to say anything. He just stands there and he makes me feel bad.

DOROTHY: Victor? Listen to me. Things are good now. It hasn't been easy, but it's good now. For both of us. You know that, right? Look, look around—you get to work on the house all day long. And you have a job now, too. And now that Mat's back it's going to be even better. You'll see. You'll see, Victor.

VICTOR: Maybe he can help out then. You know, so you can stay home with Papa. So you don't have to work so late all the time.

*(*VICTOR *and* DOROTHY *stare at each other for a beat.* VICTOR *exits. Lights come up full on rest of house and* MAT *as* DOROTHY *watches* VICTOR *leave.)*

MAT: I was in the middle of a scene, this was on the second day of shooting. This weird kitchen scene, the director's idea. And I was feeling kind of funny about it. When the smells of this house . . . You know, like during Thanksgiving—the turkey, stuffing, steamy rice smothered in your gravy, and Papa's striped bass sashimi that he'd just caught laid out next to Auntie Lila's apple pie—it all came flooding back to me. And I used it, the memory, put it into my character, played it right to the camera—and I nailed it. I nailed it. *(Beat)* When I saw the rough cut, though. My face wasn't even part of the scene. *(Pause)* I thought about this house a lot. This house. You.

DOROTHY: Why didn't you just come home then?

MAT: I couldn't.

DOROTHY: You didn't want to.

Fish

Head

Soup

MAT: I couldn't, not until now.

DOROTHY: What do you mean, "couldn't"? I don't understand you, Mat.

(Pause.)

MAT: My work, Mama? In the industry? It's not easy, okay?

DOROTHY: Well, nothing is easy, I've told you that, Mat. You can't be afraid to work . . .

MAT: No, no, this has nothing to do with that, please . . . I want to ask you something. *(MAT guides her to a seat.)*

DOROTHY: You okay? You all right, Mat? You in trouble?

MAT: No, no, nothing like that. *(Pause. Seated.)* I got this thing I want to do. *(Beat)* I want to make a movie. A small independent feature, nothing too extravagant. And it can be good, good, Mama.

DOROTHY: But you already made one.

MAT: Yeah, but not my own. See, see everybody uses you, makes you do things you don't want to . . .

DOROTHY: No one can make you do something if you don't . . .

MAT: I WANT TO MAKE . . . *(Beat. Tries to calm down.)* I want to make my own movie. Okay? About people like you and me. Japanese Americans. I want people to see us. Know who we really are. And you can't wait for someone else to do it for you because they don't know how—they twist it up, make it something they want to see, make it a lie . . .

DOROTHY: Nobody's lying, why would they lie . . .

MAT: Mama? Mama? Like home movies, like our own home movies of this family. Everybody else, they look at the screen, it can be their family. What about us? Dad's Papa? Your Mama? Up there, our own home movies. *(Beat)* I need some money.

DOROTHY *(cautious)*: All right. How much?

MAT: A hundred thousand dollars.

DOROTHY: What?

MAT: I know it's a lot, but it's only a loan.

DOROTHY: You want how much—a hundred thousand dollars? *Fish*

(We hear VICTOR *hammering, coming from deep in the* *Head* *house.* MAT *pulls out loan papers.)*

MAT: A mortgage, you take a second mortgage, you'll get *Soup* it back, I promise. And the timing is right for something like . . . *(Continues.)*

DOROTHY *(overlapping)*: What, a mortgage—what are you . . .

MAT: . . . this, Japan is emerging—and I can play the lead, ME, I'd be perfect for it. I've been to the bank already and talked to them. All we *(pulls out papers)* need to do is shoot ten minutes of the film, then we show it to PBS and our Japanese investors and they'll put up . . . *(Continues.)*

DOROTHY *(overlapping)*: What? What's this? . . . *(Calling)* Victor! Victor, stop it! I can't sign this, Mat. I can't . . . *(Continues.)*

MAT: . . . the rest of the money and I can pay you right back. I just need you to sign the papers and we'll . . .

DOROTHY: . . . sign this, PAPA'S GOT TO SIGN IT! *(Silence.)*

MAT: Yeah, but Papa . . . He can't sign . . .

DOROTHY: I'm not going to sign something like this, I can't. What's gotten into you, Mat? Look at you, look at the way you're . . . What's gotten into you?

*(*DOROTHY *exits.* MAT *turns to look at* PAPA. *Dim to darkness.)*

*(*VICTOR *lit. Wearing dark suit, on limo phone.)*

VICTOR: No, no, this group didn't want to—Jesse, I'm not going to force them if they don't want to go. I mean, not all Japanese men wanna look at naked white women, okay? I'll pick them up later at the golf course. What? Yes, yes, I like my job, Jesse. I like it a lot. I'm sorry, okay? It's my fault, all right? "We all have to make a living," yes, I know—What? The college girls? Yeah, they were very nice, I took them all over—they just wanted to go shopping so I—I know I don't speak Japanese, but they spoke English so—I mean, we laughed about it—I try to speak and it comes out all mixed up, I look Japanese but I act kinda funny—what? They thought I was—what? Retarded? *(Dim to darkness on* VICTOR.*)*

(Lights up on the house. Early evening. MAT *puts a pen into* PAPA's *hand, carefully closing his fingers around it. Notices the loan papers need a backing, looks around. Sees his picture sitting on the* obutsudan *[Buddhist shrine] and grabs it, placing the papers on top of his photo. Sets them in* PAPA's *lap.* MAT *taps the papers to get* PAPA's *attention.* PAPA *looks down, stares for a beat. Then drops his pen hand and looks at* MAT *with a blank expression.* MAT *in frustration yanks the loan papers off his photograph.* PAPA *looks down at the photo of* MAT *and begins to move his hands up and down as if snagging.* MAT *notices. Gets an idea. Takes the photo, puts it in front of his own face and moves to the center of the room.* PAPA *leans forward following the photo, continuing to snag.* MAT *pulls the photo away, revealing his face.* PAPA *stares. Then starts slowly to snag again.* VICTOR *enters and sees him. Stands by the entrance to see what* MAT's *going to do.* MAT *starts to get down on his hands and knees.)*

VICTOR *(entering)*: What are you going to do?

*(*MAT *realizes* VICTOR's *there.)*

MAT: I just want to try something.

VICTOR: Where's Mama?

MAT: She's in the back.

*(*VICTOR *moves to protect* PAPA.*)*

MAT: Just let me try something, okay, Victor? All right? I just want to try one thing.

(Pause. VICTOR *moves back.* MAT *slowly begins to crawl towards* PAPA.*)*

MAT: Papa? Papa? You caught me. Look, it's Mat, your son. You caught me, reel me . . . *(Continues.)*
(MAT on knees in front of PAPA wiggling like a hooked fish.)
PAPA *(overlapping, upset)*: No, no, Mat's not my son, Mat's NOT my son. Victor's my son, Victor's my son . . .
MAT: . . . in! Reel me in, Papa! You hooked me good, drag me in kicking and . . .
VICTOR *(overlapping, pushing MAT away)*: Get away from him! Get the hell away from him! *(VICTOR goes to comfort the upset PAPA.)*
MAT: I just want to try something, Jesus, what's the problem, huh?
PAPA *(clinging)*: Victor, Victor . . . *(Continues.)*
VICTOR *(overlapping)*: You're getting him upset. It's okay, Papa. It's okay.
MAT *(overlapping)*: So he gets upset, so what? He's crazy now, Victor. Why not try anything, huh? Maybe he needs to get upset, shook up?
PAPA: . . . Victor, Victor, Victor . . .
(MAT shoves his face right in front of PAPA's.)
MAT: AHHH!
PAPA: AHHH! Mama?! Mama?! I want . . . *(Continues.)*
VICTOR *(shoving him away)*: Mat! Get the hell away!
MAT: Why not shock him? Why not . . . *(Continues.)*
PAPA: . . . Mama home! I want Mama home! Mama! Mama . . .
VICTOR *(overlapping)*: Shhh, shhh, it's okay, Papa, it's okay, I'm here, Victor's here.
MAT: . . . shock therapy? What do we got to lose, Victor? Why the hell not try anything? Huh? Anything?
(Silence. MAT watches VICTOR embracing PAPA and rocking him in his arms.)
MAT: You like him like this.
(VICTOR stares at MAT.)

MAT: No, no, you do.

VICTOR: You're nuts.

MAT: Christ, you like him just this way, don't you?

VICTOR: Just stay away from him, okay? You stay away from him.

    (MAT starts to move between VICTOR and PAPA.)

MAT: Victor and Papa, hiding out at home. You're both happy as clams, huh? Don't have to go anywhere, don't have to see anybody.

(VICTOR tries to get back next to PAPA but MAT won't let him.)

VICTOR: I don't like him like this.

(MAT begins to shove VICTOR with his chest each time VICTOR tries to get to PAPA. The shove quickly develops into a form of chest butting. This goes on while they continue to talk. VICTOR holds his own all through the following and even challenges MAT, though it is clear MAT has the psychological edge.)

MAT: Yes you do, admit it.

VICTOR: No, I don't, Mat, no, no, I don't.

MAT: Yes you do.

VICTOR: I don't.

MAT: You do . . .

(They are now fully into butting chests. They stop after each encounter, pulling back to opposing positions. Stare at each other for a beat, then charge. Arms pulled back, bumping each other more and more violently until they are jumping into the air and ramming into each other's bodies.)

DOROTHY *(off)*: Mat? Victor? What's going on? I don't want you kids breaking anything out there. Victor, you're the older one, you make sure Mat doesn't get into trouble. And Mat, don't you hurt your older brother. You hear me? Mat? Victor?

(VICTOR, who has been getting the worst of this, suddenly explodes and knocks MAT down, using what is

▲

obviously a trained combat maneuver. DOROTHY *enters just at this moment.)*

VICTOR: You fucking asshole! You goddamn fucking asshole! DIE, YOU FUCKING GOOK!

*(*VICTOR *has* MAT *in a stranglehold.* DOROTHY *looks on in horror. Blackout.)*

*(*PAPA *lit.)*

PAPA: Fish? Hah! When my own papa and I fished we'd chum with everything—throw in old rotten potatoes, fish guts, corn, old hamburger—hell, they'd have to come around. But sometimes they just wouldn't bite. Nothing would work. Then my old man would start to sing this song. He had a big voice, it could fill up a room. But this song was quiet, very old. And when he sang it, it was like someone else was singing. And it came from someplace so deep inside of him I was scared I would fall in and get lost. *(Starts to sing. Then stops abruptly. Upset.)* That's my land! That's my land! Get off my land! Get off my— *(Abruptly stops. Transition into talking.)* He used to say if you sing good enough, then all the fish would come out of hiding. Yeah, come right out. And then you catch 'em, take 'em home, and eat the damn suckers! *(*PAPA *laughs loudly. Dim to darkness.)*

(Lights up on the house. MAT *and* VICTOR *jerk away from each other and go sprawling onto the ground. Silence.* MAT *rubs his neck,* VICTOR *sits in a daze.* PAPA *sits in his chair.* DOROTHY *moves between them.)*

MAT *(catching breath)*: It's okay, it's okay, Mom.

DOROTHY: Victor?

MAT: Mom, it's okay, I can handle him.

DOROTHY: Victor? You all right?

MAT: Mom, I can . . .

DOROTHY: Shut up, Mat. Victor?

VICTOR: Go, Mama, get out. Just get outta here. Go.

(Silence. DOROTHY *stares at them, then exits.)*

MAT: Victor? Victor? Just a little roughhousing. Brothers having a little fun. We just got a little carried away, that's all. But it's all right, it's all right, Victor. I know, I know. You don't have to be a gook. You don't have to think of yourself like Papa does. You don't have to be like him. You don't. *(Beat)* I was in Japan. Japan. And I had an incredible experience there. You wouldn't believe what . . .

VICTOR: "Hakujin manko shitai?" Do you like white pussy?

MAT: What?

VICTOR: You don't know anything.

MAT: It's an incredible country, Victor. Okay, okay, I was only there five days, but . . .

VICTOR *(overlapping, muttering)*: Five days, five days . . .

MAT *(continuing)*: . . . everyone, everyone—get this—looks like us. Yeah, just like us. It's wild. Black hair and everything, just like you and . . .

VICTOR: They're assholes. They're ass—

MAT: What do you mean, assholes? We got the same blood. The same blood. Our father's father's father was the same father. Some guy like Mifune, wielding . . . *(Continues.)*

VICTOR *(overlapping)*: He was a poor starving farmer clawing at the ground.

MAT: . . . his sword around, "Hah! Hah!" Our mother's mother's mother was the . . . *(Continues.)*

VICTOR *(overlapping)*: Eating insects and roots because the land was dried up and dead.

MAT: . . . the same mother. Reaching across—kimono gently flapping in the breeze. We're family. Don't you see, Victor? We're all the same . . .

VICTOR: Family? Family? What about this family? THIS family. Not those goddamn Japanese. They don't care about you, Mat. You're just a retarded JA gook to them. And I am not a gook. I am not a . . . *(Blackout.)*
(Viet Cong soldier lit. Raised gun, about to shoot

VICTOR. VICTOR, *in pool of light, stares wide-eyed
with terror. Blackout.)*

(Lights up full on VICTOR, MAT, *and house.)*

VICTOR *(mumbling rapidly to himself a Buddhist prayer)*:
Namu Amida Butsu, Namu Amida Butsu, Namu Amida
Butsu . . .

MAT: Victor? Victor? *(No response)* Victor.

*(*VICTOR *stops and turns to* MAT.*)*

MAT: Picture this, picture this. When I get off the plane in
Tokyo, I'm hit by a sea of faces. These faces. Everywhere I
look. The cab driver yelling at me, the bar hostess trying to
pick me up, the cop telling me to move along—listen to me,
listen to me—in the newspapers, on magazine covers, up
on the billboards . . . yellow skin, flat noses, tight eyes,
everywhere, everywhere I fucking look! Victor, Victor, I
can't take it, I nearly pass out. I stumble into the hotel,
stagger to my room, close the curtains, turn out the lights.
My mind is swimming, I need to unwind. I flick on the TV.
I can't believe it. A baseball game and Dwight Gooden is
Japanese! I run to the bathroom and throw water on my
face. I look into the mirror. The face, the face staring back
at me. Who is this guy? The nose, the nose . . . It's not
pointy and huge, but it has a subtle turn and a size that is
just right. And the black hair. It seems strong, the deep
richness so potent—a lighter color would seem washed
out. And the eyes, the single fold. How clever, how perfect.
A double eyelid seems overdone, gauche—less is more.

*(*VICTOR *touches his own face.)*

Who is this good-looking guy staring back at me? He
could be a movie star. *(Beat)* We could be movie stars, Victor. You and me, we can be movie stars, not gooks, movie
stars.

*(*VICTOR *stares at* MAT. *As lights face to black,* MAT *is
isolated in a light.)*

[END OF ACT ONE]

Saturday night.
VICTOR *lit in pool of light. Sits bolt upright in bed with a*
Viet Cong soldier pointing a gun in his face. Blackout.

VICTOR *lit in pool of light. Sits bolt upright in bed with* MAT
standing over him, shaking him by the collar.

MAT: Victor, Victor, I got it—I couldn't sleep so I been drinking coffee, you know, drinking, thinking about stuff and I
got it. Carp blood. Yeah, carp blood. *(Continues.)*
  *(*VICTOR *tries to orient himself.)*
  I was talking to this Japanese guy in a bar—he's a priest
or something of one of those new religions—he said the
blood of Japanese carp, you know, koi, the real old ones,
has special chemical properties. Special chemical properties that heal certain types of mental illness. Papa? Papa's
problem? Maybe we can help him. I mean, I didn't believe
him, "Nah, come on." He said, "Hey, then how come these
damn fish live to be a hundred years old?" Huh, Victor,
huh?
  *(*VICTOR *starts to pay attention.)*
MAT: Victor? Remember that old koi in the fishpond at the
Buddhist Church? You used to be able to make him come
to you like a pet dog—what was its name, what the hell
was its . . . Moe! Yeah, Moe, that was it, 'cause its head
looked like Moe's hair cut. It's an old Japanese koi, Victor.
Brought from Japan. And its blood, maybe it can heal
Papa.
  *(*MAT *stares at* VICTOR. *Dim to darkness.)*

PAPA *lit, picking up earth and feeling it, inhaling its rich smell.*

Fish

PAPA: They said nothing would grow here. But my papa? Jinzo Iwasaki, fresh off the boat? He had dreams so big and *Head* a heart so full, not even the hakujin* landowners could turn him away. "Here's a few worthless acres, go 'head and *Soup* farm it," they laughed. Papa took some seed, put it into his clenched brown fist and drove it into the soil. The black peat dirt swirled up around his head like a swarm of friendly butterflies. "This is good, this is good growing soil," he thought to himself. He raised his fist and drove it in again. Up sprang tomatoes! Asparagus! And potatoes, bigger and tastier than anyone had ever seen! Acres and acres of potatoes as far as the eye could . . .

(DOROTHY lit upstage from him.)

DOROTHY: Papa, Mrs. Davidson called. She said you didn't show up. You keep doing that you're going to lose another house. We can't afford that . . . *(Notices* PAPA *trying to hide his hands full of soil)* You went out to the farm again, didn't you? They're going to have you arrested if you go out there, they warned you . . .

PAPA: From over there, to over there, that's all Grandpa's . . .

DOROTHY: Papa, Papa, please! *(Beat)* I know you tried. But there were only a few acres left after the war, what could you do with them? And with your father, the way he was . . .

PAPA: It's my land, it's my land, Mama.

DOROTHY: It's not your land, Papa. *(Beat)* You're a gardener now. A gardener.

(DOROTHY turns and exits. PAPA *senses that there is something diseased about the soil. Drops it and tries frantically to wipe it off his hands.* PAPA *dims to darkness.)*

*Caucasian.

Fish

Head

Soup

"Like A Rolling Stone" brought up loud over the house speakers. Lights up on MAT *and* VICTOR *cruising along in* MAT's *convertible. Night. Both wearing dark sunglasses, heavy coats. Wind blowing in their faces.* MAT's *laughing, singing along with the radio, having a grand time.* VICTOR *is trying to have a good time, mumbling the words and moving awkwardly to the rhythm.*

MAT: You feel good? You feel good? I feel good, real good. Victor? You feel good? You feel goooood!! . . . *(*MAT *turns hard into a turn at high speed, wheels screeching. Then back onto a straightaway.)* Ha-hah! You feel good, you feel good?

VICTOR *(cautiously)*: Yeah, yeah, I do.

MAT: Ah, I feel great. I feel really . . . GREAAAT!! . . . *(Turns hard into another turn. Then back onto a straightaway.)* Ahhh! . . . Like old times, huh? Just like old times . . .

*(*MAT *takes his hands off the wheel and slaps* VICTOR *affectionately on the back.* VICTOR *notices and grabs the wheel.)*

MAT *(laughing, taking the wheel back)*: Ah man, I feel great . . .

*(*MAT *brings the car to a screeching halt. Turns radio off. They admire the night vista.)*

MAT *(taking off his dark glasses)*: Whew! Would you look at that. Huh? Look at that. City lights!

VICTOR: Not too much tule fog, huh.

*(*MAT *notices* VICTOR *still has his dark glasses on, leans over and taps them gently.* VICTOR *sheepishly takes them off.* MAT *lights up a cigarette.)*

MAT *(laughing)*: 'Member that time Mom and Dad took us to the drive-in to see that movie *The Mole People*? 'Member, 'member, *The Mole People*? And how we were so scared we couldn't sleep, so I crawled into your bed?

VICTOR: That was scary. They were all bumpy looking.

MAT: We went to sleep holding onto each other for dear life. The next morning when Mom found us we were still hold-   *Fish* ing each other.

VICTOR: Yeah.   *Head*

(They share a quiet laugh.)

MAT: You want a smoke?   *Soup*

VICTOR *(shaking head)*: Un-uh.

(Pause.)

MAT: You weren't really scared, were you?

(VICTOR doesn't follow.)

MAT: You weren't scared. Of the mole people.

VICTOR: Yeah, I was.

MAT: Nah, nah—you just pretended to be so I wouldn't feel bad. You let me crawl into bed with you. Hold onto you. *(Beat)* Hell, I was scared shitless—those mole people, whoa, get outta here—they looked ugly, man, ugly!

(They laugh. Calm down, stare out at the vista, enjoying the moment.)

VICTOR: Mat? Do you sometimes . . . Do you sometimes kinda not know where you . . . *(VICTOR is silent.)*

MAT: Victor?

(Slight pause.)

VICTOR: When I was in 'Nam? You know when I was hit by some Viet Cong mortar fire? They wouldn't pick me up, the medics. I was lying there, bleeding all over, they were picking everyone else up. I kept screaming, "I'm an American, I'm a Japanese American, I'm not VC." But they wouldn't pick me up. They walked right past me. They thought I was . . .

(A carload of youths drives by.)

YOUTHS *(voices all overlapping)*:

  (Youth 1) Hey Japs, it's some Jap boys. Don't you know it's freezing, dumbshits!? It's NIPPY! It's NIPPY!!

  (Youth 2) Fuckin' Vietnamese, we should've killed you all over there. Gooks! Gooks! Gooks!

(Youth 3) We don't want your fucking slant-eyed
Fish   money! This is America not JAPLAND—go buy Mexico!
       MAT *(out of control)*: FUCK YOU! GET OUTTA THAT
Head   CAR AND I'LL BREAK YOUR FUCKIN' FACE.
       YEAH YOU, FUCK YOU! COME ON— *(MAT notices*
Soup   VICTOR *is silent.)* Victor, come on, tell 'em "Fuck you!" Go
       on, say it! Say it, Victor, say it!
       (VICTOR can't. The youths drive away, shouting.)
       MAT: FUCK YOU! *(MAT is shaking. Trying to calm down.)*
       Victor, what the hell's wrong with you? Huh? What the
       hell's wrong with you? You don't have to be scared of those
       punks. You can speak up, you don't have to be silent. I was
       in Japan. Hey, we're a part of a voice the whole world is
       listening to. If they give you a bad time, just say, "Fuck
       you."
       (VICTOR remains silent and rigid. MAT eases off.)
       MAT: Victor? Victor, you okay? Victor?
       (VICTOR is silent. MAT feels bad.)
       MAT: I'm sorry I yelled at you, okay? I shouldn't have yelled
       at you. You're all right. Don't worry, you're all right. Vic-
       tor? Victor?
       (Pause.)
       VICTOR *(quietly)*: I'm glad you're back. Mat? I'm glad.
       MAT: Like old times, huh. The Iwasaki Brothers.
       (VICTOR nods.)
       MAT: I'm going to make everything right, too. For you,
       Mama and Papa—the whole family. Okay? And I'm not
       going to leave you behind. I'm not going to forget you. You
       don't have to be afraid. *(Starting up engine. Putting sun-
       glasses on* VICTOR *and himself.)* Hey, I was a little worried
       about coming back. Well, because of the way I left and
       everything. But you know, maybe me dying was the best
       thing. I mean it, really, maybe it was the best thing for the
       family. Yeah, the best thing.
       (VICTOR's mood changes, upset. Takes off sunglasses.)

MAT: Besides, we're movie stars now, Victor. Movie stars . . . (MAT *turns up the radio and revs up the engine. The Doors' "Break on Through" comes on.* MAT *shouts over the sound.*) And stars do only one thing . . . (*Pulls out flashlight and shines it on themselves*) Shine! Shine! Shine! (*Dim to darkness on* MAT *and* VICTOR. *"Break on Through" transitions into sutra chanting.*)

Fish

Head

Soup

(*Night. The Buddhist Church koi pond. We hear Buddhist sutra chanting.* MAT *enters, flashing his light around.* VICTOR *follows, silent and preoccupied. He holds a bag of potato chips.*)

MAT: There must be some kind of service going on. What is it, a funeral or something? God, this is weird, this is really weird. I haven't been back here in years. I think the last time was Uncle Gordon's omairi service or whatever you call that three-year thing after someone dies—Hey, remember Obon, all the dancing and fat cousin Brenda in her kimono trying to do those Japanese moves? She looked like fuckin' Godzilla out there. (*Noticing*) All right, here we go, here we go—yeah, the pond. Old Moe's here, he's here—I can feel it . . . (*Hears something, grabs* VICTOR *and pulls him into the shadows*) Shhh! (*Checking, decides it's clear.* VICTOR *jerks his arm away from* MAT's *clutch.*) We're all right as long as we don't make too much noise. Okay, go ahead.

(MAT *pushes* VICTOR *forward.*) Go ahead and call him. Go on, call him.

(VICTOR *is silent.*)

MAT: Call him, Victor. Call him—you know, with the song, the song.

VICTOR: What song?

MAT: Jesus fucking Christ—the song, remember the song Papa used to say would make the fish come out. You used to sing it. Moe would come tearing out from under the lilies, tongue hanging out—and he'd come right up to you and you'd pet him. Yeah, you'd goddamn pet him.

(VICTOR is silent.)

MAT *(angry)*: Give me the carp food. Come on, come on, give me the potato chips. Give me the goddamn potato chips! *(Grabs them from VICTOR. Starts angrily to toss the chips into the pond.)* Moe! Moe! Get your butt over here. It's Larry and Curley! *(Frustrated, crumples the bag)* I know he's out there, Victor. He's out there. You gonna do it or what? Huh? You gonna do it?

(VICTOR is silent.)

MAT: Okay, okay, be that way—I'll do it myself. You just stand there like an asshole, I'll do it. Get some rocks and bombard him *(exiting while speaking)* in the deep end, scare the shit out of him and he'll jump right out of the water!

(MAT exits. The sutra chanting continues in background. VICTOR stands for a moment staring out into the darkness. Then, slowly begins to sing the song. Softly, barely audible, then growing in volume. It seems to weave in and out of the sutra chanting. VICTOR spots Moe. Bends down, carefully reaches out, and begins to pet the fish. Continues to sing, his voice intoning a song that melds with the sutra chanting. MAT appears and stops when he sees VICTOR. Starts to approach but VICTOR motions him to stay back.)

MAT *(whispering)*: Grab him! Grab him!

VICTOR: Why?

MAT: Why? So we can make Papa well, dummy.

VICTOR: Why do you want to do that?

MAT: Why, why?—grab the thing before it gets . . .

VICTOR *(threateningly)*: I'll scare it away.

MAT: Jesus, don't, don't—for the family, for the family— okay? okay?—grab it now.

VICTOR: You don't care about the family. When . . .

(Continues.)

MAT *(overlapping)*: Victor, I'm the one, I'm the one who can
make us all proud of the Iwasaki name . . .   *Fish*

VICTOR: . . . did you ever care about this family? Huh?

MAT: I need the money, okay, I need the money! *(Pause)* I need   *Head*
the money to make a movie. If we're going to be movie
stars, you gotta make a movie, right? That thing that hap-   *Soup*
pened to me in Tokyo? That's the story—a Sansei discovers
his roots. I need Papa to get well so he can sign these
papers. *(Pulling them out)* I talked to Mom about it, it's all
okay, now grab the fish, Victor, grab . . .

VICTOR: Stay back! You talked to Mama? Wait, what are
those?

MAT: Jesus Christ, Jesus Christ, to the house—it's only a
loan, a temporary thing.

VICTOR: The house?

MAT: Yeah, yeah—a loan on a second mortgage, everybody does it all the time. It's no big deal—once this movie
breaks . . .

VICTOR *(splashing the water, scaring the fish away)*: AHH!
(Sutra chanting stops. Silence.)

MAT *(incredulous)*: Why? Why'd you do that, Victor? *(No
response)* Victor, why'd you do it? Huh? Why the hell . . .

VICTOR: They dragged that river for one week. One whole
week before they gave up. They wanted to quit but Papa
wouldn't let them. He kept hollering and screaming . . .
(Continues.)

MAT *(overlapping)*: Victor, what the hell you talking about?
Victor? Victor?

VICTOR: . . . that he wasn't going to let the river take his son.
"I want him back, I want my son back." I think all the skin-
divers and people with equipment felt sorry for him so they
kept on. Mama and I thought it was no use but we were too
scared to say anything . . . *(Continues.)*

MAT *(overlapping)*: Victor, I don't want to hear this. I don't
want to hear this right now. Victor? Victor? Not now . . .

VICTOR: . . . By the end he had no voice. Just a raspy wheeze that came out of his mouth. Finally we got him home but he wouldn't sleep. He just sat by the window holding your fishing pole.

(Sutra chanting begins again.)

VICTOR: I got up during the night to check on him. He was gone. I figured he went back to the river, so I went down there. It was so foggy but I could see him. He was . . . *(Continues.)*

(PAPA lit, standing on his overstuffed chair. Mimes casting out, begins snagging. VICTOR and MAT turn and watch as VICTOR describes the action.)

VICTOR: . . . out on the boat. His Coleman lamp was burning so it cast this strange glow around him, like watching him in his own dream. And as I watched him I could see he had his line in and was snagging. He would reel a bit, then snag. Reel a bit, then snag. And then it dawned on me. He was trying to catch you. I just watched. All night. I just stood and watched him. Standing there with this vacant look in his eyes, snagging away.

(PAPA dims to darkness. Sound cue ends.)

VICTOR: And that's the way he's been, Mat, ever since then. Ever since you killed yourself. So don't you come back here and tell me how you care about this family. How you . . .

MAT *(overlapping)*: No, no, you can't blame me, he was heading that way all along . . .

VICTOR *(continues)*: . . . want to make Papa well. You don't care about this . . .

(PAPA lit in chair.)

PAPA: MAT, VICTOR, WAIT!

(MAT and VICTOR turn toward PAPA.)

PAPA: I see you playing with the kids in the new neighborhood. It's all right to do things together. Have hakujin friends. But if anything ever happens, they'll turn on you. You can't trust white people. *(Beat)* Now, go play.

(MAT and VICTOR *look at each other. As they dim to darkness,* PAPA *goes to half-light.* DOROTHY *lit.* PAPA *watches.* DOROTHY *removes her robe to reveal a nightgown.)*

DOROTHY: It's hard to explain. I guess when I'm with you I feel . . . I feel things are right. *(Listening)* Well, yeah, "right"—I said it's hard to explain . . . *(Pause. Uncomfortable.)* When I was in camp, relocation camp? You don't mind if I talk about this, do you? I mean, you asked so . . . *(Pause. Difficult.)* I was only a young girl—nine, ten years old. And I remember thinking, "We must have done something wrong." Everyone kept saying, "How come we're in here, we didn't do anything." But at night, as I lay in bed, I kept thinking, "We must have done something. Something bad. I mean, why else would they punish us like this?" I know that's stupid, I was only a kid . . . *(Shrugs, embarrassed)* When I'm with you I feel . . . I feel things are the way they're supposed to be. Right. Safe. I feel special.

(DOROTHY *dims to darkness. Then,* PAPA *follows.)*

MAT *lit on phone, holding a gift-wrapped box. Later that same night at the Iwasaki house.*

MAT: What? The Japanese have pulled out? But you said . . . Yeah, I know these things change quickly but . . . We still have PBS, right? We still have them, they're still interested in the idea? Good, good . . . Don't worry, please, okay, please, I'm working on 'em, I'm working on 'em. Okay, I'll call you later, bye.

(Hangs up. DOROTHY *enters from the back. Dressed in robe.)*

DOROTHY: Where's Victor?

(MAT's *startled.)*

MAT: Don't scare me like that, okay? *(Composing himself)* Sorry about, you know, earlier. We didn't break anything, did we?

DOROTHY: Un-uh. I heard the car drive off. I came out to check and you were both gone. Where'd you go at this hour?

MAT: We had to work some things out. Victor and me. *(Noticing* DOROTHY's *hair and earrings)* You go out again?

DOROTHY: I couldn't sleep. I ran some errands. Where is he? Is he okay?

MAT: He's fine, Mama.

DOROTHY: Where is he, then? I don't want you getting him into any trouble. The way he is and everything.

MAT: I'm not going to get him into any trouble. He's just walking back.

DOROTHY: Why's he walking back?

MAT: He wanted some fresh air, okay? Trust me, he's fine— he doesn't need my help and I don't need his. *(Awkward pause.* MAT *remembers the box and offers it to* DOROTHY.) It's for you. I forgot about it in all the excitement, coming home and everything.

*(*DOROTHY *doesn't move.)*

MAT: Go on, take it. It's for you, Mama. I got it for you special.

*(*DOROTHY *reluctantly takes it.)*

MAT: It's from L.A. I bought it down there, Rodeo Drive. The latest. A Hanae Mori. I thought it would look good on you.

*(*DOROTHY *still hasn't moved to open it.)*

MAT: Please? Mama? Please open it.

*(*DOROTHY *finally gives in and opens it.)*

MAT *(gesturing towards it)*: The color and everything, I thought, you know . . .

(Silence. DOROTHY *fingers the fabric.)*

MAT: You like it?

*(*DOROTHY *is lost in her thoughts.)*

MAT: Mama?

DOROTHY: Yes, I do, yes.

MAT: You like it then? Huh? You like it, Mama?

DOROTHY *(moved)*: Yes, I like it. I like it very much, Mat.
(*Pause.*)
MAT: Try it on.
DOROTHY: Now?
MAT: Yeah, yeah, try it on. I want to see how it looks on you.
DOROTHY: I don't know . . .
MAT: Come on, come on. If you look good enough, you can
be my date.
DOROTHY: For what?
MAT: The Academy Awards.
(*They both laugh.* DOROTHY *decides to try it on. As she
goes to the hallway, she stops.*)
DOROTHY: Mat?
MAT: Yeah?
DOROTHY: I've been thinking about the money? You know
the loan? For the movie? I've got another idea.
MAT: Great, great, ah great, Mama. I knew you'd come
through for me.
(DOROTHY *turns and exits.*)
DOROTHY *(off)*: The house thing can't work, okay? But,
maybe we can talk to this friend of mine. Maybe he can
advise you. He's very good at these things.
(MAT *stares for a long moment in* DOROTHY's *direction.
Then begins to wander slowly around the house looking,
touching things.*)
DOROTHY *(off)*: How'd you know my size?
MAT: Still the same?
DOROTHY *(off)*: Yes. You remembered.
(MAT *continues to feel the textures of things, to inhale
their smells.*)
DOROTHY *(off)*: You know the movie? Mat?
(MAT *hears but doesn't respond.*)
DOROTHY: Mat?
MAT: Yes?
DOROTHY *(off)*: Your movie? Maybe you shouldn't do it just

about Japanese Americans. I mean, we were talking about
Fish　　this, my friend and I—who's interested in that kind of
thing? You should do a regular story. A more normal one.
Head　　Then people will want to go see it. Not just about Japanese
Americans, who's going to want to go see it, anyway. At
Soup　　least . . . *(Entering)* One white character, huh? You could
be his assistant or his best friend or something . . . *(DOR-
OTHY is quite stunning.)* What do you think?
(Pause.)
MAT: Nice, very nice.
(DOROTHY is feeling good. A small turn.)
MAT: The dress you had on last night? When you came in?
DOROTHY: Un-huh?
(MAT shakes head disapprovingly.)
MAT: You should never shop at the local mall here.
(DOROTHY moves to MAT.)
DOROTHY: Let's dance.
MAT: What?
DOROTHY: Like we used to. I want to dance.
*(Pause. MAT hesitates but is taken in by DOROTHY's
playfulness. She moves into his arms, and they dance
for a moment in silence.)*
DOROTHY: Remember Victor? He just couldn't ask a girl to
dance. He'd try and try . . .
MAT: Yeah, I remember.
DOROTHY: He wasn't like you, you were so popular with the
hakujin girls. Calling all hours of the day and night. I had
to call their parents, Papa wouldn't. Imagine, Caucasian
girls chasing my boy. *(Dancing, DOROTHY stares at MAT's
face.)*
MAT: What are you looking at?
DOROTHY: I just can't believe you're back. I'm sorry.
MAT: No, that's okay.
(DOROTHY adjusts his collar, straightens his hair.)

DOROTHY: We have to get you to shave, clean up . . . *(Staring, touching)* Your face—everything about it . . .

MAT: My face is your face.

DOROTHY *(laughing)*: Yes. *(DOROTHY whirls MAT around.)*

MAT: Whoo! That was an interesting move.

(DOROTHY laughs.)

MAT: Did he teach you that?

DOROTHY: What?

MAT: Did he teach you that move? When you were out dancing together?

(DOROTHY stops dancing.)

DOROTHY: I don't know what you're talking about.

MAT: Who is this guy you go out dancing with till all hours of the night?

DOROTHY: I have to work late at the restaurant.

MAT: Leaving Papa at home. I mean, what if he has an accident, falls over, or . . .

DOROTHY: Victor stays home with him. He takes care . . .

MAT: Victor can't take care of himself, how the hell is he going to take care of Papa?

DOROTHY: He's working now, he does all kinds of things around the house. He's . . . *(Continues.)*

MAT *(overlapping)*: I don't see anything. What the hell has he done? I don't see anything different. The only . . .
(Continues.)

DOROTHY: . . . always hammering away all the time, ripping things out and putting things in.

MAT: . . . thing I see is you running around like some goddamn seventeen year old in heat!

(Silence.)

DOROTHY: What was I supposed to do after you left, Mat? After you died? Talk to Victor? He just wants to bang away at the walls all day long. Talk to Papa? Hmph . . . Mama raised me for more refined things in life than taking food orders from people who don't even know what the food is.

Fish

Head

Soup

MAT: I'm back now and you stay at home. You stay at home
Fish   with Papa. I'm back and . . . *(Continues.)*

DOROTHY *(overlapping)*: What about Papa, Mat? What
Head   about Papa? You did that and the house isn't the same anymore. It's . . . *(Continues.)*

Soup   MAT: . . . everything's going to be just like it was. Just like it
was.

DOROTHY *(continuing)*: . . . never going to be the same. And
I like it this way, I like it just the way it is.

MAT: Who is this guy? Is this the guy you were going to introduce me to, huh? Who's supposed to help me make my
movie? Who is he, huh? Who is he?

DOROTHY: He takes me dancing, takes me to the best Japanese restaurants, we eat fugu—do you know what fugu
is, do you? It's poisonous blowfish. And that dress? You
said I bought at the local mall? He brought it back from
Tokyo, not L.A., Tokyo where he goes all the time to visit
the home office. *(Beat)* Mr. William Odell, William
Odell—he distributes Japanese ice cream. He collects Japanese swords, he studies . . . *(Continues.)*

(MAT starts to rip the dress off DOROTHY.)

MAT *(overlapping)*: Mama. Mama. Mama! I want *Mama*! I
WANT MAMA!

DOROTHY: . . . kendo. He looks like William Holden. William Holden and he knows more about Japanese culture
than I do. HE'S MORE JAPANESE THAN YOU ARE!

(Silence. DOROTHY stands there, dress torn.)

DOROTHY: I was standing there. The air was so still. I could
hear the voices of the workers calling to each other, they
seemed so far away. And I was so cold. The wet fog had
seeped into my bones, so cold. And I wanted to die. Not
Mat. Not my son. Me. I wanted to take your place. And I
kept thinking if I could only make myself smaller and
smaller it would be easier to die. And all the time I had this
image in my head of myself holding you in my arms, a little

baby, rocking you back and forth, back and forth . . . I
didn't have much—I wait on tables—but what I did have
I gave to you. Not Victor, I gave to you. Because I could see
the spark in your eyes, the Akari brightness, a willingness
to live, not be afraid. I remember holding your hand and
walking you through this house, you were five, six years
old. And as we walked I handed you things. This vase, it
was my ohi-ojiisan's, my great-grandfather's. I had you
hold it, feel it. This kakeji, this scroll, has been in my family
for generations. And this . . . I had you touch it, smell it, so
you would remember, so you would always know who you
were, where you came from. It wasn't much, but it was all
I had to give and I offered it to you. To you. And what did
you do? You threw it away. You killed yourself. You gave
me a terrible gift, but I accepted it. I lived. I survived, to
carry on the Akari name so these can be remembered, cher-
ished. You can't stop me from feeling this. You can't make
me die now. Not now. I am alive. *(Dim to darkness on* DOR-
OTHY *and* MAT.*)*

Fish

Head

Soup

We hear VICTOR's *voice softly singing. Sutra chanting
gradually brought up.*
    VICTOR *lit at pond, petting Moe.*

VICTOR: We're being overrun. I'm hit. Lying against a dirt
    ravine. And this young VC is coming towards me. He's all
    out of control, shooting everything—Bam! Bam! Bam!
    Wounded GIs, dead bodies—Bam! Bam! Bam! He's
    totally jacked up. I see him coming towards me and I can't
    move, my leg . . . Bam! Bam! He hits Jackson, blows half
    his body away. He looks at me. Our eyes lock. He raises his
    gun. He's terrified. He's looking at me. His gun is aimed
    right at my face. He's going to shoot, he's going to blow my
    fucking head off . . . *(Beat)* He lowers his gun, still looking
    at me, staring at me, at my face. My face. He runs off. He

didn't shoot me. He didn't kill me . . . *(Pause)* I am not the enemy. I am not the . . . *(Continues.)*

(VICTOR begins to beat himself more and more violently with his fists.)

VICTOR *(continuing)*: . . . enemy. I am not the enemy . . .

Lights up on the Iwasaki house. MAT *and* VICTOR.

VICTOR *(mumbling)*: Namu Amida Butsu, Namu Amida Butsu, Namu Amida Butsu . . .

MAT: How long has this thing with Mom been going on?

(VICTOR continues to mumble to himself.)

MAT: Victor!

(VICTOR stops, noticing MAT.)

VICTOR: It makes me feel good.

MAT: What?

VICTOR: "Namu Amida Batsu," that thing we used to say in church. I don't even know what it means, it just makes me feel . . .

MAT: Victor. How long has this thing with Mama been going on?

(Pause.)

VICTOR: What thing?

MAT: AAHH! *(Beat)* It's 3:00 in the morning and she went out again. She just ups and goes out. Where do you think she goes, Victor?

VICTOR: Ice cream?

MAT: Victor, Victor, Victor—what the hell's wrong with you? I mean, first you don't want to help Papa and now you pretend like you don't know Mom's stepping out on him. Mom and Papa used to have a good thing. We used to all sit down to dinner. We used to talk about this and that. It used to be good. What happened to this family, Victor? I leave and the whole goddamn thing falls apart.

VICTOR: I don't like you anymore.

MAT: What?

VICTOR: I said, "I don't like you anymore."   *Fish*

MAT: Ah, Jesus, not now, Victor, not now. I don't want to
hear this, I don't have time for . . .   *Head*

VICTOR: Fuck you.

MAT *(moving towards the bedroom)*: Great, great, you don't   *Soup*
like me, I get the picture.

(VICTOR *blocks* MAT's *way.*)

MAT: I want to check on Papa.

(VICTOR *doesn't move.*)

MAT: I was making some headway. He's going to sign the
papers, I'm going to make this movie.

(VICTOR *is silent.*)

MAT: GET OUT OF MY WAY! *(No response)* Okay, okay,
I'm through messing around. Get out of my way.

(VICTOR *pushes* MAT *back into the dining room table.*)

MAT: I don't want to hurt you. I'm warning you.

(VICTOR *begins to strangle* MAT.)

MAT: Victor? Victor, you're hurting me.

(VICTOR *pushes* MAT *down on the table continuing to
strangle the struggling* MAT.)

MAT: I can't breathe, Victor. I can't breathe . . . Victor, let
go . . . Victor . . .

(Blackout.)

(Lights up on MAT *and* VICTOR. MAT *is lying on the
table. He appears to be dead. Silence.* VICTOR *stares at*
MAT's *body.*)

VICTOR: "He's all right, he's going to be all right." They're
pulling the car out of the river. "He's all right, he always
lands on his feet." They find your jacket. "He's all right, he
always gets out of trouble." They find your shoes. "He's all
right, you'll see, you'll see" . . . *(Pause)* I believed in you. I
would've done anything for you, Mat, anything. Because
you were the one. I mean, no one had to point it out to me,
make me see it. You were better in school, better in sports,

better looking. You just were always the better one as long as I could remember. And as we got older? I mean everybody loved you. Not just Mom and Papa anymore, but the kids at school. I always used to think, "How does he do it? How come he's so comfortable with all those kids? I always feel intimidated around them. Like they have something over me—like everything they do is somehow the right way and I'm . . . less than them." But you? No, not Mat. Mat just struts in there one of the "in" crowd. Laughing loudly, making too much noise, drawing attention to himself. I don't want people to notice me, I want to blend in. But you, you were so good at it, sometimes I used to think, "My god, he's even out-whiting the other white kids." *(Pause)* I wanted to be just like you. I mean, you were beating them at their own game. But I couldn't be like you. I couldn't then, I can't now. *(Beat)* Stop making me feel so, so . . . Just go away. Just go away, Mat. *(Pause.* VICTOR *looks away from* MAT's *body.)*

Aaron Copland's Clarinet Concerto is gradually brought up. It evokes a mood of beautiful sadness. Lighting change. MAT, on the table, turns over onto his downstage side as if turning in his sleep. PAPA and DOROTHY enter. PAPA, appearing healthy and vigorous, playfully tousles VICTOR's hair. VICTOR in turn laughs at the teasing gesture and the two exchange a few playful boxing jabs. As a smiling DOROTHY moves to the table with the food, PAPA embraces her from behind and kisses her on the cheek. They take no notice of MAT on the table. PAPA, DOROTHY, VICTOR—all normal, happy, around the dinner table about to enjoy a meal. No utensils, everything mimed.

    MAT awakens and moves away from the table. For a moment he stands and watches, unsure of what to make of the situation. The other family members notice him and motion for him to join them. As MAT sits, they hand him food and he soon finds himself drawn into the activity of this warm family gathering. PAPA stops everyone and has them all join hands in

appreciation of the moment, then return to their meal. MAT is
overcome with joy. They're the perfect Japanese American   Fish
family. Perfect. They pass food, smile warmly at each other,
eat . . .   Head
    Then, slowly, MAT's expression changes to despair. He
leans back away from the table. As he does, the other family
members, who talk among themselves, go to half-light as MAT   Soup
remains lit in an isolated pool. He sadly watches them. The
music swells. Slow fade to black.

[END OF ACT TWO]

Sunday. DOROTHY *lit. Back turned, pulling a kimono on. Talking to her friend. In a "sex" hotel. Uncomfortable, but hiding it.*

DOROTHY: You want me to wear this? This is what you like? No, no, if this is what you want. I just didn't think—no, no, I like it, I like it, too. *(Adjusting the kimono)* My mother wanted me to marry him. It was always her idea. She wanted me to. "See this dish in front of you," she'd say—it was old hand-me-down stuff. "Don't believe your eyes. It's not cheap everyday ware, no, no, but an Imari plate—a high-toned, expensive Japanese plate. That's what you're really eating off of" . . . *(Interrupted by friend's suggestion. Uneasy.)* Okay . . . *(As she begins to loosen her hair, she continues.)* "Marry Togo Iwasaki's son, marry him, marry him. So they don't have as much as they used to. It's in the blood. The Iwasaki blood" . . . *(She is now very uneasy. She lets her hair loose so it falls to her shoulders.)* I'm just a little uncomfortable. Wearing this. Being in this kind of place. No, no, I don't mind, if this is what you want . . . What? The movie?
    *(*DOROTHY *picks up the remote and presses the button. We hear the sounds of a cheesy low-budget sound track.)*
FEMALE VOICE *(overtly sexual)*: Oooo . . . Come to Mama-san, big boy. Oooo . . .
    (DOROTHY *sees something on the TV screen that disturbs her. We begin to hear the sounds of love-making. She stares bewildered at the screen.)*
DOROTHY: Mat? Mat? . . .

(DOROTHY dims to darkness.)

Lights up on the house. MAT *on phone holding a towel around his tender neck.*

MAT: No, no, I don't want to hear this. Don't tell me this. You said PBS was interested, you said it was a done deal. "Redress"? So we're getting redress money for the camps, so what? "We're not politically hot anymore"? You're doing the *what*? The Black-Korean grocer controversy, it's more sexy? What is this, a beauty contest? Two minorities are better than one? Yeah, yeah, I'll bet you are. Well, you go 'head, go 'head and do it. I don't need you, I don't need PBS, I don't need the Japanese! *(MAT slams phone down.)*
    (VICTOR enters pushing PAPA in a wheelchair. VICTOR is very distracted.)
VICTOR: Mat? Mat? . . .
    (MAT ignores VICTOR and steers a clear path around him into the hallway.)
    (Pause.)
MAT *(off)*: Goddamnit, goddamnit!
    (MAT reenters.)
MAT: The toilet doesn't work, Victor. I thought you fixed the damn thing.
VICTOR: Mat?
MAT *(feeling his neck)*: Stay away, stay away from me . . . *(MAT goes to the sink to wash his hands. Turns the faucet, nothing comes out.)* No water, Victor, no water. This is a water faucet—water's supposed to be coming out of it. *(MAT goes over to pour himself some cold coffee.)*
VICTOR: You know what my job is? Mat, know what it is?
MAT: You drive people around, right?
VICTOR: At the Japanese hotel—you know what my job really is?
MAT: I'm happy you're working, okay, I've told you that.

VICTOR: They don't want to go see the port. They don't want to go see the Japanese American Cultural Center. You know where they want to go?

MAT: I don't have time for this, Victor. I don't . . . *(Continues.)*

VICTOR *(overlapping)*: They all want to go to those hotels. To go . . . *(Continues.)*

MAT *(overlapping)*: . . . want to hear this, I don't care about your sex life. Whatever you like is . . . *(Continues.)*

VICTOR: . . . into those rooms with those women. They have these TV screens and sometimes I watch. I watch . . .

MAT: . . . fine by me, guy, I don't care, I don't give a damn! *(Silence.)*

VICTOR: Mat, Mat, I'm ready to help Papa. I'm ready now. I think we should make him well, make Papa all right so Mama will come home. Mama will stay at home. Mama has to stay at home. Mat? What do you say, huh? What do you say?

(Silence. MAT *stares at* VICTOR.*)*

MAT: Now? You want to help him now? Just go away, just go . . . *(Continues.)*

VICTOR *(overlapping)*: Mat? Please? Mat . . .

MAT: . . . away, Victor. Just . . . fuck you. *(Beat, quietly)* "Fuck you"?

*(*VICTOR *stares at him for a moment. Then, turns and exits.* MAT *looks at* PAPA.*)*

Cross-fade to river area. As lights come up, MAT *wheels* PAPA *downstage to the river's edge.*

MAT: Well, here we are. God, it's cold. You okay? That's where Grandpa's farm used to be. *(Turning)* And the river. *(Pause, looking. Starts to laugh.)* Remember how Mama had me in that harness and she'd walk me around on the end of that dog leash. You, Victor, and Mama sitting there trying to quietly fish and I'd be pulling at the end of the leash trying to get away. She was afraid I'd wander off and fall in the water.

(MAT looks at PAPA, who stares out.)

MAT: The film deal is dead, Papa. You did it to me again, you satisfied? *(Beat)* Talk to me. Please. I know you can hear me. I know you can. You've got to talk to me. You've got to—Stop this! Stop fucking with my head! I know you can hear me! I know you're in there, so talk! TALK!

PAPA: Where's Victor? Where's Victor? Where's Victor?

(MAT stares at PAPA.)

PAPA: Where's Mama? Where's Mama? Mama? Mama?

MAT: She's out. She's out, Papa. She just stepped out for a bit but when we get back she'll be there. I'm sure of it.

PAPA *(upset)*: Mama? Mama?

MAT: Papa, don't worry, she'll be right back, don't worry. It's Mat. Your son. Mat, your son.

PAPA: Mat's not my son. Mat's not my son. Victor's my son. Victor's my son. Mat's not my son.

(Silence. MAT stares at PAPA.)

MAT: Remember that time downtown? Are you listening to me? Are you listening? Remember that time downtown when that big guy came up to you? "Hey, you a China-man?" You mumbled something and pushed Victor and me into the backseat of the car. You had this funny look on your face all tight. "No, no, excuse me." Victor and I had our noses pressed against the window waiting for you to yell at this ugly man. To put this ugly mean man in his place. "What, you one of those people from Ja-pan? You a Jap?" He was laughing and having a good time, a crowd had gathered. You finally got in the car but the man was lying on the hood now. I kept thinking, "Why isn't Papa yelling like he does at home or when Mr. Nakamura fixes the car wrong?" But you just sat there, stiff, staring ahead. Are you listening to me?

Fish

Head

Soup

Fish

Head

Soup

All the way home, no one said anything. And I remember my face feeling all hot. Feeling ashamed. Victor and I never talked about it. And I began to hate you. Hate you because you were my daddy and every time I looked at you I saw you being humiliated, shuffling like a houseboy in front of that man. And you made me feel that same feeling.

So, I hung out with whites. Yes, I made fun of other "oriental" kids, cracked jokes about them—hell, I wasn't one of them. I mean, why would I want to be like one of those quiet shuffling cowards? Why would I want to be like my papa? Papa who sits here while Mama goes off and . . .

And so one night I left. Nah, one night I killed myself. Yes, I just killed myself off.

(Pause.)

But Papa? I'm back. And you gotta help me this time. This time, you gotta help me, you can't leave me in the backseat. Papa? You owe *(grabbing* PAPA *by shirt and shaking him)* me. *You owe me!* YOU OWE ME!

(Silence. PAPA *stares at* MAT. MAT *gives up and lets go of* PAPA. MAT *and* PAPA *dim to darkness.)*

Koi pond. VICTOR *enters with a flashlight. Stops, stares out at the pond. Agitated. Proceeds to take off his shoes and socks, to roll up his pant legs. Now he's ready. Takes out a white towel and holds it in front of him, the ends gripped with both hands. Looks out at the water for a beat. Then, he quickly jerks both ends making a snapping sound. Blackout.*

Lights up at the Iwasaki house. MAT *throws his clothes into his carry bag.* DOROTHY *watches him.*

DOROTHY: I know about the "movie."

MAT: Yeah? It doesn't matter anymore, Mom.

DOROTHY: I know about the "movie."

MAT: I don't care, though. I don't need this family's help. I'll figure out a way to do it on my own. I don't need . . .

DOROTHY: The one you did in Japan. I know about it. Someone told me, Mat. The movie you did in Tokyo. Someone told me all about it.

Fish

(Silence. DOROTHY *and* MAT *stare at each other.)*

Head

MAT *(going back to packing)*: Independent films can show things big-budget movies can't show. I mean, European films show that kind of stuff . . . *(Continues.)*

Soup

DOROTHY *(overlapping)*: Stop it, all right, Mat, stop it, will you? *(Beat)* Just stop lying, stop lying to me, please . . .

MAT: . . . all the time, it's an art film. It's not for everybody—I mean, most people aren't accustomed to seeing that kind of thing but in the independent film industry it goes on all the . . .

DOROTHY *(slapping* MAT *hard)*: STOP IT! *(Silence)* How could you? Mat? How could you?

MAT: Mama, you don't know. You don't . . . *(Picking up the vase)* The "Akari brightness" . . . *(Can't finish line)* I get to Hollywood—ah man, I'm finally free. I'm free to be anyone I want to be now. But they don't want Paolo. They don't want Joaquim. They don't even want Mat Iwasaki. No, no, they want this . . . *(Pulls the sides of his eyes upwards and makes his teeth appear bucktoothed)* But after a while they don't even want me for that anymore. Why should they, Mama? They got white guys playing me now. I mean, I killed myself for this? For this? And then I get this phone call. I can't believe it. And I get to be—what? The lead? Opposite a beautiful woman? In a romantic love story? AHHH! Yes, yes, finally the clouds have parted and Buddha has reached out and tapped me. ME. Because I'm the golden boy—right, Mama?—as I'm pulling down my zipper. I'm the one who's supposed to carry on the family name—my pants bunched up around my feet. I'm Mama's boy, Mama's boy—see, see the "Akari brightness." I'm shining, shining—I'm a movie star.

(Dim to darkness on MAT *and* DOROTHY.)*

Fish

Head

Soup

Sutra chanting. VICTOR *lit at koi pond holding the white towel. Staring at the water and humming the song. He slowly wades into the pond of bluish watery lights. Plunges the cloth into the water and pulls up a struggling Moe covered in the dripping white towel. He stands for a moment, holding the flopping fish in his hands, trying to summon the will for what he must do next. Then, grabbing Moe's head, he jerks it back. Moe stops moving.* VICTOR *holds the fish tightly to himself. Dim to darkness on* VICTOR.

Cross-fade to VICTOR *and* PAPA. VICTOR *approaches* PAPA. *In his hands he is holding Moe wrapped in the white towel.*

VICTOR: Papa? Papa? Here. I won't walk away. I'm not going to leave you behind. This is for you. I got it for you. (VICTOR *is extending it to* PAPA. *But he doesn't move to take it.* VICTOR *sets it in his lap.)* Papa? Please? You have to take this. You have to . . .
    (VICTOR, *frustrated, stares at the unmoving* PAPA.)
VICTOR *(becoming angry)*: It's your fault, Papa. It's your fault Mama's acting this way. You gotta open your mouth, make words come out, make everything all right again. Papa? Papa?
    (VICTOR *gives up. Turns and exits.* PAPA *sits for a moment unmoving. Then, slowly looks down at Moe and picks the fish up. Holds it with both hands in front of him. Begins to hum the song. Dim to darkness on* PAPA.)

The sound of a large truck horn. DOROTHY *lit driving a car. With her friend. Thick fog. The truck roars by, passing them.*

DOROTHY: No, you don't understand. I wear the kimono for work, only for work—I don't even know how to tie the obi right anymore—this fog, I hate this fog. *(Beat)* Why do you like me, huh? I mean, what do you want from me? No, no, I don't want to go there, I said I don't want to . . . You

see this, this woman who's supposed to be the answer to
all your fantasies—waiting on you hand and foot, giving   *Fish*
in to your every wish, and in bed I'm supposed to know
everything, be dirty and still be innocent—but I'm not   *Head*
that, I'm not yet, I find myself . . . What do you want from
me, huh? What the hell do you want from me? *(Listening)*   *Soup*
"What do I want from you?" . . . *(Dim to darkness.)*

Lights up on the Iwasaki household. VICTOR *is already
seated at the dinner table, his hammer in front of him. And
an animated* PAPA *is dragging* MAT, *who was just about to
leave with his bag, to the table. Both* VICTOR *and* MAT
stare at PAPA.

PAPA *(shoving* MAT *along)*: I caught me a big one, a real big
one. Couldn't believe my luck. First cast, hauled that
sucker in. Bled it right there in the boat. Decided to come
right home. No use *(*PAPA *has pushed* MAT *into his seat.)* letting the meat sit all day out in the open. Scaled and gutted
it right in the kitchen sink. The meat should be so tasty.
*(*DOROTHY *enters. She appears very upset.)*
PAPA: Mama! Mama, just in time. Sit, sit, sit . . .
DOROTHY *(overlapping, being dragged to the table)*: What's
going on? Papa? Papa, what's—Victor? What is . . .
PAPA: . . . right over here where you always sit. There. Everyone ready? *(*PAPA *rushes to the stove and brings over a big
pot.)* Fish head soup. *(Starts to ladle it out)* Just like old
times, huh? Your grandpa used to make this dish for the
family on special occasions. Soup. Fish soup. It's made
from all the leftovers. After you clean the fish, fillet it good,
what's left? The real good stuff. Tail, bones—but it's still
got meat on it—and the best part, the head. Fish head.
My papa would throw that stuff in a big pot, cook it and
cook it—and no salt, no MSG, nothing—only the natural
flavors coming out. And then we'd all sit down to eat. He

got first pick and he always took the head. Best part, he'd say. Pop out the eyeballs, suck the meat off the lips, and the cheeks. Ahh, the cheek meat was the best part of all. Delicacy.

Otosan said, fish head soup, when it's good and the family is all sitting around eating together—Mama, Papa, the kids—a man can never feel alone. You can feel your entire family all there. Even the dead ones, Ojiisan, Obaasan, and back and back, all your ancestors from the old country sitting around inhaling the good smell of that fish soup just like they used to make it. And the babies that are going to be born tomorrow and the years to come—they're all sitting around the pot, too. All there, everyone there. Sharing this one pot of soup.

(The food has been ladled out and PAPA *begins to eat. The others sit, unsure as to what to make of his behavior.)*

PAPA *(noticing)*: Eat! Eat!

(They all begin to eat in silence, stealing glances at PAPA *and each other.* PAPA *eats without looking up.* MAT *watches him.)*

MAT: He's still crazy.

VICTOR: Don't say that.

MAT: Look at him, he doesn't know we're here. Papa? Papa? See. He's just reliving some memory or something.

*(*DOROTHY *starts to giggle. It's almost on the verge of becoming a crying jag.)*

DOROTHY: I'm sorry, it's just—forget it. No, no, I should share this. Papa? Victor? A friend saw Mat's movie. You know the one he did in Tokyo? You know what kind of movie it is? A pornographic one. X-rated. Mat's a porno star . . . *(Stops giggling)* I'm sorry. There, I'm okay now.

VICTOR: I saw you.

*(*DOROTHY *doesn't understand.)*

VICTOR: I saw you. With your friend. I followed you. And

you know where you went? To the same place I take my
customers. Those hotels. I saw you, Mama.

*(DOROTHY stares at VICTOR. MAT starts to laugh as he
makes the realization.)*

MAT: Some friend told you? Hah, you saw me, not some
friend, *you* saw me. And you saw me in my moment of
glory after all. How'd I look? Huh? You're disgusted,
you're ashamed? Mama, you're my biggest fan! *(Beat)* I
only act, Mama. I don't live this shit.

DOROTHY: What? You expect me to be with this man? I'm
supposed to sleep with this child, with this . . .

VICTOR: Say something, Papa. Papa? Please say something . . .

DOROTHY: Oh, he won't say anything.

VICTOR: He used to. He used to talk all the time. Tell me
stories about Grandpa and . . .

DOROTHY: He never talked to me. He grunted. He pointed.
He . . .

*(DOROTHY breaks down. For a moment all we hear is
DOROTHY's crying. Turns to PAPA.)*

DOROTHY: He never wanted me, he never touched me. He
drove me away . . .

PAPA *(mumbling to himself)*: Rumors, rumors . . .

DOROTHY: He drove me away with his silence . . .

PAPA: Rumors, rumors—they're going to ship us back to
Japan, rumors, rumors, put us in prison camps. But Papa
just laughs. So Japan attacks Pearl Harbor—he's a big-
shot farmer with connections. He just laughs. All his
friends are big-shot farmers. And they're hakujin, white.

Then the notice comes. He gets mad. He doesn't laugh,
he gets so mad. He's going to get his farmer friends to sign
a petition and he's going to send it to the governor himself.
Hell, they aren't going to kick Togo Iwasaki off his farm—
no, no, no.

"Come, you come with me. I'll show you how it's done."

We drive to Mr. Crawford's. We sit down in his living room. Papa asks him to sign the petition so he can stay. But Mr. Crawford says no. He's very sorry, he keeps apologizing. But Papa gets so mad, he cusses the man up and down.

We drive to the next friend's farm. This man says no, too. "No, no," all these hakujin friends speaking such good English—"No, no," to my papa. And Papa so proud, so proud, getting smaller and smaller, getting bent over and old like the sickness is getting into him, eating him up.

(Pause.)

I don't want to see it, but I see it, the sickness. I see it everywhere. In the eyes, the eyes of Papa's farmer friends, smiling, filled with so much smiling hate. The newspapers, the newspapers, Mr. Lippmann, Mr. Lippmann, the newspapers screaming all ripped up and shredded with lies—we don't signal submarines, we aren't spies, and the voice on the radio—Mr. Hughes, Mr. Hughes, filled with disease, all lies making us sick. And the long train ride, the train ride to the camp, the camp, the barbed wire, twisting, crawling with it. And Mama looking at Papa, "The camp did that, the camp did it," and me knowing it's not true, it's not true, because I could always see it. It was always there, the sickness. A part of the land. The land itself. And the moment you leave your mama's stomach it begins to feed on you. Entering your body, your blood, your mind—so that your thoughts, your thinking, it's all filled with the sickness. The sickness that is pushing and moving your life with its silent hands. Cutting its way into your skin with the lies, into your body, all inside of me. Eating me up, like a cancer, eating me away . . .

(Pause.)

My children. My sons . . . Mat, Mat doesn't have it, the sickness. "Stay away." He's my hope. "Don't come near me, you'll get it!" He doesn't carry it. He's not my son. He's my hope. Mat's not my son. Victor. Victor's Papa's child.

Victor's my son. And this is his house. I'm sorry. I'm sorry.

(Pause. To DOROTHY.*)*

"Mama, see! See!" But Mama can't see it. "Look, look,

it's everywhere!" Mama can't see it, Mama can't see it.

(Beat) But Mama has it. Mama has it.

DOROTHY *(resisting)*: I don't have it, I don't have it, I don't

have the disease. I don't. I don't . . . *(Continues.)*

(While DOROTHY *speaks,* VICTOR *starts banging his*

hammer against the walls.)

VICTOR *(overlapping)*: I'm fixing the house, ripping out

all the no-good stuff. I'm fixing the house. I'm fixing the

house . . . *(Continues.)*

*(*MAT *grabs his carry bag.)*

MAT: This is just too much. It's just too goddamn much. I'm

dead, okay? I'm not your son. I'm gone . . .

(As MAT *steps up onto the dining room table, he's lit in a*

pool of light. Rest of the stage goes to half. MAT *looks out*

as he hears someone yell at him.)

MAT *(speaking to some toughs, challenging them)*: What'd you

say? What'd you say to me? What the hell did you say!

*(*MAT *is suddenly struck, then hit again and again.*

The violent beating is underscored by loud percussive

sounds. The rest of the family members watch in horror.

Then, the beating done, MAT *stumbles off the table as*

lights are brought up on the house. He's bleeding,

shirt ripped. He can barely walk and stumbles around

knocking things over. These actions echo a bit of his

earlier "becoming a fish" sequence.

As MAT *speaks,* PAPA, DOROTHY, *and* VICTOR *"hear"*

his words. It touches something deep within. They begin

to shake, moans begin to come from them. Their sound

grows louder, turning into a wail. The group wail is

punctuated by angry cathartic shouts. Their wail is

underscored by the whirling sound of wind building

to a roar. In the final climax, the house is blown apart

by blowers upstage.)

MAT: They get out of the car, these three guys. They surround me. They think I'm going to back down. No, no, no . . . I get right in their faces. Right in their faces. I ain't no coward, Papa. And I begin to beat on them. All three of them. I'm pounding their faces in . . .

And then I hear this tiny voice. Coming from somewhere deep inside me. I couldn't recognize it before. And I wouldn't put a name to it because I knew if I listened to it I would die. But this time. This time I had to listen to it. And I knew what it was. It was you, Papa, you. And as I listened to you inside me, I felt the fear. The intimidation. The sickness. And I began to cower in front of these white men. And as they began to hit me and kick me I still had to listen. To let your voice grow and grow and fill me with its sound . . .

I felt you inside of me. But Papa, it wasn't just the sickness. No, no, it was much, much more. *(PAPA, DOROTHY, and VICTOR begin to moan.)* It was the ability to see it, give the sickness a name. You didn't know that, Papa, did you? To know its face and be able to hurl it back out of one's soul. Shout it out of one's being. *(Growing louder, becoming a wail)* And if we do? When we do? They'll run, Papa. They'll have to run because it won't be just my voice, or your voice all alone, no, no, no. It will be our voice—yours and mine, Mama's and Victor's, Ojiichan's and Obaachan's, on and on! GATHERING LIKE A STORM DEEP DOWN INSIDE AND HURLING OUT WITH A FURY OF BEATINGS, HOWLS AND SCREAMS! THEY'LL HAVE TO RUN—CUT, BOUND, RIPPED TO SHREDS BY ITS FORCE!! . . .

(Silence. Everything subsides.)

I felt you inside and I did not die. I am your son. I am your son, Papa. And this, this is my family . . .

(The walls of the house have collapsed, blown away by the fury of the wails, revealing the clean framework of the

*house—pipes, wiring—pristine and glowing. A large full
moon is lit upstage. The family members all look out.)* Fish

PAPA: It's a clear night.

DOROTHY: The moon . . . Head

MAT: A huge glowing heart . . .

DOROTHY: No, more like a . . . Soup

MAT: Yes?

VICTOR: A window . . .

MAT: Into? . . .

DOROTHY: Yes? . . .

PAPA: A house . . .

VICTOR: Of dreams . . .

DOROTHY: Yes, dreams, a house of dreams . . .

MAT: Forgotten, buried, lost . . .

DOROTHY: And then remembered . . .

VICTOR: Remembered . . .

(Pause. The family members all look at each other.)

PAPA: It's a clear night.

VICTOR: I see . . .

DOROTHY: I see . . .

*(MAT finds an imaginary pole in his hands and he's getting
a bite. MAT snags and he's caught something, something
big. As he begins to reel it in, it fights and struggles
against him. They all continue to gaze out.*

*As the lights fade, the structure of the house, along
with the moon, continues to glow for a beat. Then
fade to black.)*

[END OF PLAY]

▲

Yankee

Dawg

You

Die

Yankee Dawg You Die had its world premiere at the Berkeley
Repertory Theatre (Sharon Ott, artistic director; Mitzi Sales,
managing director) in Berkeley, California, in February 1988.

DIRECTOR. Sharon Ott
ASSISTANT DIRECTOR. Phyllis S. K. Look
SET AND LIGHTING DESIGN. Kent Dorsey
COSTUMES. Lydia Tanji
SOUND DESIGN. James LeBrecht
ORIGINAL MUSIC. Stephen LeGrand and Eric Drew Feldman
STAGE MANAGER. Michael Suenkel

The production was subsequently moved to the Los Angeles Theater
Center in May 1988; the lighting co-designer was Douglas Smith.

Cast

VINCENT CHANG. Sab Shimono
BRADLEY YAMASHITA. Kelvin Han Yee

Yankee Dawg You Die was presented by Playwrights Horizons (Andre Bishop, artistic director) in New York City in April 1989.

DIRECTOR. Sharon Ott
SET DESIGN. Kent Dorsey
COSTUMES. Jess Goldstein
LIGHTING DESIGN. Dan Kotlowitz
MUSIC AND SOUND DESIGN. Stephen LeGrand and Eric Drew
   Feldman
PRODUCTION STAGE MANAGER. Robin Rumpf
PRODUCTION MANAGER. Carl Mulert

Cast

VINCENT CHANG. Sab Shimono
BRADLEY YAMASHITA. Stan Egi

Characters

VINCENT CHANG, actor, in his mid to late sixties, former hoofer
BRADLEY YAMASHITA, actor, in his mid to late twenties

Set

Minimal, with a hint of fragmentation and distortion of perspective to
allow for a subtle, dream-like quality. Upstage, high-tech shoji screens
for title and visual projections. Set should allow for a certain fluidity
of movement. Allow for lights to be integral in scene transitions.
Suggested colors—black with red accents.

Lighting

Fluid. Interludes should use cross-fades. Dream sequences might
experiment with color and shafts of light cutting at askew angles,
as in film noir.

Music

Minimal instrumentation. Classical in feel.

Settings

ACT ONE
Scene 1. Balcony of a house in the Hollywood Hills; party in progress.
Scene 2. Audition waiting room at a theater.
Scene 3. After acting class.
Scene 4. A bar, after acting class.

ACT TWO
Scene 1. Acting class.
Scene 2. Vincent's apartment.
Scene 3. An outdoor shelter.
Scene 4. The Hollywood Hills house balcony, six months later.

Darkness. Filmic music score enters. Then, on the projection screens upstage we see emblazoned the following titles:

"[Name of Producing Theater] PRESENTS . . ."

"VINCENT CHANG . . ."

VINCENT *lit in pool of light, staring pensively into the darkness. The music dips and we hear the faint beating of a heart. A hint of blood red washes over* VINCENT *as he lightly touches his breast over his heart. Fade to black.*

"AND INTRODUCING . . ."

"BRADLEY YAMASHITA"

BRADLEY *lit in pool of light. Restless, shifting his weight back and forth on his feet. The music dips and we hear the light rustling of large wings. As he looks skyward, a large shadow passes overhead. Fade to black.*

"IN . . ."

"YANKEE DAWG YOU DIE"

The entire theater—stage as well as audience area—is gradually inundated in an ocean of stars. Hold for a moment, then a slow fade to black.

Lights come up. VINCENT *portrays a "Jap" soldier. Lighting creates the mood of an old 1940s black-and-white movie. He wears thick, "Coke-bottle" glasses, holds a gun. Acts in an exaggerated, stereotypic—almost cartoonish—manner.*
    Sergeant Moto pretends to be falling asleep while guarding American prisoners. The snakelike lids of his slanty eyes droop into a feigned slumber. Suddenly Moto's eyes, spitting hate and bile, flash open, catching the American prisoners in the midst of their escape plans.

VINCENT *(as Moto)*: You stupid American GI. I know you try and escape. You think you can pull my leg. I speakee your language. I graduate UCLA, Class of '34. I drive big American car with big-chested American blonde sitting next to . . . Heh? No, not "dirty floor." Floor clean. Class of '34. No, no, not "dirty floor." Floor clean. Just clean this morning. Thirty-four. No, no, not "dirty floor." Listen carefully. Watch my lips. *(He moves his lips but the words are not synched with them, à la poorly dubbed Japanese monster movie.)* Thirty-four. Thirty-four! Thirty-four!!! *(Pause. Return to synched speaking.)* What is wrong with you? You sickee in the head? What the hell is wrong with you? Why can't you hear what I'm saying? Why can't you see me as I really am? *(*VINCENT *as Sergeant Moto dims to darkness.)*

[END OF INTERLUDE]

Scene One

You Looked Like a Fucking Chimpanzee

Night. Party. House in Hollywood Hills. VINCENT CHANG, *a youthful, silver-maned man, in his late sixties, stands on the back terrace balcony sipping a glass of red wine. Stares into the night air.* BRADLEY YAMASHITA, *twenty-seven, pokes his head out from the party and notices* VINCENT. *Stops, losing his nerve. Changes his mind again and moves out on the terrace next to* VINCENT. BRADLEY *holds a cup of club soda.*
   Silence. VINCENT *notices* BRADLEY, BRADLEY *smiles,* VINCENT *nods.*
   Silence. They both sip their drinks.

BRADLEY: Hello. *(*VINCENT *nods.)* Nice evening. *(Silence)* God. What a night. Love it. *(Silence. Looking out.)* Stars. Wow, would you believe. Stars, stars, stars. *(Pause.)*
VINCENT: Orion's belt. *(*BRADLEY *doesn't follow his comment.* VINCENT *points upwards.)* The constellation. Orion the Hunter. That line of stars there forms his belt. See?
BRADLEY: Uh-huh.
   (Pause. BRADLEY *sips his drink.* VINCENT *points to another part of the night sky.)*
VINCENT: And of course, the Big Dipper.
BRADLEY: Of course.
VINCENT: And, using the two stars that form the front of the lip of the dipper as your guide, it leads to the . . .
BRADLEY: The North Star.
VINCENT: Yes. Good. Very good. You will never be lost.
   (Both quietly laugh.)
BRADLEY: Jeez, it's a bit stuffy in there. With all of them. It's nice to be with someone I can feel comfortable around. *(*VINCENT *doesn't understand.)* Well, I mean, like you and

Sab Shimono (right) *and Kelvin Han Yee*
in Yankee Dawg You Die
Courtesy Berkeley Repertory Theatre

Sab Shimono (right) *and Kelvin Han Yee in* Yankee Dawg You Die
Photo by Fred Speiser, courtesy Berkeley Repertory Theatre

Yankee

Dawg

You

Die

me. We're—I mean, we don't exactly look like . . . *(Nods towards the people inside.)*

VINCENT: Ahhh.

(BRADLEY laughs nervously, relieved that VINCENT has understood.)

VINCENT: Actually, I had not noticed. I do not really notice, or quite frankly care, if someone is Caucasian or oriental or . . .

BRADLEY *(interrupts, correcting. Vincent doesn't understand)*: It's Asian, not oriental. *(VINCENT still doesn't follow.* BRADLEY, *embarrassed, tries to explain.)* Asian, oriental. African American, negro. Woman, girl. Gay, homosexual . . . Asian, oriental?

VINCENT: Ahhh. *(Pause)* Orientals are rugs? *(BRADLEY nods sheepishly.)* I see. *(VINCENT studies him for a moment, then goes back to sipping his red wine.)* You don't look familiar.

BRADLEY: First time.

VINCENT: You haven't been to one of these parties before? *(BRADLEY shakes his head.)* Hah! You're in for a wonderful surprise. Everyone here is as obnoxious as hell.

BRADLEY: I noticed.

VINCENT *(extends his hand)*: Vincent Chang . . .

BRADLEY: *(overlapping)*: Chang!

(BRADLEY grabs VINCENT's hand and manipulates it through the classic "right-on" handshake. VINCENT watches it unfold.)

BRADLEY: You don't have to tell me. Everybody knows who you are. Especially in the community. Not that you're not famous—I mean, walking down the street they'd notice you—but in the community, whew! Forget it.

VINCENT: Ahhh. And you?

BRADLEY: What?

VINCENT: Your name.

BRADLEY: Oh. Bradley Yamashita.

(Pronounced "Yamasheeta" by him. BRADLEY *shakes his*

hand again. VINCENT *repeats name to himself, trying to remember where he's heard it. He pronounces the name correctly.)*

BRADLEY: This is an amazing business. It really is. It's an amazing business. One moment I'm this snotty-nosed kid watching you on TV and the next thing you know I'm standing next to you and we're talking and stuff and you know . . . *(Silence. Sips drink. Looks at stars.)* Mr. Chang? Mr. Chang? I think it's important that all of us know each other. Asian American actors. I think the two of us meeting is very important. The young and the old. We can learn from each other. We can. I mean, the way things are, the way they're going, Jesus. If we don't stick together who the hell is going . . .

VINCENT *(interrupts, waving at someone)*: Ah, Theodora. Hello!

BRADLEY: Wow . . .

VINCENT: Theodora Ando. The *Asian American* actress.

BRADLEY: God, she's gorgeous.

VINCENT *(coldly)*: Don't turn your back on her. *(BRADLEY doesn't follow.* VINCENT *mimes sticking a knife in and twisting it.)*

BRADLEY *(staring after a disappearing Theodora)*: Oh . . .
(Silence. They sip and stare out into the darkness.
BRADLEY *begins to turn and smile at* VINCENT *in hopes that* VINCENT *will recognize his face.* VINCENT *does not.)*

BRADLEY: New York. Jesus, what a town. Do you spend much time out here? *(*VINCENT *shrugs.)* Yeah. I've been out in New York. That's where they know me most. Out in New York. I come from San Francisco. That's where I was born and raised. Trained—A.C.T.* But I've been out in New York. I just came back from there. A film of mine

Yankee

Dawg

You

Die

---

*American Conservatory Theatre.

opened. New York Film Festival. Guillaume Bouchet, the
Yankee   French critic, loved it.

VINCENT *(impressed)*: Guillaume Bouchet.

Dawg   BRADLEY: Uh-huh. Called it one of the ten best films of the
year.

You   VINCENT: It's your film? You . . . directed it? *(BRADLEY
shakes his head.)* Wrote it?

Die   BRADLEY: No, no, I'm in it. I'm the main actor in it.

VINCENT *(mutters under his breath)*: An actor . . .

BRADLEY: It's a Matthew Iwasaki film.

VINCENT: I have heard of him, yes. He does those low-
budget . . .

BRADLEY *(interrupts, correcting)*: Independent.

VINCENT: Ahhh. *Independent* movies about . . .

BRADLEY *(interrupts, correcting again)*: Films. Independent
films, they play in art houses.

VINCENT: Ahhhh. *Independent films* that play in *art houses*
about people like . . . *(Nods to BRADLEY and to himself)*

BRADLEY: Uh-huh.

VINCENT: I see. Hmmm.

BRADLEY: I'm in it. I star in it. Eugene Bickle . . .

VINCENT *(interrupts)*: Who?

BRADLEY: Eugene Bickle, the film critic on TV. You know,
everybody knows about him. He used to be on PBS and
now he's on the networks with that other fat guy. He said
I was one of the most "watchable" stars he's seen this year.

VINCENT: Really?

BRADLEY: He said he wouldn't mind watching me no matter
what I was doing.

VINCENT: *Really?*

BRADLEY: Well, that's not exactly—I'm sort of paraphras-
ing, but that's what he meant. Not that he'd wanna watch
me doing anything—you know, walking down the street.
But on the screen. In another movie.

VINCENT: Film.

BRADLEY: What?

VINCENT: You said "another movie." *Yankee*

BRADLEY: Film.

VINCENT: Ahh. *Dawg*

BRADLEY: My agent at William Morris wanted me to come
to L.A. I have an audition on Monday. One of the big *You*
theaters.

VINCENT *(impressed, but hiding it)*: William Morris? *Die*

BRADLEY *(notices that* VINCENT *is impressed)*: Uh-huh.
(Pause) Who handles you?

VINCENT: Snow Kwong-Johnson.

BRADLEY: Oh. *(Pause)* I hear they handle mainly . . .

VINCENT *(interrupts)*: She.

BRADLEY: Oh, yes. *She* handles mainly . . . *(Motions* VIN-
CENT *and himself.)*

VINCENT: Yes. Mainly . . . *(Motions to* BRADLEY *and to
himself.)*

BRADLEY: Ahhh, I see. Well.
(Silence.)

VINCENT: It's a bit warm tonight.

BRADLEY: I feel fine, just fine.
*(*VINCENT *takes a cigarette out and is about to smoke.*
BRADLEY *begins to steal glances at* VINCENT'*s face.*
VINCENT *remembers to offer one to* BRADLEY.*)*

BRADLEY: I don't smoke.
(The mood is ruined for VINCENT. *He puts the cigarette
away. About to take a sip of his red wine.* BRADLEY
notices VINCENT'*s drink.)*

BRADLEY: Tannins. Bad for the complexion. *(Holds up his
drink)* Club soda.

VINCENT: I imagine you exercise, too?

BRADLEY: I swim three times a week. Do you work out?

VINCENT: Yes. Watch.
(Lifts drink to his lips and gulps it down. Pause.
VINCENT *notices* BRADLEY *looking at his face.*
BRADLEY *realizes he's been caught, feigns ignorance,*

Yankee

Dawg

You

Die

and looks away. VINCENT *touches his face to see if he has a piece of food on his cheek, or something worse on his nose.* VINCENT *is not sure of* BRADLEY*'s intent— perhaps he was admiring Vincent's good looks.* VINCENT*'s not sure.)*

VINCENT: Bradley? Was there something? You were . . . looking at me?

*(*VINCENT *motions gracefully towards his face. Pause.* BRADLEY *decides to explain.)*

BRADLEY: This is kind of personal, I know. I don't know if I should ask you. *(Pause)* Okay, is that your real nose?

VINCENT: What?

BRADLEY: I mean, your original one—you know, the one you were born with?

VINCENT *(smile fading)*: What?

BRADLEY: Someone once told me—and if it's not true just say so—someone once told me you hold the record for "noses." *(Barely able to contain his giggling)* You've had all these different noses. Sinatra, Montgomery Clift, Troy Donahue—whatever was *in* at the time. Sort of like *The Seven "Noses" of Dr. Lao* . . . *(Notices* VINCENT *is not laughing)* That's what they said. I just thought maybe I would ask you about . . .

VINCENT *(interrupts)*: Who told you this?

BRADLEY: No one.

VINCENT: You said someone told you.

BRADLEY: Yes, but . . .

VINCENT *(interrupts)*: Someone is usually a person. And if this person *told you*, it means he probably has lips. Who is this person with *big, fat, moving* lips?

BRADLEY: I don't know, just someone. I forget—I'm not good at remembering lips.

VINCENT: No. *(*BRADLEY *doesn't follow.)* No, it is *not* true. This is my natural nose. As God is my witness. *(Silence.* VINCENT *sips drink. Turns to look at* BRADLEY. *Repeats the*

name to himself.) Yamashita . . . Ya-ma-shita . . . You
worked with Chloe Fong in New York? *(BRADLEY nods.)*　　Yankee
Ahhh.

BRADLEY: What?　　　　　　　　　　　　　　　　Dawg
　　(VINCENT ignores BRADLEY's query and goes back to
　　staring out at the night sky. Occasionally, glances at　　You
　　BRADLEY knowingly.)
BRADLEY: What?　　　　　　　　　　　　　　　　Die
　　(Pause.)
VINCENT: Now this is kind of personal. And tell me if I am
　　wrong. I heard you almost got fired in New York.
BRADLEY: Who said that—what?
VINCENT: You are the fellow who was out in that play in
　　New York, correct? With Chloe?
BRADLEY: Yeah, so?
VINCENT: I heard—and tell me if I am wrong, rumors are
　　such vicious things—I heard they were not too happy with
　　you, your work.
BRADLEY: What do you mean, "not happy with me"?
VINCENT: Now, this is probably just a rumor—I do not
　　know—But, that is what I . . .
BRADLEY *(interrupts)*: That's not true. That's not true at
　　all. I was a little nervous, so was everybody. And I never
　　"almost got fired." Did Chloe say that?
VINCENT: No, no, no.
BRADLEY: 'Cause I was okay. Once I got comfortable I
　　was good. You ask Chloe. The director came up afterwards
　　and congratulated me, he liked my work so much. White
　　director. — ~~lve that is better~~
VINCENT: Ah, rumors.
BRADLEY *(mutters under his breath)*: Bullshit . . .
　　(Silence. VINCENT takes a cigarette out, lights it, and
　　takes a deep, satisfying drag.)
VINCENT: Ahhh. I needed that.
　　(Pause.)

Yankee

Dawg

You

Die

BRADLEY: Who said I almost got fired? Was it Chloe? She wouldn't say something like that. I know her. *(Beat)* Was it her?

VINCENT: It is just a rumor. Take it easy. Just a rumor. Remember this? *(Taps his nose)* Dr. Lao? It comes with the terrain. You must learn to live with it. It happens to everyone. Sooner or later. Everyone. You are walking along, minding your own business, your head filled with poems and paintings—when what do you see coming your way? Some ugly "rumor," dressed in your clothes, staggering down the street impersonating you. And it is *not* you but no one seems to care. They want this impersonator—who is drinking from a brown paper bag, whose pant zipper is down to here and flapping in the wind—to be you. Why? They like it. It gives them glee. They like the lie. And the more incensed you become, the more real it seems to grow. Like some monster in a nightmare. If you ignore it, you rob it of its strength. It will soon disappear. *(Beat)* You will live. We all go to bed thinking, "The pain is so great, I will not last through the night." *(Beat)* We wake up. Alive. C'est dommage. *(Pause)* Have you seen my latest film? It has been out for several months.

BRADLEY: Was this the Ninja assassin one?

VINCENT: No, that was three years ago. This one deals with life after the atomic holocaust and dramatizes how post-nuclear man must deal with what has become, basically, a very very hostile environ—

BRADLEY *(interrupts)*: Oh, the one with the mutant monsters—they moved all jerky, Ray Harryhausen stuff—and the hairy guys eating raw meat? You were in that film? I saw that film.

VINCENT: I got billing. I got . . .

BRADLEY: You were in it?

VINCENT: . . . the box.

BRADLEY: I'm sure I saw that film. *(Looking at* VINCENT's *face.)*

VINCENT: I came in after everyone signed so my name is in that square at the bottom. My name . . .

BRADLEY: Nah, you weren't in it. I saw that film.

VINCENT: . . . is in all the ads. There is a big marquee as you drive down Sunset Boulevard with my name in that box.

BRADLEY *(staring at* VINCENT's *face, it's coming to him)*: Oh, oh . . . You were the husband of the woman who was eaten by the giant salamander? *(*BRADLEY *is having a hard time suppressing his laughter.)*

VINCENT *(shrugging)*: It was a little hard to tell, I know. The makeup was a little heavy. But it was important to create characters that in some way reflected the effects . . .

BRADLEY *(overlapping, can no longer contain himself and bursts out laughing)*: Makeup a little heavy? Jesus Christ, you had so much hair on your face you looked like a fucking chimpanzee!

> *(*BRADLEY *stops laughing as he notices* VINCENT's *pained expression. Awkward silence.* VINCENT *smokes his cigarette.* BRADLEY *sips on his soda.* BRADLEY *occasionally steals a glance at* VINCENT. VINCENT *watches the North Star. Dim to darkness.)*

[END OF SCENE]

Yankee

Dawg

You

Die

− rude!

Scene Two

Win One for the Nipper

Audition waiting room at a theater. VINCENT *is seated, reading a magazine.* BRADLEY *enters, carrying script.*

BRADLEY *(calls back):* Yeah, thanks, ten minutes. *(*BRADLEY

Yankee   *sees* VINCENT, *cautiously seats himself.* VINCENT *pretends*
not to notice BRADLEY *and turns away from him, still buried*

Dawg   *in his magazine. They sit in silence.* BRADLEY *breaks the ice.)*
Mr. Chang, I'm sorry. I really didn't mean to laugh . . .

You   VINCENT *(interrupts):* Excuse me, young man, but do I know
you?

Die   BRADLEY: Well, yes . . . we met at that party over the week-
end in the Hollywood Hills . . .

VINCENT *(interrupts):* What did you say your name was?

BRADLEY: Bradley. Bradley Yamashita.

VINCENT: And we met at that party?

BRADLEY: Yeah. On the balcony.

    *(*VINCENT *stares intently at* BRADLEY, *who is becoming*
uncomfortable.)

VINCENT: You look familiar. You must forgive me. I go to so
many parties. Did I make a fool of myself? I do that sometimes. I drink too much and do not remember a thing. That
makes me an angel. You see, angels have no memories.
    *(*VINCENT *smiles and goes back to reading.)*

BRADLEY: Look, whether you want to remember or not,
that's your business. But I'm sorry, Mr. Chang. I sincerely
apologize. I can't do more than that. I shouldn't have
laughed at you.
    (Silence.)

VINCENT: You say your name is Bradley? Bradley Yamashita? *(*BRADLEY *nods.)* Which part in the play are you
reading for?

BRADLEY: The son.

VINCENT: They want me for the part of the father. I am meeting the director. We could end up father and son. It might
prove to be interesting.

BRADLEY: Yeah.

VINCENT: Then again, it might not. *(Silence. Awkward*

moment. VINCENT *studies* BRADLEY.) Maybe they will cast
Theodora Ando. As your sister. Make it a *murder* mystery.
(VINCENT *mimes stabbing with a knife and twisting the
blade.* BRADLEY *recalls* VINCENT's *earlier reference to
Theodora at the party and laughs.* VINCENT *laughs, also.
Pause.)*

BRADLEY: You know, Mr. Chang, when I was growing up
you were sort of my hero. No, really, you were. I mean, I'd
be watching TV and suddenly you'd appear in some old
film or an old "Bonanza" or something. And at first something would always jerk inside. Whoa, what's this? This is
weird, like watching my own family on TV. It's like the first
time I made it with an Asian girl—up to then only white
girls. They seemed more outgoing—I don't know—more
normal. With this Asian girl it was like doing it with my
sister. It was weird. Everything about her was familiar. Her
face, her skin, the sound of her voice, the way she smelled.
It was like having sex with someone in my own family.
That's how it was when you'd come on the TV. You were
kind of an idol.
(Pause.)

VINCENT: You know who I wanted to be like? You know
who my hero was? Fred Astaire. *(Noticing* BRADLEY's
look) Yes, Fred Astaire.

BRADLEY: You danced?

VINCENT *(nods)*: Uh-huh.

BRADLEY: I didn't know that.

VINCENT: Yes, well . . .
*(Awkward pause. Both want to pursue conversation but
unsure how to.* VINCENT *starts to go back to script.)*

BRADLEY: Would you show me something? *(*VINCENT
doesn't follow.) Some dance moves.

VINCENT: Now? Right here?

BRADLEY: Yeah, come on, just a little.

VINCENT: No, no, I haven't danced in years.

Yankee

Dawg

You

Die

BRADLEY: Come on, Vincent. I'd love to see you . . .

Yankee   VINCENT *(overlapping)*: No, no, I can't.

BRADLEY: . . . dance. No one's around. Come on, Vincent,

Dawg   I'd love to see it.

VINCENT: Well. All right. *(He gets up.)* A little soft-shoe rou-

You   tine . . . *(VINCENT does a small sampling of some dance moves ending with a small flourish.)*

Die   BRADLEY *(applauds)*: Great! That was great!

VINCENT: Back then you did everything. Tell jokes, juggle, sing—The Kanazawa Trio, great jugglers. Oh, and Jade Wing, a wonderful, wonderful dancer. The Wongettes— like the Andrews Sisters. On and on, all great performers. We all worked the Chop Suey Circuit.

BRADLEY: Chop Suey Circuit?

VINCENT: In San Francisco you had, of course, Forbidden City, Kubla Khan, New York's China Doll—some of the greatest oriental acts ever to go down. That's my theater background. *(VINCENT tries to catch his breath.)* See, there was this one routine that Jade—Jade Wing, she was my partner—and I did that was special. We had developed it ourselves and at the end we did this spectacular move where I pull her up on my shoulders, she falls back, and as she's falling I reach under, grab her hands and pull her through my legs thrusting her into the air . . . And I catch her! Tadah! We were rather famous for it. This one night we performed it—we were in town here, I forget the name of the club—and as the audience began to clap, these two people at one of the front tables stood up, applauding enthusiastically. Everyone followed. It was an amazing feeling to have the whole house on their feet. And then we saw the two people leading the standing ovation. We couldn't believe our eyes—Anna Mae Wong, the "Chinese Flapper" herself, and Sessue Hayakawa. The two most famous oriental stars of the day. They invited us to their table, Hayakawa with his fancy French cigarettes and his thick accent. It was a good thing that I spoke Japanese.

Yankee

BRADLEY: You speak Japanese?

VINCENT: A little, I speak a little. But Anna Mae Wong spoke impeccable English. In fact, she had an English accent, can you believe that? "Vincent, you danced like you were floating on air." We nearly died then and there. Jade and I sitting at the same table with Anna Mae and Sessue.

Dawg

You

Die

BRADLEY: God, wasn't Anna Mae gorgeous.

VINCENT: Yes. But not as pretty as Jade Wing. I think Anna Mae Wong was a little jealous of all the attention Sessue was paying to Jade. God, Jade was beautiful. She was twenty-three when I met her. I was just nineteen. She was a burlesque dancer at the Forbidden City.

BRADLEY: What? Did you two have a thing going on or something?

VINCENT: For a while. But things happen. You are on the road continuously. She wanted one thing, I wanted another. I was pretty wild in those days. There were things about me she just could not accept. That was a long, long time ago.

BRADLEY: What happened to her?

VINCENT: I do not know. I heard she ended up marrying someone up in San Francisco who owned a bar in Chinatown. I forget the name of the bar—Gumbo's or some such name. I always meant to go and see her.

BRADLEY: I've been there a couple of times. There's . . .

VINCENT *(overlapping)*: I think she may have passed away. She was . . .

BRADLEY: . . . this old woman who runs it, a grouchy old bitch . . .

VINCENT: . . . so beautiful . . . *(Awkward pause.* VINCENT *had heard* BRADLEY *speak of the old woman.)* Remember this? *(Reenacting a scene from his most famous role)* "A sleep

that will take an eternity to wash away the weariness that
I now feel."

BRADLEY: I know that, I know that . . . *Tears of Winter,*
opposite Peter O'Toole. You were nominated for best sup-
porting actor! It's out on video, I have it. I know it by heart.

(VINCENT *feels good. Decides to launch into the whole
scene. Saki is mortally wounded.)*

VINCENT *(as Saki):* "Death is a funny thing, Master Abrams.
You spend your entire life running from its toothless grin.
Yet, when you are face to face with it, death is friendly. It
smiles and beckons to you like some long-lost lover. And
you find yourself wanting, more than anything in the
world, to rest, to sleep in her open inviting arms. A sleep
that will take an eternity to wash away the weariness that
I now feel." (VINCENT *stumbles towards* BRADLEY.)

BRADLEY: Vincent?

(VINCENT *collapses into* BRADLEY's *unexpecting arms.
They tumble to the ground.* VINCENT, *cradled in*
BRADLEY's *arms, looks up at him.)*

BRADLEY: You surprised me.

VINCENT: "Don't speak."

BRADLEY: What?

VINCENT: "Don't speak." That's your line, Peter O'Toole's
line. "*Don't speak.*"

BRADLEY: Oh, oh. "Don't speak, Saki. You must save your
strength. We did the best we could. All is lost, my little 'nipper.' The dream is dead."

(*Saki is fading fast. Starts to close eyes. Then, suddenly—)*

VINCENT: "No! A dream does not die with one man's death,
Master. Think of all the women, children, and babies who
will suffer if we are defeated. You must smash the enemy!
You must win! (*Pause. Coughs up blood. Continues with
heroic efforts.)* Then I can sleep the final sleep with only one
dream, the most important dream to keep me company on

my journey through hell." (VINCENT *nudges* BRADLEY *to feed him his line.*)
BRADLEY: "What dream is that, Saki?"
VINCENT: "The dream of *victory!*" *(Saki gasps for life.)* Master . . ."
BRADLEY: "Yes?"
VINCENT: "Win one for the . . . nipper." *(Saki dies in his master's arms.)*
BRADLEY: "Saki? Saki?" *(He bows his grief-stricken head to Saki's breast. Then, recovering—)* Oh, you were great in that film. Great.
VINCENT: You weren't so bad yourself. *(*BRADLEY *helps* VINCENT *to his feet.)* I'm ready for the director now.
BRADLEY: Can I run my audition piece for you? This is the first Asian American play I ever saw. Characters up there talking to me, something inside of me, not some white guy. I'd never experienced anything . . .
VINCENT *(interrupts)*: Just do it, do it. Don't explain it away. *(*BRADLEY *stands in silence. Closes eyes. Shrugs, fidgets, clears throat. Opens eyes, finally, and begins.)*
BRADLEY: "It was night. It was one of those typical summer nights in the valley. The hot dry heat of the day was gone. Just the night air filled with swarming mosquitoes, the sound of those irrigation pumps sloshing away. And that peculiar smell that comes from those empty fruit crates stacked in the sheds with their bits and pieces of mashed apricots still clinging to the sides and bottom. They've been sitting in the moist heat of the packing sheds all day long. And by evening they fill the night air with that unmistakable pungent odor of sour and sweet that only a summer night, a summer night in the San Joaquin Valley, can give you. And that night, as with every night, I was lost. And that night, as with every night of my life, I was looking for somewhere, someplace that belonged to me. I took my dad's car 'cause I just had to go for a drive. 'Where you

Yankee

Dawg

You

Die

Yankee

Dawg

You

Die

going, son? We got more work to do in the sheds separating out the fruit.' 'Sorry, Dad . . .' I'd drive out to the Yonemotos' and pick up my girl, Bess. Her mother'd say, 'Drive carefully and take good care of my daughter—She's Pa and me's only girl.' 'Sure, Mrs. Yonemoto. . . .' And I'd drive. Long into the night. Windows down, my girl Bess beside me, the radio blasting away . . . But it continued to escape me—this thing, place, that belonged to me . . . And then the D.J. came on the radio, 'Here's a new record by a hot new artist, "Carol" by Neil Sedaka!' Neil who? Sedaka? Did you say, 'Sedaka'? *(Pronunciation gradually becomes Japanese.)* Sedaka. Sedaka. Sedaka. *Sedaakaa.* As in my father's cousin's brother-in-law's name, Hiroshi Sedaka? What's that you say—the first Japanese American rock-'n'-roll star? Neil Sedaka! That name. I couldn't believe it. Suddenly everything was all right. I was there. Driving in my car, windows down, girl beside me—with a goddamn Buddhahead singing on the radio . . . Neil Sedaakaa! I knew. I just knew for once, wherever I drove to that night, the road belonged to me." *(Silence.)*

BRADLEY: Bradley? Neil Sedaka is not Japanese.

BRADLEY: Yes, I know.

VINCENT: I have met him before. He's Jewish, or was it Lebanese. Very nice fellow. But definitely not Japanese.

BRADLEY: Yes, yes, I know. It's by Robinson Kan, the Sansei playwright. It shows the need we have for legitimate heroes. And how when you don't have any, just how far you'll go to make them up.

VINCENT: Yes, yes. Well . . . *(Awkward pause)* Say, do you sing?

BRADLEY: Sukoshi, a little.

VINCENT: Do you know the musical I was in, *Tea Cakes and Moon Songs?* Sure you do. Let's do Charlie Chop Suey's love song to Mei Ling. I'll play Charlie the Waiter and you play Mei Ling.

BRADLEY: Mei Ling?

VINCENT *(dragging* BRADLEY *about)*: Your part is easy. All *Yankee* you have to do is stand there and sing, "So Sorry, Charlie." You hit the gong. *(Standing side by side.* VINCENT *provides* *Dawg* *classic singsong intro.)* Da Da Da Da—Dah Dah Dah Dah Dah Da Da Da Dah Dah DAH! *(*VINCENT *looks expec-* *You* *tantly at* BRADLEY, *who doesn't have a clue and is feeling ridiculous.)* You hit the gong. You hit the gong. *Die* *(*VINCENT *demonstrates, then quickly hums intro and starts the song.* BRADLEY *feels awkward but is swept along by the enthusiasm of* VINCENT.)

VINCENT *(singing)*:
> Tea cakes and moon songs,
> June bugs and love gongs,
> I feel like dancing with you.
> Roast duck and dao fu
> Lop chong and char siu,
> Strolling down Grant Avenue,
> Chorus: Da Da Da Da—Dah Dah Dah Dah Dah
> So Solly Cholly."

(As they dance around, BRADLEY *coquettishly hiding behind a fan,* VINCENT *urges him to make his voice more female sounding.)*

VINCENT: Higher, make your voice higher! Da Da Da Da— Dah Dah Dah Dah Dah.

BRADLEY *(struggling to go higher)*: So Solly Cholly!

VINCENT: Higher! Higher!

BRADLEY *(falsetto)*: So Solly Cholly!
(They are whirling around the stage. VINCENT *singing and tap-dancing with* BRADLEY *in tow singing in a high-pitched falsetto. Both are getting more and more involved, acting out more and more outrageous stereotypes.* BRADLEY *slowly starts to realize what he's doing.)*

BRADLEY: Wait, wait, wait, what is this—WAIT! What am I doing? What is this shit? *(Then accusingly to* VINCENT *who has gradually stopped—)* You're acting like a Chinese

(handwritten: they always have awkward entrances)

▲

Yankee

Dawg

You

Die

Stepinfetchit. That's what you're acting like. Jesus fucking Christ, Vincent. A *Chinese Stepinfetchit.*

(BRADLEY *exits.* VINCENT *glares in the direction of his exit.)*

[END OF SCENE]

Interlude Two

VINCENT *lit in pool of light accepting an award.*

(handwritten: acts even if it's a stereotype & becomes full with any...)

VINCENT: This is a great honor. A great honor, indeed. To be recognized by my fellow Asian American actors in the industry. I have been criticized. Yes, I am aware of that. But I am an actor. Not a writer. I can only speak the words that are written for me. I am an actor. Not a politician. I cannot change the world. I can only bring life, through truth and craft, to my characterizations. I have never turned down a role. Good or bad, the responsibility of an actor is to do that role well. That is all an actor should be or has to be concerned about. Acting. Whatever is asked of you, do it. Yes. But do it with dignity. I am an actor.

(VINCENT dims to darkness. Flash! BRADLEY lit in pool of light, holding a camera that has just flashed, wearing stereotypic glasses. He is at an audition for a commercial.)

BRADLEY: What? Take the picture, then put my hand like this—in front of my mouth and *giggle?* Yeah, but Japanese men don't giggle. How about if I shoot the picture and like this . . . Just laugh. *(Listens)* I'm sorry, but I can't do that. Look, it's not truthful to the character. Japanese men don't

(handwritten margin notes: points the point ethnicity stereotypes to... Give Francisco from Chizan's play)

94

giggle. What? *(Listens. Turns to leave.)* Yeah, well the same
to you, Mr. Asshole Director.
(Dim to darkness on BRADLEY. *We hear a glitzy, Las
Vegas version of* Tea Cakes and Moon Songs. VINCENT
*lit in a pool of light, wearing a big cowboy hat. He is the
master of ceremonies at a huge Tupperware convention in
Houston. Holding mike.)*

VINCENT: Howdy! Howdy! It is good to be here in Houston,
Texas. In case you don't know me, I'm Vincent Chang.
(Applause) Thank you, thank you. And if you do not know
who I am, shame on you! And, go out and buy a copy of
Tears of Winter. It is on video now, I understand. Hey, you
know what they call Chinese blindfolds? *Dental floss!*
(Laughter) And I would especially like to thank Tupper-
ware for inviting me to be your master of ceremonies at
your annual nation—no, I take that back—your *interna-
tional* convention. *(Applause, and more applause)* Yeah!
Yeah! What's the word? *(Holds mike out to audience)* TUP-
PERWARE! Yeah! What's the word?
*(*VINCENT *holds mike out to the audience. Blackout on
*VINCENT. BRADLEY *lit talking to his Asian actor
friends.)*

BRADLEY: I can't believe this business with the Asian American awards. I mean, it's a joke—there aren't enough
decent roles for us in a year. What? An award for the best
Asian American actor in the role of Vietnamese killer.
(Mimicking sarcastically) And now in the category of "Best
Actress with Five Lines or Less . . ." That's all we get.
Who're we kidding? This business. This goddamn fucking
business. And I can't believe they gave that award to Vincent Chang. *Vincent Chang.* His speech—"I never turned
down a role." Shi-it!
(Dim to darkness.)

[END OF INTERLUDE]

Yankee

Dawg

You

Die

Scene Three

    They Edited It Out

    After an acting class. VINCENT *is upset.* BRADLEY *is packing his duffel bag.*

VINCENT: You do not know a thing about the industry. Not a damn thing. Who the hell . . .

BRADLEY *(interrupts, calling to someone across the room)*: Yeah, Alice—I'll get my lines down for our scene, sorry.

VINCENT *(attempts to lower his voice so as not to be heard)*: Who the hell are you to talk to me that way. Been in the business a few . . .

BRADLEY *(interrupts)*: Look, if I offended you last time by something I said I'm sorry. I like your work, Mr. Chang. You know that. I like your . . .

VINCENT *(interrupts)*: A "Chinese Stepinfetchit"—that is what you called me. A "Chinese Stepinfetchit." Remember?

BRADLEY: I'm an angel, okay, I'm an angel. *No memory.*

VINCENT: And you do not belong in this class.

BRADLEY: My agent at William Morris arranged for me to join this class.

VINCENT: This is for *advanced* actors.

BRADLEY: I've been acting in the theater for seven years, Mr. Chang.

VINCENT: Seven years? Seven years? Seven years is a wink of an eye. An itch on the ass. A fart in my sleep, my fine-feathered friend.

BRADLEY: I've been acting at the Theater Project of Asian America in San Francisco for seven years—acting, directing, writing . . .

VINCENT: Poppycock, cockypoop, bullshit. Theater Project
of Asian America—"Amateur Hour."　　　　　　　*Yankee*
BRADLEY: "Amateur Hour"? Asian American theaters are
where we do the real work, Mr. Chang.　　　　　*Dawg*
VINCENT: The business, Bradley, I am talking about the
business, the industry. That Matthew Iwasaki movie was　*You*
a fluke, an accident . . .
BRADLEY *(interrupts)*: Film, Mr. Chang.　　　　　　*Die*
VINCENT: *Movie!* And stop calling me Mr. Chang. It's Shi-
geo Nakada. "Asian American consciousness." Hah. You
can't even tell the difference between a Chinaman and a
Jap. I'm Japanese, didn't you know that? I changed my
name after the war. Hell, I wanted to work . . .　　*Sell-out*
BRADLEY *(mutters)*: You are so jive, Mr. Chang . . .
VINCENT: You think you're better than I, don't you? Somehow special, above it all. The new generation. With all
your fancy politics about this Asian American new-way-
of-thinking and seven long years of paying your dues at
Asian Project Theater or whatever it is. You don't know
shit, my friend. You don't know the meaning of paying
your dues in this business.
BRADLEY: The business. You keep talking about the business. The industry. Hollywood. What's Hollywood? Cutting up your face to look more white? So my nose is a little
flat. Fine! Flat is beautiful. So I don't have a double fold in
my eyelid. Great! No one in my entire racial family has had
it in the last ten thousand years. My old girlfriend used to
put Scotch tape on her eyelids to get the double fold so she　*Saw this*
could look more "Cau-ca-sian." My new girlfriend—she　*on Oprah*
doesn't mess around, she got surgery. Where does it begin?
Vincent? All that self-hate, *where does it begin?* You and
your Charley Chop Suey roles . . .
VINCENT: You want to know the truth? I'm glad I did it. Yes,
you heard me right. I'm glad I did it and I'm not ashamed,
I wanted to do it. And no one is ever going to get an apol-

ogy out of me. And in some small way it is a victory. Yes, a
victory. At least an oriental was on screen acting, being
seen. We existed.

BRADLEY: But that's not existing—wearing some goddamn
monkey suit and kissing up to some white man, that's not
existing.

VINCENT: That's all there was, Bradley. That's all there was!
But you don't think I wouldn't have wanted to play a better
role than that bucktoothed, groveling waiter? I would have
killed for a better role where I could have played an honest-
to-god human being with real emotions. I would have
killed for it. You seem to assume "Asian Americans"
always existed. That there were always roles for you. You
didn't exist back then, Buster. Back then there was no
Asian American consciousness, no Asian American actor,
and no Asian American theaters. Just a handful of "orientals" who for some godforsaken reason wanted to perform. *Act.* And we did. At church bazaars, community
talent night, and on the Chop Suey Circuit playing China-
towns and Little Tokyos around the country as hoofers,
jugglers, acrobats, strippers—anything we could for anyone who would watch. You, you with that holier-than-
thou look, trying to make me feel ashamed. You wouldn't
be here if it weren't for all the crap we had to put up with.
We built something. We built the mountain, as small as it
may be, that you stand on so proudly looking down at me.
Sure, it's a mountain of Charley Chop Sueys and slipper-
toting geishas. But it is also filled with forgotten moments
of extraordinary wonder, artistic achievement. A singer,
Larry Ching, he could croon like Frank Sinatra and better
looking, too. Ever heard of him? Toy Yet Mar—boy, she
could belt it out with the best of them. "The Chinese
Sophie Tucker." No one's ever heard of her. And Dorothy
Takahashi, she could dance the high heels off of anyone,
Ginger Rogers included. And who in the hell has ever

heard of Fred Astaire and Dorothy Takahashi? Dead
dreams, my friend. Dead dreams, broken backs, and long-
forgotten beauty. I swear, sometimes when I'm taking my
curtain call I can see this shadowy figure out of the corner
of my eye taking the most glorious, dignified bow. Who
remembers? *Who* appreciates?

BRADLEY: See, you think every time you do one of those
demeaning roles, the only thing lost is *your* dignity. That
the only person who has to pay is you. Don't you see that
every time you do that millions of people in movie theaters
will see it? Believe it. Every time you do any old stereotypic
role just to pay the bills, someone has to pay for it—and it
ain't you. No. It's some Asian kid innocently walking
home. "Hey, it's a Chinaman gook!" "Rambo, Rambo,
Rambo!" You older actors. You ask to be understood, for-
given, but you refuse to change. You have no sense of social
responsibility. Only me . . .

VINCENT *(overlapping)*: No . . .

BRADLEY: . . . me, me. Shame on you. I'd never play a role
like that stupid waiter in that musical. And . . .

VINCENT: You don't know . . .

BRADLEY: . . . I'd never let them put so much make-up on
my face that I look like some goddamn chimpanzee on the
screen.

VINCENT *(overlapping)*: You don't know . . .

BRADLEY: I don't care if they paid me a million dollars, what
good is it to lose your dignity? I'm not going to prostitute
my soul just to . . .

VINCENT *(overlapping)*: There's *that* word. I was wondering
when we'd get around to that word. I hate that word!
I HATE THAT WORD!

BRADLEY: . . . see myself on screen if I have to go grunt-
ing around like some slant-eyed animal. You probably
wouldn't know a good role if it grabbed you by the balls!

VINCENT: I have played many good roles.

Yankee

Dawg

You

Die

BRADLEY: Sure, waiters, Viet Cong killers, chimpanzees, *Yankee* drug dealers, hookers . . .

VINCENT *(interrupts)*: I was the first to be nominated for an *Dawg* Academy Award.

BRADLEY: Oh, it's pull-out-the-old-credits time. But what *You* about some of the TV stuff you've been doing lately? Jesus, TV! At least in the movies we're still dangerous. But TV? *Die* They fucking cut off our balls and make us all houseboys on the evening soaps. *(Calls out)* "Get your very own, neutered, oriental houseboy!"

VINCENT: I got the woman once.

(BRADLEY *doesn't understand.*)

VINCENT: In the movie. I got the woman.

BRADLEY: Sure.

VINCENT: And she was *white.*

BRADLEY: You're so full of it.

VINCENT: And I kissed her!

BRADLEY: What, a peck on the cheek?

VINCENT: ON THE LIPS! ON THE LIPS! *I GOT THE WOMAN.*

BRADLEY: Nah.

VINCENT: Yes.

BRADLEY: Nah?

VINCENT: *YES.*

BRADLEY *(pondering)*: When was this? In the thirties? Before the war?

VINCENT *(overlapping)*: No.

BRADLEY: Because that happened back then. After the war, forget it. Mr. Moto even disappeared and he was played by Peter Lorre.

VINCENT: No, no. This was the fifties.

BRADLEY: Come on, you're kidding.

VINCENT: 1959. A cop movie. *(Correcting himself)* Film. *The Scarlet Kimono.* Directed by Sam Fuller. Set in L.A. Two police detectives, one Japanese American and one Caucasian. And a beautiful blonde they both love.

BRADLEY: Yeah . . . I remember. And there's this violent kendo fight between you two guys because you both want the woman. *(Realizing)* And you get the woman.

VINCENT: See, I told you so.

(Pause. BRADLEY *seats himself.)*

BRADLEY: Except, when I saw it you didn't kiss her. I mean I would have remembered something like that. An Asian man and a white woman. You didn't kiss her.

VINCENT: TV?

BRADLEY: Late night.

*(*BRADLEY *nods.* VINCENT *makes the realization.)*

VINCENT: They edited it out.

(Silence. VINCENT *is upset.* BRADLEY *watches him. Dim to darkness.)*

[END OF SCENE]

Interlude Three

Darkness. BRADLEY *lit in pool of light. Silently practicing tai chi, with dark glasses on. His movements are graceful, fluid. Stops. Poised in silence like a statue. Suddenly breaks into savage kung fu kicks with the accompanying Bruce Lee screams. Stops. Silence.* BRADLEY *shakes himself as if trying to release pent-up tension. Quietly begins the graceful tai chi movement.* BRADLEY *dims to darkness as* VINCENT *lit in pool of light.*

VINCENT *(on the phone to Kenneth)*: I cannot. You know

Yankee

Dawg

You

Die

why. Someone might see us together. *(Listens)* You do not know. People talk. Especially in this oriental community and then what happens to my career? I am a leading man. *(Kenneth hangs up on him.)* I am a leading man. *(Dim to darkness.)*

[END OF INTERLUDE]

Scene Four

The Look in Their Eyes

After acting class, VINCENT *and* BRADLEY *in a crowded, noisy bar having a drink. They play a raucous verbal game.*

BRADLEY: Mr. Chang, it's a . . .

VINCENT *(interrupts, calls to a waitress)*: Excuse me! Tanqueray martini, straight up with a twist. Dry.

BRADLEY *(pretending to be a casting agent making an offer)*: Mr. Chang, it's a two-day contract.

VINCENT *(no accent, straight, not much effort)*: Yankee dog, you die.

BRADLEY *(trying to suppress his laughter)*: Mr. Chang, it's a one-week contract. And don't forget the residuals when this goes into syndication.

VINCENT *(big "oriental" accent. Barely able to contain his laughter)*: Yankee dawg, you die!

BRADLEY: Mr. Chang, it's a three-month shoot on location in the Caribbean Islands. Vincent, we're talking a cool six figures here. You can get your condo in Malibu, your silver Mercedes, you'll . . .

VINCENT (*overlapping. An outrageous caricature, all the while barely containing his laughter*): YANKEE DAWG YOU DIE! YANKEE DAWG YOU DIE! YANKEE DAWG YOU DIE!

BRADLEY: . . . BE LYING ON SOME BEACH IN SAINT-TROPEZ, GETTING A TAN, HAVING A GOOD OLE TIME! . . .

VINCENT: My drink . . .

(Both calm down.)

BRADLEY: I talked my agent into getting me an audition. It's that new lawyer series. He was very reluctant, the role wasn't written for an Asian. I said, "Jason, just get me in there." I showed up for the audition. I said, "I can do it, I can do it." They said, "No, the character's name is Jones." I said, "I can play a character named Jones." They said, "No." "I was adopted." "No." "I married a woman and gave up my name." "No." Hell, if some white guy can play Chan, some yellow guy can play Jones.

(Pause. They sip their drinks.)

VINCENT: Do you remember that film *Bad Day at Black Rock?*

BRADLEY (*remembering*): Yeah, yeah . . .

VINCENT: That role, that role that Spencer Tracy plays?

BRADLEY: Yeah, but it's about some Nisei 442* vet, right?

VINCENT: That's who the story revolves around, but he does not appear. He's dead. Got killed saving Tracy's life in Italy. After the war Tracy goes to the dead soldier's hometown to return a war medal to his Issei parents. Only they don't appear either. Their farm is burned down, they are missing, and therein lies the tale. I should have played that role.

BRADLEY: Whose role? Spencer Tracy's?

VINCENT: It's about a Nisei.

*World War II all Japanese American U.S. Army combat unit.

Yankee

Dawg

You

Die

BRADLEY: Yeah, but none appear.

Yankee BRADLEY: But he could have been a Nisei, Tracy's character. And I have always felt I should have played it.

Dawg BRADLEY: Me. Robert De Niro, *Taxi Driver.* "You talking to me? You talking to me?"

You VINCENT: *Harvey.*

BRADLEY: Keitel?

Die VINCENT: No, no. The film with Jimmy Stewart.

BRADLEY: With the rabbit? The big fucking rabbit nobody can see?

VINCENT: God, Stewart's role is wonderful. Everyone thinks he is mad, but he is not. He is not. Original innocence.

BRADLEY: Mickey Rourke in *Pope of Greenwich Village.* "Hit me again—see if I change."

VINCENT: James Dean, *East of Eden,* Salinas, a farm boy just like me.

(As VINCENT enacts a scene from the movie, BRADLEY appears quiet and momentarily lost in thought.)

BRADLEY *(interrupts)*: Forget what I said about Mickey Rourke. He's an asshole—he did that *Year of the Dragon.* I hated that film.

VINCENT: Not that film again. It is . . . just a "movie." *(Calls after waitress, who seems to be ignoring him)* My drink!

(They sip in silence. BRADLEY reaches into his bag and pulls out a script.)

BRADLEY: Vincent? Want to work on something together?

VINCENT: We already are taking the same class . . .

BRADLEY *(interrupts)*: No, no, over at the Asian American Theater. The one here in town.

VINCENT: No, no, all those orientals huddling together, scared of the outside world—it is stifling to an actor's need for freedom.

BRADLEY: It's a workshop production, a new play by Robinson Kan—a sci-fi, political drama about . . .

VINCENT *(interrupts)*: You should be out there doing the

104

classics, Bradley. It is limiting, seeing yourself just as an Asian. And you must never limit yourself. Never.

(BRADLEY reaches into his bag and pulls out a small Godzilla toy.)

BRADLEY: It's got Godzilla in it.

VINCENT: Godzilla?

BRADLEY *(Moving it playfully.)*: Godzilla. Aahk.

VINCENT *(calling to waitress)*: My drink, *please.*

BRADLEY: You can do and say whatever you want there.

VINCENT: An actor must be free. You must understand that. *Free.*

BRADLEY: And they will never edit it out. *(Awkward silence. Sipping.)* I was in a theater in Westwood. I was there with a bunch of Asian friends. And then that "movie" starts. Rourke struts into this room of Chinatown elders like he's John Wayne and starts going on and on, "Fuck you, fuck you. I'm tired of all this Chinese this, Chinese that. This is America." And then these young teenagers sitting across from us start going, "Right on, kick their butts." I started to feel scared. Can you believe that? "Right on, Mickey, kick *their* asses!" I looked over at my friends. They all knew what was happening in that theater. As we walked out I could feel people staring at us. And the look in their eyes. I'm an American. Three fucking generations, *I'm an American.* And this goddamn movie comes along and makes me feel like I don't belong here. Like I'm the enemy. *I belong here.* I wanted to rip the whole goddamn fucking place up. Tear it all down.

(Silence. VINCENT picks up Godzilla.)

VINCENT: Godzilla? Robinson Kan, a workshop production? *(BRADLEY nods.)* Well. "I never turn down a role." *(They both laugh. VINCENT picks up script.)* Let's see what we have here.

(Dim to darkness.)

[END OF SCENE]

Yankee

Dawg

You

Die

Scene Five

Yankee   *Godzilla . . . Aahk!*

Dawg

You   *Darkness. Godzilla-like theme music. High-tension wires*
        crackle across the projection screens.

Die
        VINCENT *(voice-over)*: I can't believe I let you talk me into
        this!
        BRADLEY *(voice-over)*: Take it easy, take it easy.
        VINCENT *(voice-over)*: I should have never let you talk me
        into this Asian American thing! And this costume . . .
        BRADLEY *(voice-over interrupts)*: We're on! *(*BRADLEY *lit*
        in pool of light downstage right. He plays a reporter out of
        the fifties. He wears a hat and holds one of those vintage
        announcer microphones.) Good evening, Mr. and Mrs.
        America and all the ships at sea. Flash! Godzilla!
        VINCENT *(on tape)*: AAHK!
        REPORTER: A 1957 TOHO production. Filmed in Tokyo, to
        be distributed in Japan *and* America. Starring Kehara Ken,
        the scientist who develops the antioxygen bomb that
        wipes out Godzilla . . .
        GODZILLA *(on tape)*: AAHK!
        REPORTER: . . . And Raymond Burr, an American actor
        who was so popular as Perry Mason that he just might be
        the drawing card needed to bring in those American audi-
        ences. Godzilla! . . .
        GODZILLA *(on tape)*: AAHK!
        REPORTER: Rising, rising from the depths. In Japan it's
        released as *Gojira*. In America, it's Anglicized and mar-
        keted as *Godzilla!* . . .
            *(*VINCENT, *dressed up in a Godzilla outfit, bursts through*
            the projected high-tension wires as the projection screens
            turn to allow him to enter. Smoke and flashing lights.)

GODZILLA: AAHK!

(During the following, GODZILLA *acts out what the* REPORTER *is describing.)*

REPORTER: It breaks through the surface just off the shores of San Francisco. SPLAASSHH!!! It's swum the entire Pacific Ocean underwater and is about to hyperventilate. It staggers onto the beach and collapses. It looks like a giant zucchini gone to seed. A huge capsized pickle with legs.

VINCENT *(struggling to get up)*: Bradley! Bradley, I'm stuck!

(BRADLEY helps VINCENT up.)

REPORTER: Five days later—refreshed and revived, it continues its trek inland. It takes the Great Highway up to Geary Boulevard, hangs a right on Gough and follows that sucker right onto the Bay Bridge. It pays no toll. Cars screech, children cry, mothers with babies scream. The men don't. They're "manly." Godzilla! . . .

GODZILLA: AAHK!

(GODZILLA strolls over to the REPORTER/BRADLEY, takes the hat and mike and now he becomes the REPORTER. BRADLEY, in turn, now becomes the LITTLE BOY acting out what is said by VINCENT.)

REPORTER/GODZILLA/VINCENT: A little boy. A little boy watching TV. A little boy watching TV on Saturday night and it's "Creature Features" on Channel 2. Tonight the feature is *Godzilla* . . . *(REPORTER momentarily becomes* GODZILLA.) AAHK! *(Back to reporting)* . . . And a little boy watching, watching, has a hunger, a craving for a hero, for a symbol, for a secret agent to carry out his secret deeds . . . Godzilla!

GODZILLA/LITTLE BOY: AAHK!

(BRADLEY grabs the hat and mike back and becomes the REPORTER once again. VINCENT as GODZILLA acts out the blow-by-blow account.)

REPORTER: . . . In its anger it lashes out. It gouges out eyes

Yankee

Dawg

You

Die

of people who stare, rips out the tongues of people who
Yankee   taunt! Causes blackouts of old World War II movies! God-
zilla!...
Dawg   GODZILLA: AAHK!
REPORTER: It takes the 580 turnoff and continues to head
You   inland into the San Joaquin Valley. And there in the dis-
tance... STOCKTON! Stockton, a small aggie town just
Die   south of Sacramento, population one hundred and twenty
thousand and the home of a little boy. A little boy who
knows, understands, and needs Godzilla...
GODZILLA: AAHK!
REPORTER: And who Godzilla...
GODZILLA: AAHK!
REPORTER: ... with its pea-sized brain, regards with
supreme affection and would do anything the little boy
asked it to do. And this is what the little boy asked...
*(BRADLEY puts hat and mike aside and becomes the
LITTLE BOY.)*
BRADLEY/LITTLE BOY: Godzilla, ya know Sammy Jones.
She's this little fancy-pants girl. She said she was watching
this old war movie last night and that there was this female
nurse—the *only* female in the whole entire army—and
that a Japanese sniper shot her dead in the first ten minutes
of the movie. Then she said I was the enemy. And *then* she
called me a "dirty Jap."
(GODZILLA looks appalled, then angry.)
BRADLEY: You know what to do.
*(GODZILLA turns, picks up a "Sammy Jones" doll, looks
down, and then dramatically stomps his foot down as if
he were crushing a bug.)*
BRADLEY: OH BOY! OH BOY!
*(End of scene. BRADLEY and VINCENT laughing. They
have had a good time together. They do a "right on"
handshake. Godzilla-like music swells. Dim to darkness.)*

[END OF ACT ONE]

VINCENT *lit in a pool of light. Body microphone. Visual projections.*

VINCENT: I have this dream. In this dream there is a man. And though this man is rich, successful, famous, he is unhappy, so very unhappy. He is unhappy because the love around him, the love in the hearts of those he cared for most, was beginning to shrivel and wither away. And this, in turn, made his own heart begin to grow in order to make up for the love that was disappearing around him. And the more the love in the hearts of those around him shriveled up, the bigger his own heart grew in order to make up for the growing emptiness that he now began to feel. So the love kept withering away and his heart kept growing bigger. Until one day there was so little love around him and his own heart so big—it burst into a thousand red petals that filled the sky and fell slowly, so very slowly, to the earth. And the people, his friends, the ones who had withheld their love, began to swallow the petals, these remains of the man's glorious heart as they fell from the sky. Hungrily, they fed. Greedily, they swallowed. They pushed and shoved each other, gorging themselves on these petals because they felt that then they too would become like the man. Rich, famous, beautiful, lonely . . . *(VINCENT dims to darkness.)*

[END OF INTERLUDE]

everybody wants the things but we just want love

109

Scene One

Yankee

We Went to See the Movie

Dawg

You   BRADLEY *reading from a Shakespeare book. Rehearsing.*
          VINCENT *coaching.*

Die

      BRADLEY: "Or art thou but
        A dagger of the mind, a false creation,
        Proceeding from the heat-oppressed . . ."
        *(*VINCENT *enters, correcting.)*
      VINCENT: Oppres-sed. Oppres-sed.
        *(*BRADLEY, *frustrated, continues.)*
      BRADLEY: ". . . heat oppres-sed brain?
        I see thee yet, in form as palpable
        As this which I now draw."
        *(*BRADLEY *draws a knife. Uncomfortable holding it.)*
      VINCENT *(overlapping towards end of* BRADLEY's *speech)*:
        ". . . which now I draw."
      BRADLEY: "now I draw, now I draw."
      VINCENT: You should be elated you are doing Shakespeare.
        This is a great opportunity for you.
      BRADLEY *(holding up a script)*: But this is *Macbeth*. I'm
        doing *Romeo and Juliet*, Vincent—I'm doing Romeo.
      VINCENT *(holding his book up)*: You must learn them all
        while you are still young. "Is this a dagger which I see
        before me, the handle toward my hand? Come, let me
        clutch thee." There is music to its language and you must
        know its rhythm so you can think clearly within its verse.
        I studied Shakespeare when I was younger. And I was—all
        modesty aside—the best Shakespearean actor in my class.
        But the only role I got was carrying a spear. And here you
        are with a gem of a role and you don't want to work. Come
        on, come on, let's hear it.

(BRADLEY *puts his script aside and reads from his book.*)

BRADLEY: "Is this a dagger which I see before me,   *Yankee*
The handle toward my hand? Come, let me clutch thee.
I have thee not, and yet I see thee still.   *Dawg*
Art thou not, fatal vision, sensible
To feeling as to sight? or art thou but   *You*
A dagger of the mind, a false creation,
Proceeding from the heat-oppressed brain?   *Die*
I see thee yet, in form as palpable
As this which now I draw."

VINCENT: "Thou marshall'st me the way that I was going . . ."

(BRADLEY *lowers his knife.* VINCENT *notices.*)

VINCENT: Grip it. Hold it. You must be able to imagine it, feel it. Know the experience from the inside. Of course, you may not have wanted to kill someone. You must know the feeling.

BRADLEY (*overlapping after "kill someone"*): I'm having trouble with this one, Vincent. I just can't. I can't. Okay?

VINCENT: This is ridiculous. You're too tense, way too tense. Lie on the floor.

(BRADLEY *resists.*)

VINCENT: Lie on the floor.

(*While speaking,* VINCENT *lights up a cigarette. He needs a break and can do this rote. Not paying attention to* BRADLEY *sprawled out on the ground, trying out different shapes.*)

VINCENT: Become a . . . rock. You are a rock. Find your shape. Are you big, small, flat, oblong? Keep looking until you find your own particular shape.

(BRADLEY *slowly gets up into an upright position.* VINCENT, *puffing, doesn't notice.*)

VINCENT: Got it?

BRADLEY: Yeah.

VINCENT: What do you feel?

(VINCENT *turns to see the standing* BRADLEY.)

Yankee

BRADLEY: Alive. Conscious. But there is no hunger, no wanting. And no sense of time. It is now. Yes, that's it.

Dawg

Everything is *now*.

VINCENT: A rock that stands. With no appetite.

You

BRADLEY: No, no, really, I know. This is what a rock feels.

VINCENT: I have no reason not to believe.

Die

BRADLEY: I have been a rock before.

VINCENT: Now I have a reason.

BRADLEY: I have. On acid. LSD. The first time I dropped acid I walked into a forest in the Santa Cruz mountains and became a rock.

VINCENT: Why did you do this?

BRADLEY: I was in college.

VINCENT: All right. Let's work with it. Since we finally have something. *(Putting out cigarette)* Go with it, Bradley. Relive the experience. Relive it moment by moment. Pebble by pebble. *(Suppressing giggle)* I'm sorry.

BRADLEY: I am walking. There is a tightness I feel in the back of my neck—I guess it's the acid coming on. With each step I go deeper into the forest. And with each step I can feel the civilized part of me peeling away like an old skin. Whoa, my mind is beginning to cast aside whole concepts. God, the earth is breathing. I can feel it. It's like standing on someone's tummy. And this rock. This big, beautiful rock. Our consciousnesses are very similar. I do a Vulcan mind-meld. *(Touching the rock)* "I am waiting for nothing. I am expecting no one." *(Releases Vulcan mind-meld)* It is beautiful in its own rockness.

VINCENT: Good. Okay, let us work with . . .

BRADLEY: I begin walking again.

VINCENT: Okay.

BRADLEY: Thoughts of great insight float in and out of my mind like pretty butterflies. Skin holds the body together. And the head holds the brain together. But what holds the

mind together? *What holds the mind together?* I panic! I
feel my mind beginning to drift away. There is nothing to   *Yankee*
hold my mind together. Soon bits and pieces of my consciousness will be scattered across the universe. I'll   *Dawg*
NEVER GRADUATE! What? What's this? Cows. Ten,
twenty, sixty, hundreds. Hundreds and hundreds of cows.   *You*
Where did they come from? They spot me. They see that I
am different. One cow steps forward. She is the leader. She   *Die*
wears a bell as a sign of her authority. She approaches me
cautiously, studying me. This head cow nods in approval.
She knows I am no longer a civilized human, but somehow
different, like them. She turns and signals the others. They
all begin to move towards me. Soon I am surrounded in a
sea of friendly cows. Hello, hi—it's like old home week.
Suddenly I hear a noise coming from far away. It tugs at
something inside me. I turn to see where the noise is coming from. I see . . . I recognize . . . Jeffrey. My best friend.
Calling my name. I look at the cows. They are waiting to
see what I will do. I look at Jeffrey, his voice ringing clearer
and clearer, my name sounding more and more familiar. I
look at the cows—they are beginning to turn away. Should
I stay and run wild and free with the cows? Or should I
return to the dorms on campus? "HOWDY, JEFFREY!"
As I look back, the cows are once again pretending to be
cows. They slowly lumber away, stupid and dumb. Moo,
moo. (BRADLEY *notices* VINCENT *staring at him.*) It's a true
story.
VINCENT: Cows?
BRADLEY: Yes.
VINCENT: Cows that have a double life?
    (BRADLEY *nods.*)
VINCENT: The dumb façade they show to the outside world
    and their true cow selves that they show to one another
    when they are alone? Moo, moo? Well, back to the real
    world. Perhaps. Anyway, to the task at hand. The role you

Yankee

Dawg

You

Die

are playing. Let me rethink this. *(Holding book)* "Is this a dagger which I see before me, the handle toward my hand? Come, let me clutch thee . . ."

BRADLEY *(quietly)*: I killed someone.

VINCENT: What?

BRADLEY: I think I killed someone.

VINCENT: Like in a person? A human being?

(BRADLEY nods.)

VINCENT: My God.

BRADLEY: I'm not sure. I may have. But I'm not sure. It was stupid. So stupid. I was about sixteen. I used to hang around a lot with some Chinatown boys, gangs and that sort of thing. I was walking down Jackson Street with my girlfriend, we were going to see the movies, when these two guys—they must have been college students come to gawk at all the Chinese people—turned the corner. Well, as they walked past, one of them looked at my girlfriend and said, "Hey, look at the yellow pussy." So I walked over to the one guy, "What did you say? What did you say?" He just laughed at me. So I pulled a knife and stabbed him.

(Shocked silence.)

VINCENT: What happened then?

BRADLEY: We went to see the movie. *(Pause)* I don't know. Sometimes it just builds up. The anger. *(Pause)* That was over ten years ago. I hope he's okay. I hope with all my heart he's okay.

(Dim to darkness.)

[END OF SCENE]

Yankee

Dawg

Darkness. Over house speakers we hear: "Un bel dì vedremo"
from Madame Butterfly. VINCENT *lit in pool of light. He*
relaxes at home, wearing a velvet bathrobe. He is seated,
looking at himself in a mirror.

You

Die

VINCENT *(repeated two times with different interpretations)*:
"You will cooperate or I will kill you." *(Pause)* "You will
cooperate or I will kill you." I will take my moment. They
expect me to just read my lines and get the hell out of there,
another dumb North Vietnamese general. "You will cooperate or I will kill you." Yes, I will take my moment. And I
am not going to let the director know. I won't tell Robert.
I am just going to do it. *(Pause. Smiling to himself.)* Yes, I
will take my moment. Vincent Chang is an actor.
    (VINCENT *dims to darkness. Music lowers in volume.*
    BRADLEY *lit in a pool of light.)*
BRADLEY *(on the phone)*: But why? I don't understand,
Jason. I thought we had an agreement, an understanding.
I know the series fell through, but I'm going to get other
roles. I'm a leading man. You told me so yourself. How
many young Asian American leading men are there? *(Beat)*
I'm not *like* the rest of them. What? *(Listening)* Yeah . . .
I've heard of Snow Kwong Johnson.
    (BRADLEY *dims to darkness. Music up.* VINCENT *in a*
    pool of light.)
VINCENT: Why do you keep threatening to do it? I hate that.
You know you won't do it. Besides, I am not going to
change my mind. *(Pause)* We can still see each other. *(Beat)*
As friends.
    (His eyes follow someone out of the room. Music fades.

Yankee

Dawg

You

Die

VINCENT *dims. Music out.* BRADLEY *lit in a pool of light. He is talking to a friend.)*

BRADLEY: That's not true. Who said that about me? That's not true at all. What? I was an "excon"? I was a "hit man" for the *what*? *(Pause. Butterfly's suicide aria in.)* Who told you this? Huh? Who told you this?

(Music swells and peaks as lights go down on BRADLEY.*)*

[END OF INTERLUDE]

Scene Two

. . . *Hit Man for the Chinese Mafia* . . .

VINCENT'S *apartment.* BRADLEY *has stormed in.* VINCENT *is trying to put on his coat and pack a small duffel bag at the same time.*

VINCENT *(putting things back into bag)*: I cannot talk now. I cannot. Now, *please.*

BRADLEY *(angry)*: Who else could have told them, Vincent? You're the only one who knows.

VINCENT *(in a great hurry)*: Can't we talk about this later? I have to go somewhere. *(Pushing* BRADLEY *out of the way, he continues to pack.)*

BRADLEY: I told you in confidence. Haven't you heard of confidentiality? What do they call it, what do they call it— "privilege." Doctor-patient privilege. Lawyer-client privilege. *Actor-acting teacher privilege.*

*(*VINCENT *is all packed. Trying to get on his coat, which has been dangling off his left shoulder.)*

VINCENT: I have to go, Bradley. I have a very important
appointment.

Yankee

BRADLEY *(interrupts)*: Fuck your audition! What about *my*
career? You told him, didn't you. Goddamn it. You told
everybody I was an excon, a hit man for the *Chinese
Mafia*! *(Pause)* What if the casting agencies hear about it?
Huh? Think they'll want to hire me?

Dawg

You

VINCENT *(quietly)*: My friend is dying . . .

Die

BRADLEY *(not hearing)*: What happens to my . . .

VINCENT *(interrupts)*: My friend is dying! *(Silence)* He over-
dosed. Took a whole bottle of pills. I have to go to the hospital. Now, get out of my way, Bradley. *(Pushing a stunned
BRADLEY aside)* There are some things in this world more
important than *your* career . . . What has happened to
you, Bradley? What the hell has happened to you?

BRADLEY *(quietly)*: I just wanted to know. That's all. If you
told him. I haven't gotten a call lately and I thought, you
know . . .

(Pause. VINCENT feels bad about his remarks.)

VINCENT: Look. I am sorry . . .

BRADLEY: You better go, Vincent, your friend . . .

VINCENT *(starts to leave, stops)*: He always does this. My
friend is just . . . lonely. He wants me to come running.

BRADLEY: You said he took a whole bottle of sleeping pills?

VINCENT: Last time it was a whole bottle of laxatives. One
week in the hospital. He was so happy. He lost fifteen
pounds. *(Pause)* Maybe I did . . .

(BRADLEY doesn't follow his comment.)

VINCENT: . . . mention it. About what happened in Chinatown. Just to a few people. I just never had someone tell me
they killed . . .

BRADLEY *(overlapping)*: He's probably okay, now. I'm sure
the guy's fine.

VINCENT: . . . someone before. I had to tell somebody. And
I never said you were a hit man for the Chinese Mafia, or

whatever . . . *(Pause)* I am sorry, Bradley. Remember? *(Taps his nose)* Dr. Lao? I have to go. The nurses may need some help with the bedpans. *(Notices* BRADLEY*)* We all go through these periods when the phone does not ring. I, too, have had them. Of course, few and far between, but I, too. Try some ochazuke* with some umeboshi**—it's on the stove. My mother used to make me eat it when I was upset. Soothes the nerves. *(*VINCENT *turns to exit.)*

BRADLEY: Vincent? I was going to kick your ass. I was . . .

*(*VINCENT *stops. Stares at* BRADLEY*.)*

BRADLEY: I just sit in my room, waiting for the phone to ring. Why won't the phone ring, Vincent? Huh? Why won't the goddamn phone ring?

(Dim to darkness.)

[END OF SCENE]

Interlude Six

Darkness. We hear BRADLEY*'s voice. Gradually lights are brought up as he speaks. Upstage area lit in a pool of light. Body microphone. Visual projections.*

BRADLEY: I have this dream. In this dream, I'm lying on a park bench. I wear only a very ragged black overcoat. Then, I fall asleep. My mouth wide open. It is a kind of perfect sleep. No hunger, no desire . . . no dreams. My heart stops beating. The blood comes to rest in my veins. *(Noticing)* It's quite pleasureful. The whispering of warm breezes

*Rice with tea poured over it.
**Salted plum.

through my hair. Big, colorful maple leaves of red and orange that flutter down and cover my eyes like coins. Ahh . . . What's this? Two dark clouds circling high above. Now they swoop down, down, towards my sleeping corpse. I see what they are. Two magnificent vultures. I think of something to offer. "Here, here, take my fingers. Yes, yes . . . don't be afraid. Here, take the rest of my hand." That should be enough. No. They want more . . . They've jumped on my chest. They're beginning to rip me open. It feels . . . so . . . so . . . *(Dim to darkness.)*

Yankee

Dawg

You

Die

[END OF INTERLUDE]

Scene Three

I See Myself Thirty-five Years Ago

Thunder. BRADLEY *seated on a bench in a small outdoor shelter. Raining. Umbrella on ground.* VINCENT *runs to the shelter holding two cups of hot coffee.*

VINCENT *(hands coffee to* BRADLEY*)*: Black, right?
   *(*BRADLEY *nods, takes coffee. Sips, watches rain.)*
BRADLEY: I finally got a call. I just came from an audition. It was for one of those evening soaps, everybody was there. Butler gig, glorified extra. I didn't get the role. I walked outside and I started crying. And I was crying, not because of the humiliation. But because *I wanted the role.* I keep thinking, if I got it, the part, could I go through with it? I mean, actually show up and do that stuff?
VINCENT: When you walk on that set and there is all that

Yankee

Dawg

You

Die

expectation from everyone—the director, the writer, the other actors to be that way, it is so . . . I was watching TV last week. They had on this story about Martin Luther King. He was picked up by some nightriders. Drove him to the outskirts of town, dragged him out of the car and surrounded him. And that night he felt something inside he never felt before—impotent, like the slave, willing to go along, almost wanting to comply. After that, he realized he had to fight not only the white man on the outside, but that feeling, the slave inside of him. It is so easy to slip into being the "ching-chong-Chinaman." (VINCENT *looks at* BRADLEY, *knowingly.*) Moo, moo.

BRADLEY: It's still raining pretty hard. I felt kinda bad about last time. That's why I called you up. Your friend okay?
(VINCENT *nods. Pause.*)

VINCENT: I love the rain. It is like meditating. It seems to quiet all the distractions around you so you can better hear the voice of your own heart. The heart. A mysterious thing. Kind. Cruel. At times you would like to rip it out. It feels too much, gives you too much pain. And other times— aah, the ecstasy. You wish it were a huge golden peach so that everyone might taste of its sweetness. (*Pause. Thinks.*) It is also like a mirror. Yes, a mirror. And if one is brave enough to gaze into it, in it is reflected the truth of what we really are. Not as we would like to be, or as we would like the world to see us. But as we truly are. (VINCENT *looks at* BRADLEY *intently.*) Would you like to know what I see?
(BRADLEY *motions to himself, questioningly.* VINCENT *nods.*)

BRADLEY: That's okay, I'd rather you didn't tell me. An egomaniac, right? A selfish, arrogant, insecure actor.

VINCENT: No, no, quite the contrary. I see a sensitive, shy, and compassionate soul. (*Pause*) And I see a driven, ambitious, self-centered asshole. In other words, I see myself thirty-five years ago.

(They laugh quietly.)

BRADLEY: I know this sounds kind of silly. I've never told anyone. You know how everyone has these secret goals. You know what mine were? Obie, Oscar, Tony. OOT. *(They quietly laugh.)*

VINCENT: I was so cocky after my Oscar nomination. No more of those lousy Chinaman's parts for me anymore. This was my ticket out of there. Hell, I might even call my own shots.* My agent kept warning me, though. "Vincent, you're an oriental actor. It's different for you." I said, "No way. Not anymore. From now on only good roles are coming my way."

BRADLEY: Did the offers for good roles come in?

VINCENT: No. *(Pause)* I have this dream. I am standing in the middle of a room with all these people staring at me. At first I think they are friendly towards me. Then I think, "No, they are evil people out to get me." Then, suddenly again, I think this is exactly where I want to be, it feels wonderful. Then I am seized with a strange fear and I feel I must get the hell out of there. A spotlight flashes on me. I am disoriented. Someone hands me a script. *(VINCENT glances at the lines.)* "Why do I have to do this?" Then this warm, soothing voice says, "Is there a problem, Vincent? All we want you to do is fuck yourself. Take all the time you want. We'll get the most expensive lubricant if you need. Vincent, is there a problem? We hear Sly Stallone's doing it, so it must be okay. Okay? Read the lines this way." *(Pause)* I know what is going on, Bradley. I am not stupid. I know what I am doing. That is the problem.

(They sip their drinks in silence. Watch the rain.)

BRADLEY: Maybe you should call Gumbo's, that bar in San Francisco. Right now. Come on, let's be crazy!

VINCENT: What? And find out that my beautiful memory of

---

*Dialogue based on a scene from the film *Yuki Shimoda* by John Esaki and Amy Kato.

Yankee

Dawg

You

Die

Jade Wing has turned into—what did you say? A grouchy old bitch? No. I could not bear to kill any more of my dreams.

BRADLEY: That was probably just the bartender. Jade is probably rich, still beautiful, living in some expensive home in Pacific Heights, wondering this very instant, "What ever happened to Shig Nakada?"

(VINCENT sadly shakes his head.)

VINCENT: We were married. Jade and I. No one ever knew that. Just us. We were so young. *(Pause)* She left me one night. Never saw her again. I don't blame her. She caught me in bed with someone.

BRADLEY: Vincent.

VINCENT: Actually, she did not mind the idea of me playing around. Or rather she minded but she could live with it. What she could not stomach was who I was playing around with. *(Pause)* Well. It is getting late. And the rain seems to have finally abated. *(Both get up.)* Bradley? Would you like to come over to my place? For a drink?

(Awkward pause.)

BRADLEY: No, Vincent. No, I can't.

VINCENT: Right. Well. Good night.

(Pause)

BRADLEY: It's okay.

(VINCENT doesn't follow.)

BRADLEY: It's okay, Vincent. It doesn't matter to me.

VINCENT: I do not know what you are talking about.

BRADLEY: It doesn't matter, Vincent. People don't care nowadays.

VINCENT: I do not know what you are talking about, Bradley. I do not. It is late. Good-bye.

BRADLEY: Good night, Vincent.

(BRADLEY sadly watches VINCENT exit. Dim to darkness.)

[END OF SCENE]

Interlude Seven   *Yankee*

Dawg

BRADLEY *lit in pool of light, sitting.*
                                           You

BRADLEY *(bragging)*: They want me to play this Chinese
waiter. I'll go, okay, take a look. I get there and look at the   *Die*
script. Jesus. I read the lines straight. No accent, no nothing. They say, "No, no, we need an accent." You know,
THE accent. I told my agent—What? No, I quit them—if
they pay me twice the amount of the offer, okay. I'll do it
any way they want. Otherwise forget it. They paid it. The
dumb shits. They paid it. *(Laughing smugly)* On top of it,
they liked me. Yeah, they liked me.
   (Cross-fade to an empty pool of light. The aria from
   Madame Butterfly *softly underscores this scene.*
   VINCENT *enters dancing. He is wearing headphones*
   with a Walkman and is practicing one of his old rou-
   tines. Gradually the TV light and sound are brought up.
   We hear the Sergeant Moto monologue. VINCENT
   stops dancing, takes off headphones, and watches the
   TV light. He is upset by what he sees and hears.)
VINCENT'S VOICE ON TV: You stupid American GI. I know
you try and escape. You think you can pull my leg. I
speakee your language. I graduate UCLA, Class of '34. I
drive big, American car with big-chested American blonde
sitting next to—Heh? No, no, not "dirty floor." Floor
clean. Class of '34. No, no, not "dirty floor." Floor clean,
just clean this morning. *Thirty-four.* No, no, not "dirty
floor." Listen carefully. Watch my lips. Thirty-four.
Thirty-four! Thirty-four!!! What is wrong with you? You
sickee in the head? What the hell is wrong with you? Why

can't you hear what I'm saying? Why can't you see me as I

Yankee really am?

(Dim to darkness on VINCENT *dialing the phone.)*

Dawg [END OF INTERLUDE]

You

Die

Scene Four

Ahhh . . . The North Star

Six months later. Party at the same home in the Hollywood Hills. Balcony. Night. VINCENT *sips on a drink and stares into the night sky.* BRADLEY *appears. Walks over and stands beside him. They watch stars in silence.*

VINCENT *(notices* BRADLEY'S *drink)*: Tannins are bad for your complexion.

(They both laugh, clink glasses, and sip.)

VINCENT: It's been a while. What, six months or so? I tried calling your service.

BRADLEY: It's been a little hectic. My girlfriend moved down from San Francisco.

VINCENT: Oh, I didn't know. I've been seeing more of my friend . . . Kenneth.

BRADLEY: Ahh, Kenneth.

(Pause.)

VINCENT: You look good. Different. *(Looking closer at* BRADLEY*)* What is it? Your hair? Your nose?

BRADLEY: Oh, yeah. I was having a sinus problem, so I thought, you know, while they were doing that they might as well . . .

VINCENT: Ahhh. It looks good.

BRADLEY: You look good.

VINCENT: Always.

BRADLEY: God. The night air. Ahhh. It was getting a bit stuffy in there.

VINCENT: I thought you liked being around Asians.

BRADLEY: Yeah, but not a whole room full of them. *(They both laugh.)* No way I can protect my backside. *(Mimes jabbing a knife)*

VINCENT: Ahhh.

(Awkward pause. BRADLEY *embarrassed that* VINCENT *didn't laugh at the knife joke.* VINCENT *looks up at the night sky. Pointing.)*

VINCENT: The Big Dipper. Follow the two stars that form its lip and . . .

BRADLEY: The North Star.

VINCENT: *Voilà!* You will never be lost, my dear friend. Never.

(Silence. They sip their drinks.)

VINCENT: Something interesting happened to me last week. I was offered a really well paying job in that new film everyone is talking about, *Angry Yellow Planet.*

BRADLEY: I read for that movie, too.

VINCENT: Playing Yang, the "Evil One."

BRADLEY: Yang! Hah! I read for the part of Yang's number one son. We could be father and son. Might be interesting.

VINCENT: Yes.

BRADLEY: Then again it might not.

(Both laugh at the old joke.)

BRADLEY: You know what, Vincent? You won't believe this . . .

VINCENT: I turned it down. *(No response)* I just could not do it. Not this time. *(Pause)* It feels . . . it feels good. Almost. I turned it down to be in Emily Sakoda's new film. It is about a Japanese American family living in Sacramento before the war. Just like my childhood. Sixteen millimeters, everyone deferring pay. And my role, it's wonderful. I get to play my father. *(Mimics father)* "Urusai, yo!" That. It's my father. And this . . . "So-ka?" I mean, it's so damn exciting, Bradley. I had forgotten what it feels like. What it is supposed to feel like. Do you know what I mean?

BRADLEY: I took it.

(VINCENT doesn't follow.)

BRADLEY: I took *it*. The role.

VINCENT: Oh . . .

BRADLEY: I took the role of Yang's number one son. He's half Chinese and half rock.

VINCENT: I see.

BRADLEY: It's a science fiction movie.

VINCENT: Ahhh.

BRADLEY: I figure once I get there I can change it. I can sit down with the producers and writers and explain the situation. Look, if I don't take it, then what happens? Some other jerk takes it and plays it like some goddamn geek.

VINCENT: Yes. Well.

BRADLEY: I'll sit down and convince them to change it. I will. Even if it's a bit. Just a small change, it's still something. And, even if they don't change it, they'll at least know how we feel and next time, maybe next time . . .

VINCENT: Yes.

BRADLEY: And in that sense. In a small way. It's a victory. Yes, a victory. *(Pause)* Remember this? *(Sings)* "Tea cakes and moon songs . . ."

(They both laugh. Pause. BRADLEY looks at VINCENT.)

BRADLEY: Moo, moo. *(Muttering to himself)* Fucking cows.

VINCENT: Remember this? *(Starts Sergeant Moto monologue with the same stereotypic reading as in the opening interlude, but quickly loses accent. And, ultimately, performs with great passion.)* You stupid American GI. I know you try to escape. You think you can pull my leg. I speakee your language. *(Accent fading)* I graduated from UCLA, the Class of 1934. I had this big car . . . *(Accent gone)* What? No, no, not "dirty floor." The floor is clean. Class of '34. No, no, **Yankee** not "dirty floor." Listen carefully and watch my lips. Thirty-four. Thirty-four! Thirty-four!!! What is wrong **Dawg** with you? What the hell is wrong with you? I graduated from the University of California right here in Los Angeles. **You** I was born and raised in the San Joaquin Valley and spent my entire life growing up in California. Why can't you hear **Die** what I'm saying? Why can't you see me as I really am?

(VINCENT stops. BRADLEY is truly moved. BRADLEY quietly applauds his performance. They smile at each other. They turn to look out at the night sky. They are now lit in a pool of light. BRADLEY points to the lip of the Big Dipper and moving his hand traces a path to the North Star.)

VINCENT: Ahhh. The North Star.

(VINCENT and BRADLEY begin a slow fade to black. At the same time, the theater is again filled with a vast array of stars. The music swells in volume. As VINCENT and BRADLEY fade to black, the stars hold for a beat. Then, surge in brightness for a moment. Then, blackout. Screen: "THE END." Screen darkens.)

[END OF PLAY]

Property Plot

OFF, DOWN RIGHT
Plastic train
Cordless microphone with stand
Award
Two cordless telephones
Beer bottle (open, with water half full)
Cowboy hat
Reporter/Godzilla hat
Vintage announcer's microphone
"Sammy Jones" doll
Black motorcycle jacket
Sides of The Wash
Moto outfit:
　hat
　gloves
　glasses
　gun
　riding crop
Hairbrush
Ashcan

OFF, RIGHT PORTAL
Ashcan with water
Tea towel
Plastic cup of club soda
Red T-shirt
Black suit jacket
Two cassette tapes in cases
Duffel bag with:
　gray sweatshirt
　pack of gum

small pad with pencil in ring
comb
eyedrops
miscellaneous items
man's ring in outside pocket
Godzilla toy
Hairbrush
Check tray with check

OFF, UP RIGHT
Lawn chair with attached footrest, attached padding, and outdoor
    ashtray on seat
One iron chair
Canvas bag with:
    bag of chocolates
    contact lens solution
    mini-Walkman with cassette
    one pair of socks
    a crystal
    comb
    pen/pencil
    thermos of warm ginger tea
    bound script
    notepad
    empty cassette case

KITCHEN
Indoor ashtry
Martini glass
Generic bar drink glass
Two cappuccino cups
Two wine glasses
Drink mixtures:
    red wine
    club soda
    coffee
    cola

tea (in thermos)
Olives
Ice
Cigarettes
Lighter or matches

OFF, DOWN LEFT
Camera set with flash
Stereotypic glasses
Stack of goodies:
    pajamas
    slippers
    shaving kit
    toothbrush
    toothpaste

OFF, LEFT PORTAL
Sunglasses
Cordless phone
Iron chair with script of The Wash

OFF, UP LEFT
Ashcan with water
Tea towel
Glass of red wine
"Sammy Jones" doll
Hairbrush

▲

The

Wash

The Wash was first produced at the Eureka Theatre, San Francisco, California, in 1987.

DIRECTOR. Richard Seyd
SCENIC DESIGN. Barbara Mesney
LIGHTING DESIGN. Ellen Shireman
COSTUME DESIGN. Roberta Yuen
MUSIC AND SOUND DESIGN. Steve Weinstock
STAGE MANAGER. Timber Weiss
DRAMATURGE. Oskar Eustis

Cast

NOBU MATSUMOTO. Hiroshi Kashiwagi
MASI MATSUMOTO. Nobu McCarthy
SADAO NAKASATO. Woody Moi
KIYOKO HASEGAWA. Diane Emiko Takei
MARSHA MATSUMOTO. Sharon Omi
JUDY ADAMS. Judy Momii Hoy
CHIYO FROELICH. Amy Hill
CURLEY SAKATA. Art Lai

The end production was a coproduction between the Mark Taper Forum and the Manhattan Theatre Club in 1991.

DIRECTOR. Sharon Ott
SCENIC DESIGN. James Youmans
COSTUME DESIGN. Lydia Tanji
LIGHTING DESIGN. Paulie Jenkins*
MUSIC AND SOUND DESIGN. Stephen LeGrand and
Eric Drew Felman
STAGE MANAGER. Cari Norton**

Cast

NOBU MATSUMOTO. Sab Shimono
MASI MATSUMOTO. Nobu McCarthy
SADAO NAKASATO. George Takei
KIYOKO HASEGAWA. Shizuko Hoshi
MARSHA MATSUMOTO. Diane Emiko Takei
JUDY ADAMS. Jodi Long
CHIYO FROELICH. Carol A. Honda
CURLEY SAKATA. James Saito†

*Dan Kotlowitz at Manhattan Theatre Club
**Renee Lutz at Manhattan Theatre Club
†Played by Marshall Factora at Manhattan Theatre Club

Author's thanks to Gordon Davidson, Lynne Meadow, Nobu McCarthy, Mako, Richard Seyd, Sharon Ott, Barbara Damashek, John Levey, Jonathan Alper, Karen Mori, and Oskar Eustis.

Characters

NOBU MATSUMOTO, Nisei (second generation Japanese American).
Sixty-eight years old. Retired produce man. Separated from wife,
MASI. Lives alone in the family house

MASI MATSUMOTO, Nisei. Sixty-seven years old. Left NOBU.
Does housework for a living. Lives in a small apartment by herself

KIYOKO HASEGAWA, in her mid-fifties. Originally from Japan.
Previously married to an American soldier, now a widow.
Seeing NOBU. Owns and runs a small Japanese restaurant

SADAO NAKASATO, Nisei. Sixty-five years old. Widower.
Seeing MASI. Retired pharmacist

MARSHA MATSUMOTO, Sansei (third generation Japanese
American). Thirty-three years old. Single. Older daughter of NOBU
and MASI. Works as a dental hygienist in a nearby big city

JUDY ADAMS, Sansei. Twenty-nine years old. Married to James, and
has a baby. Younger daughter of NOBU and MASI. Fifth-grade
teacher. Not working at present

TIMOTHY, JUDY's baby

CHIYO FROELICH, originally from Japan, but has lived most of her
adult life in the U.S. Late forties. Divorced. Friend of KIYOKO.
Owns and runs small beauty salon next door to KIYOKO's
restaurant

CURLEY SAKATA, Hawaiian Nisei in his mid-fifties. Speaks with a
thick pidgin that comes and goes at his convenience. Works as the
cook at KIYOKO's restaurant

Place

Center stage is NOBU's place, the old family home. Stage right is
KIYOKO's restaurant. Stage left is MASI's small apartment. The
clothesline is in the upstage area. The downstage area is used to play
several scenes that take place elsewhere.

The set should be realistic but elemental, allowing for an underlying
abstract feeling. NOBU's place is the most complete, with MASI's and
KIYOKO's places more minimal.

Time

The play takes place in the present over a period of six months—July to
January. Clothing that reflects the seasonal changes might assist in
showing the passage of time.

Settings

Act One

Scene One

NOBU's *place, the old family home. Along the upstage area is the kitchen. Stage left is a door that leads to the outside, the proverbial side-door entrance into the kitchen that everyone uses. Stage right of the kitchen, along the upstage side, is a door leading to the hallway and bedrooms, a sink, refrigerator, stove. There is a kitchen table with a pile of dirty clothes on it. On the stove, a pot of water is boiling.*

In the dish rack there are a teapot, some dishes, chopsticks, etc. Down right a TV is on quietly. A long couch is angled facing the TV, with a long coffee table in front of it. On the table sits the yet undeveloped skeleton of a large kite NOBU *is building. Throughout the course of the play, the kite becomes more and more pronounced in its construction.*

The pile of dirty clothes is lit in a shaft of light. Lights come up to half on NOBU's *place.* NOBU *asleep, lengthwise on the couch, facing the TV. Newspaper is sprawled over his chest. Mouth open, snoring loudly. TV lights come up.* NOBU *can be seen in the flickering light of the television screen. Lights come full up.* NOBU *awakens with a start, newspaper falling to the floor. Pulls himself upright and just sits and stares into space for a moment, trying to awaken.*

Then he picks up the newspaper, tosses it in a heap on the couch. Checks to examine the progress he's making on the kite. Carefully sets the kite back on the table and shuffles over to the stove to shut the boiling water off. He gets a plate and a pair of chopsticks from the dish rack, puts the two hot dogs that had been boiling onto the plate. Then he gets some tea out and puts it into the teapot which he has taken from the rack. About to throw out the hot-dog water to boil some new water, then stops, thinks. Proceeds just to pour the hot-dog water into the teapot and use it to make tea.

Nobu McCarthy (left) *and Sab Shimono in*
The Wash, *Mark Taper Forum, Los Angeles*
Photo by Jay Thompson,
courtesy Hereford/Mark Taper Forum

(Left to right, seated) *Sab Shimono and Jodi Long*. (Standing) *Diane Takei, Shizuko Hoshi, James Saito, and Carol A. Honda, in* The Wash
Photo by Jay Thompson, courtesy Hereford/Mark Taper Forum

George Takei and Nobu McCarthy in The Wash
Photo by Jay Thompson, courtesy Hereford/Mark Taper Forum

NOBU *reaches into the refrigerator and pulls out a bowl of cold rice, covered over in cellophane, and a small bottle of French's mustard. He uncovers the rice, scoops some of it into a rice bowl using his chopsticks, pours hot tea over it. The tea starts to spill, and he quickly bends down and slurps up the excess. He opens the mustard and, using his chopsticks again, shovels a healthy portion of mustard onto his hot dogs. Licks the mustard off his chopsticks. Then he carefully makes his way back to the couch with the plate of hot dogs and bowl of rice. Sets the food down on the coffee table and begins to eat while working on the kite and watching television.*

While he is eating, MASI *enters through the side door with two large brown paper bags. She's struggling to open and close the door with both hands so full.* NOBU *turns around and notices her but gives no greeting and makes no effort to help her. Instead, goes back to eating, working on the kite, and watching TV. She is not upset by his actions. She has no expectation of assistance from him. Business as usual.* MASI *sets both bags on the kitchen table and catches her breath. She proceeds to put vegetables from one of the bags into the refrigerator. Tomatoes and Japanese eggplant.*

MASI *(putting vegetables into refrigerator)*: If you have any more dirty clothes I can take them now. Nobu? Is this everything?

NOBU *(not turning, eating)*: Want some hot dog?

MASI: No, I ate before. Got these from Mr. Rossi. The tomatoes are soft, so eat them right away. *(Folds bag and puts it into drawer. She knows this place well. Walks over and checks his shirt collar from behind.)* No more clothes?

NOBU *(brushing her hand away)*: No, already.

> *(*MASI *goes over to the other bag and begins unpacking the freshly washed clothes in neat piles on the kitchen table.)*

MASI *(unpacking)*: I just finished cleaning Dr. Harrison's place. You should see the bathrooms. If you see the family

walk down the street, they look so clean and neat. But the
toilets, kitanai.*

(Finished unpacking, MASI *takes a cup out of the rack
and pours herself a cup of tea. She walks over to the couch
and sits down next to* NOBU *and watches TV. She takes a
sip of tea and makes a face.* NOBU *notices.)*

NOBU: Hot-dog water.

*(*MASI *decides not to drink. She looks at the unfinished
kite frame.)*

MASI: You gonna fly this one? *(Picking up the kite)* Nobu,
why don't you at least try a different design this . . .

NOBU: My old man did it this way. *(Mutters)* Jesus Christ . . .

MASI *(gathering clothes):* Have you talked to the kids? *(No
response)* Marsha said she stopped by. *(Beat)* You know if
you don't see Judy's baby soon he's going to be all grown
up. Nobu?

NOBU: No.

*(*MASI *gives up trying to talk to him at all.)*

MASI: No more dirty clothes, Nobu?

*(*NOBU *shakes his head without turning away from the
TV.)*

MASI: All right, then I'm going.

*(*MASI *leaves with the bag of old clothes.* NOBU *continues
to watch TV for a few moments. Then, turns and stares at
the door. Dim to half, with the TV light illuminating* NOBU.
MARSHA *lit in pool of light looking towards* NOBU.*)*

MARSHA: Dad?

*(*NOBU *turns to look at* MARSHA *momentarily, then back
to the television.* JUDY *is lit in a pool of light, holding*
TIMOTHY.*)*

*Dirty.

JUDY: Mom?

(MASI *moves away.* MASI *turns to look at* JUDY *momentarily, then exits.* MARSHA *and* JUDY *dim to darkness.* NOBU *and* MASI *dim to darkness. We hear Japanese restaurant Muzak.*)

[END OF SCENE]

Scene Two

KIYOKO'S *restaurant. Afternoon, next day. Lights come up.* KIYOKO *struggling to move* CHIYO'S *Karaoke* equipment out of the way.*

KIYOKO *(calling)*: Curley! Curley! Can you help me with this!
   (CURLEY SAKATA *enters, wiping face with towel and holding beer. Speaks in a Hawaiian pidgin. He can lose it if he wants to.*)
CURLEY: Easy, easy, no go break da speaker. Bumbai** Curley's sweet sounds no can come out. *(Helping her move the equipment)*
KIYOKO *(struggling)*: Why can't Chiyo keep this at her place?
CURLEY: Hey, cannot sing Karaoke at a beauty shop. Has to be nightclub place like dis.
KIYOKO: This is a restaurant . . .
   (*As they finish moving the equipment,* KIYOKO *notices* CURLEY'S *beer. Stares at him.*)
CURLEY *(feigning innocence)*: What'sa matta?

*Japanese singing accompaniment machine.
**Hawaiian for "by and by."

KIYOKO: Curley.

CURLEY: It makes my cooking mo' betta.

(KIYOKO *continues to stare.*)

CURLEY: I'm thirsty, I wanted a beer.

KIYOKO *(taking his beer)*: No more drinking on the job, I told you.

CURLEY: But it makes my cooking mo' betta. If I feel betta, my cooking mo' betta. No bull lie yo.

KIYOKO *(scooting* CURLEY *back to the kitchen)*: Your face turns red like a tomato and everything tastes like shoyu.*

CURLEY *(exiting into the back, scratching his behind)*: This place no fun no mo'.

KIYOKO: And don't scratch your oshiri,** you're the cook, remember?

(*As* KIYOKO *goes back to wiping,* NOBU *enters and walks up to* KIYOKO. *She notices.*)

KIYOKO: Irasshaii, welcome.

NOBU *(holds out his hand to her)*: Excuse me. Here.

(KIYOKO *doesn't know what's going on.* NOBU *takes* KIYOKO'*s hand and gives her money.*)

NOBU: Here, here, you gave me too much. You gave me too much change. When I paid my bill. I was emptying out my pockets at my house when I noticed.

KIYOKO *(looking at the money)*: Twenty-five cents?

NOBU *(nodding)*: Un-huh. It cost six seventy-five, I gave you seven bucks, and you gave me back fifty cents. So . . .

(NOBU *nods toward the money. He's not sure what to do next. Awkward beat. Then turns to leave.*)

KIYOKO: Wait, wait.

(NOBU *stops. Beat. For a moment* KIYOKO *doesn't know what to say.*)

KIYOKO: You walked all the way back here to give me twenty-five cents?

*Soy sauce.
** Backside.

NOBU: You gave me too much. So I . . .

(KIYOKO *doesn't know what to say.*)

NOBU: All right then.

(NOBU *turns to leave again.*)

KIYOKO: No, wait, wait. Sit, sit, please sit. I'll get you some tea.

(KIYOKO *guides him to a seat and goes to get his tea.*
CURLEY *has been watching the action. Sipping on a new beer.*)

CURLEY: Eh, Mr. Abe Lincoln? You come in a lot, huh. For lunch.

NOBU: Almost every day.

CURLEY *(approaching)*: And dat's your seat, huh? All da time you gotta sit in dat same seat. Last week Mr. Koyama was sitting dere—I saw you come in—you left and came back later when dat seat was open. What'sa matta, your butt got a magnet for dat seat?

KIYOKO *(bringing tea, shooing* CURLEY *away)*: Curley. Go, go . . .

CURLEY *(moving away, to* NOBU*)*: And you always order da same thing.

NOBU: The combo plate.

KIYOKO: And you like the eggplant pickle.

NOBU: Un-huh.

KIYOKO: Kagoshima style.

NOBU: Kagoshima ka? My family's from there.

KIYOKO: Ara, Kagoshima? Honto, yo?* Doko kara, where?

NOBU: The, uh, southern part.

KIYOKO: Ahhh. Watashi no, north part, Yokokawa. *(Awkward beat. Motioning to his tea.)* Dozo.** (NOBU *sips the tea.)*

KIYOKO: What is your name?

NOBU *(Getting up)*: Nobu. Nobu Matsumoto.

*From Kagoshima? Really?
**Please.

KIYOKO: Ah, Matsumoto-san. Kiyoko. Kiyoko Hasegawa. Dozo yoroshiku?*

(As NOBU *starts to bow awkwardly,* KIYOKO *extends her hand to shake. He's caught off guard and both are slightly embarrassed.* NOBU *recovers and reaches out to shake* KIYOKO's *hand.* CURLEY *watches, amused. Dim to darkness.)*

[END OF SCENE]

Scene Three

MASI's *place. Three weeks later. Small apartment with bedroom downstage from main room.* SADAO *is lit seated on sofa in a pool of light.* MASI *is in half-light at counter fixing coffee.*

SADAO: We were all sitting around in somebody's living room, when someone said, "How come you still wear your wedding ring?" They weren't being mean. That's why we were there. To ask those kinds of things. I didn't know what to say. Speechless. Then someone else said, "Sadao, you always complain about not meeting people, not being able to start a new life—how come you still wear your ring?" I began to cry. Like a little boy. I remember thinking, "How strange. I am crying in front of all these people that I don't know. And yet I feel no shame." The room was so still. All you could hear was my crying. Then I heard a tapping sound. I looked up and noticed a woman sitting across from me, slapping the sandals she was wearing

*How do you do?

against the bottom of her feet. Tap, tap, tap . . . I said I
didn't know why. It just never crossed my mind to take it *The*
off. "Why should I take the ring off?" Then one of the wid-
ows, the one who formed the group, said, "Because you're *Wash*
not married anymore."

(Lights come up on the rest of the apartment area. MASI
*is at the small kitchen counter fixing two cups of Sanka
coffee. She wasn't quite prepared for him sharing such
personal details of his life and is a bit unsure how to
respond.* SADAO *in turn fears he may have gotten a bit
carried away.)*

MASI *(bringing coffee over)*: Cream? It's nondairy creamer.
*(*SADAO *shakes head.)*

MASI: If you want tea?

SADAO: No, this is fine. I ran on a bit, didn't I?

MASI: No, no, it's all right. *(Pause)* It's just Sanka.

SADAO: Good. Otherwise the caffeine keeps me up all night.
Have you tried decaffeinated coffee?

*(*MASI *motions to the Sanka, unsure of what he means.)*

SADAO: No, the bean. They actually make a decaffeinated
bean.

MASI: No, we never did anything like that. Just instant.
Yuban makes a good instant coffee. That's what I usually
drink, but I don't have any since I moved over here.

SADAO: No, I've never tried it.

MASI: I'll have to get some next time I go shopping.

SADAO: They have this process they use. On the bean. I mean
they don't grow a decaffeinated bean. I don't know what's
worse. The caffeine in it or the chemicals they use to get the
caffeine out. *(Laughing at his own joke. Gathering momen-
tum.)* I have a little grinder. Braun? You know a Braun?

*(*MASI *doesn't know what it is. Awkward pause.)*

MASI: We never did anything like that. We just drink instant.

SADAO: I like Sanka. I have to drink it all the time. Doctor's
orders. *(Imitating)* "If you drink coffee, Sadao, drink

The Wash

Sanka!" *(Laughs valiantly at his attempt at humor.* MASI *stares at her cup.* SADAO *notices and offers a feeble explanation.)* Blood pressure . . .

(They both drink in silence. Suddenly, SADAO *remembers something.)*

SADAO: Oh. I forgot. *(SADAO reaches down and picks up a fishing pole and reel wrapped up like presents.)*

MASI *(surprised)*: Sadao, what's this?

(SADAO holds out pole.)

MASI: I can't.

(NOBU lit in half-light at his place watching TV. His face illuminated by the flickering screen's glow.)

SADAO: No, no, it's for you.

MASI: But Sadao . . .

SADAO: No, no, it's for *you.*

MASI *(one hand on it)*: Sadao, you shouldn't have.

SADAO: Go 'head. Open it up.

MASI *(takes it and begins unwrapping it)*: No, I can't accept this. I don't have anything for you.

(MASI unwraps pole, which is broken down into pieces. SADAO *sets reel on table and takes pole from* MASI *and proceeds to put it together.)*

SADAO: See, it goes like this. And then you're all set to catch fish. *(Hands it back to* MASI*)* I told you I was going to take you. Now you can't refuse.

MASI: Yeah, but . . .

SADAO: Thought I was kidding, huh?

MASI: But this is so expensive. I know how much these things cost, 'cause of Nobu. I don't know anything about fishing. He's the fisherman. I just pack the lunch and off he goes.

SADAO: Well, this time you're going and it's lots of fun. Economical, too. You get to eat what you catch.

MASI: But you have to do all that walking.

SADAO: No, who said that? We sit on the bank and fish from

148

there. We'll pack a good lunch—I'll make it—you bring
the cards so we can play blackjack. We have to practice. **The**
MASI: I don't play.
SADAO: That's why we have to practice, so we can go to **Wash**
Tahoe. If there's a good game on we'll have to watch it. I'll
bring my portable TV. I love the Giants.
MASI: What about fishing?
SADAO: Only if we have time. See, this is how you cast out.
(Demonstrating) You hook your index finger around the
line here. Turn the bail and . . . *(Casts.)*
(NOBU, still lit in half-light, gets up to phone MASI.
Phone rings. MASI goes over and answers it. It's NOBU.
Slowly lights dim on SADAO and rest of apartment. MASI
and NOBU are lit.)
MASI: Hello.
NOBU *(lit in small pool of light)*: You coming to pick up the
clothes?
MASI: Nobu? I was just there. You mean next week? Don't
worry, I'll be there. I do it every week, don't I? Nobu?
NOBU: I'm not worried. You all right?
MASI: Yes, I'm all right. Did you want something? *(No*
response) I got more vegetables. Do you need some more?
NOBU: No. *(Pause)* Can you bring more eggplant?
MASI: I don't have any more.
NOBU: All right then.
MASI: I'll ask Mr. Rossi. He can always get lots more. *(Pause)*
Nobu, I have to go now.
NOBU: I went fishing so I got a lot of dirty clothes.
MASI: All right. Don't worry, I'll be by.
NOBU: I'm not worried.
MASI: Bye.
NOBU: Bye.
(Dim to darkness.)

[END OF SCENE]

Scene Four

The

Wash

Poker game. CURLEY *is setting up Karaoke machine.* CHIYO *and* KIYOKO *are at the table.* CHIYO *is dealing out cards. Wears a poker visor. They are playing five-card stud, one card down and one up.*

CHIYO: Kiyoko, I never said I didn't like him.

CURLEY *(fiddling with the machine)*: Test, test.

KIYOKO: Curley, you in this game or not?

CURLEY *(singing into microphone)*: "Tiny bubbles . . ."

CHIYO: I just don't think he's right for you, that's all. He's too old.

KIYOKO: Curley, we're waiting.

CURLEY: Okay, okay . . .

CHIYO: Dealer's high, I bet a nickel.

KIYOKO: I see you.

> *(*CURLEY *moves to table, guzzling a beer and carrying a six-pack in his other hand. They both notice* CURLEY *chugging down the rest of his beer, making loud gurgling sounds.* CURLEY *notices them staring.)*

CURLEY: You gotta drink beer when you're playing poker or you aren't playing poker. You're just playing cards. I don't like cards. Hate cards. *(Holds up another beer)* I *love* poker.

KIYOKO *(to* CURLEY*)*: Ante, ante . . .

CHIYO: Go dancing with Eddie and me. Yeah come, come . . .

KIYOKO: Chiyo, how can I do that? Who's gonna run this place, huh?

CHIYO: Come on, Kiyoko, you work too hard.

KIYOKO: The refrigeration unit's breaking down, Mr. Sato says we can't fix it anymore . . .

CHIYO: Kiyoko, I met one of Eddie's friends, Ray Jensen. He's good-looking, yo. Tall, lotsa fun to be with . . .

KIYOKO: Chiyo, Chiyo, I'm too busy. I'm not looking for that kind of thing anymore.

CHIYO: What do you mean, "that kind of thing"?

KIYOKO: That kind of thing, thinking about men and getting all . . .

CURLEY: I like it when da wahinis talk dirt.

(KIYOKO and CHIYO shoot CURLEY a dirty look.)

CURLEY: Geez, don't lose your coconut.

KIYOKO: I like Nobu, he's a nice man, Chiyo. He comes in here, we sit down and eat together and then he goes home. I like that.

CHIYO *(to KIYOKO)*: Okay, okay. Two sixes, a pair of saxophones. *(To CURLEY)* A three of diamonds gives you . . . nothing. *(To self)* Eight of puppy toes to the dealer, working on a possible club flush. *(To KIYOKO)* Pair of saxes high. He's married, Kiyoko.

KIYOKO: Ten cents. They're separated.

CHIYO: But did he tell you? Huh? I call.

KIYOKO: Curley, you in or not?

CURLEY: Don't rush me, don't rush me.

CHIYO: No, you had to hear it from me. Eighty-year-old Mrs. Nakamura with the blue hair comes to my beauty shop, "I want my perm and a blue rinse," yak-yakking away. I decide to do some snooping for my good friend. "Nakamura-san? Oh, Nakamura-san? You know this Nobu guy?"

CURLEY: Old magnet butt?

CHIYO: I know his kind, Kiyoko, old Japanese-type guys. She left him, he can't get over that. He's still thinking about her. He only wants you for one thing—your tempura. Yeah. He's over here every day, desho?* You're feeding him. He's eating up all your profits.

KIYOKO: Chiyo.

*Isn't he?

The

Wash

CHIYO *(to* KIYOKO*)*: Nine of spades. No help there. *(To* CUR-
LEY*)* A trois. Oh, a pair of threes. *(To self)* And for the
dealer . . . another club. Flush looking very possible. *(To*
KIYOKO*)* Pair of saxes still high.

KIYOKO: Check.

CHIYO: Check. He checks, too.

CURLEY: I'm thinking, I'm thinking . . .

CHIYO: I try looking out for you and what do you do? You
get mad at me.

KIYOKO: Nobu is an honest man. That's all I know. One
time I gave him too much change, he walked all the
way . . .

CURLEY *(overlapping, mimicking Kiyoko)*: . . . He walked all
the way back to return it. Twenty-five cents.

CHIYO *(overlapping* CURLEY, *mimicking* KIYOKO, *too)*:
. . . to return it. Twenty-five cents.
*(*CURLEY *and* CHIYO *laugh.)*

CHIYO: Good investment. He gets a $4.50 combo plate free
now. Last card, down and dirty.
*(*CHIYO *starts dealing as she and* CURLEY *calm down.)*

KIYOKO: Look, he's just a friend. That's all he is. I don't see
why you're all making such a fuss.

CHIYO *(showing her card)*: Another puppy toes—flush,
flush, flush.

KIYOKO: Fifty cents.

CURLEY *(surprised)*: Fifty cents.

CHIYO *(confidently)*: I see you and I bump you one dollar.

CURLEY *(in disbelief)*: One dollar . . .

KIYOKO *(eyes* CHIYO's *cards and tries to decide whether to
stay in or not)*: I call you.

CHIYO: You got the three-of-a-kind?

KIYOKO: Pair of sixes, that's all. You got the flush?

CHIYO: Pair of eights! Hah!
*(*CHIYO's *about to grab the pot when* CURLEY *puts down
his cards.)*

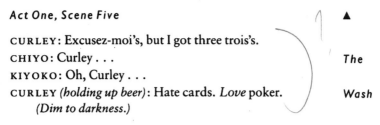

CURLEY: Excusez-moi's, but I got three trois's.

CHIYO: Curley . . .

KIYOKO: Oh, Curley . . .

CURLEY *(holding up beer)*: Hate cards. *Love* poker. *(Dim to darkness.)*

The Wash

[END OF SCENE]

Scene Five

NOBU's *place.* MARSHA's *dinner party scene.* MARSHA *busy at stove.* NOBU *seated in his chair.*

NOBU: What do you mean, "be nice to Mama"?

MARSHA: All I'm saying is just try to be nice to her when she gets here. Say something nice about the way she looks or about the way she dresses . . .

NOBU: I'm always nice to Mama. I'm always good to her.

MARSHA *(moving over to* NOBU *and adjusting his clothes)*: Dad, Dad, I just want us to have a good time tonight, okay? All of us, together. And besides, I made you your favorite. *(*MARSHA *moves back to stove.)*

NOBU: Yeah, but how come Mama has to live over there, huh? She should be at home here. How come Mama has to live way in the hell over there?

*(*MASI *enters carrying a small paper bag.)*

MARSHA: Hi, Mom. *(Taking bag)* Here, let me take that.

MASI *(to* NOBU*)*: Just some leftover fruit that was in the icebox. Starting to rot so eat it right away. And this is for you.

*(*MASI *hands package to* MARSHA. MASI *and* NOBU *acknowledge each other awkwardly.)*

153

MARSHA: Thanks, Mom. *(Takes package)* Judy and the baby couldn't make it.

MASI: She called me.

NOBU: Eh? *(NOBU's expression reveals he didn't know they had been going to come.)*

MARSHA *(offering explanation to NOBU)*: Jimmy wasn't going to come. *(Pause)* Sit down, sit down. Dinner's almost ready in a minute. Roast beef. Dad, coffee? Tea for you, Mom? *(MARSHA goes to kitchen. Silence.)*

NOBU: She wanted to eat at her place. I told her to cook dinner here.

(Pause.)

MASI: Her place is cozy, neh.

NOBU: Marsha's? Looks like the rooms back in camp.

MASI: At least she's clean. Not like the younger one.

(Pause.)

NOBU: How you been?

MASI: All right.

NOBU: Isogashii no?*

MASI: No. The usual.

NOBU: I called the other night, no one answered.

(MASI doesn't offer an explanation.)

NOBU: How you been?

(MARSHA interrupts, carrying an ashtray.)

MARSHA: Dad, look what Mom gave me. She's taking a ceramics class. Judy got her to go. *(Hands him the ashtray)* She made it. *(NOBU stares at it.)*

MASI: It's an ashtray.

NOBU: You don't smoke.

MASI: I'll get Daddy's coffee. *(MASI exits with cup.)*

MARSHA: Dad, just say you like it. That's all you have to say. Just say it's nice.

*Busy?

NOBU: Yeah, but you don't smoke. Why give an ashtray if
   you don't smoke?   *The*
   (MASI *returns with a cup of coffee for* NOBU *and tea for*
   herself. MARSHA *gives* NOBU *an encouraging nudge and*   *Wash*
   exits into kitchen.)
NOBU (*holding ashtray*): It's a nice ashtray. Is this where you
   go all the time? I call in the evening. I guess that's where
   you must be. (*Pause*) Remember those dances they used to
   have in the camps? You were a good dancer. You were. Best
   in the camps.
MASI: You couldn't dance at all. You were awful.
NOBU: Remember that fellow Chester Yoshikawa? That
   friend of yours?
MASI: He could dance so good.
NOBU: Remember that dance you were supposed to meet me
   out front of the canteen? We were all going to meet there
   and then go to the dance together. Shig, Chester, and a cou-
   ple others. Everybody else, they went on ahead. I waited
   and waited . . .
MASI: Nobu, that was forty years ago.
NOBU: Yeah, I know, but remember you were supposed to
   meet . . .
MASI (*interrupts*): That's over forty years ago. How can I
   remember something like that?
NOBU: You didn't show up. Chester didn't show up either.
   (MASI *puts cream and sugar into* NOBU's *coffee.*)
MASI: Nobu, didn't we talk about this? I'm sure we did.
   Probably something came up and I had to help Mama and
   Papa.
NOBU: Where were you, huh?
MASI: How am I supposed to remember that far back? Ches-
   ter died in Italy with the rest of the 442* boys.
NOBU: Where the hell were you?

*World War II all Japanese American U.S. Army combat unit.

MASI: How in the hell am I supposed to remember that far back!

NOBU *(notices his coffee)*: *You* put the cream and sugar in. That's not mine.

(*Pushes coffee away.* MASI *realizes what she's done.*)

MASI: That's right. You like to put the cream and sugar in yourself.

NOBU: I like to put it in myself.

MASI *(pushing cup towards him)*: It's the way you like it, the same thing.

NOBU *(pushes it back)*: No, it's not the same thing.

(MARSHA *puts her head in and watches.*)

MASI: All right, all right, I'll drink it myself. Here, you can drink mine.

(MASI *shoves her tea to* NOBU *and grabs the coffee cup.*)

NOBU: What are you doing?

MASI: I don't mind.

(MASI *starts to raise cup, but* NOBU *reaches for it.*)

NOBU: It's no good for you, Mama. Your blood pressure. Remember what Doc Takei . . .

MASI *(interrupts, clinging to cup)*: Who gives a damn? You make such a fuss about it. Monku, monku, monku.* I'll drink it.

NOBU *(struggling with* MASI*)*: It's no good for you, Mama. *(Coffee spills on the table. To* MASI.*)* Clean it up.

MASI: I'm not going to clean it up.

MARSHA *(entering)*: I'll clean it up.

(*While* MARSHA *starts to wipe the table,* MASI *grabs* NOBU's *coffee cup and exits into the kitchen.*)

MASI *(exiting)*: I'll get him more coffee.

MARSHA: Dad.

NOBU: That's the way she is.

(MASI *returns with* NOBU's *coffee and sets it down in front of him. Then, she turns and quickly exits.*)

*Kvetch, kvetch, kvetch.

156

MARSHA *(chasing after* MASI*)*: Mom . . .
*(*NOBU *is left alone with his cup of coffee.* MARSHA
*reenters and watches him. He slowly puts in the cream
and sugar himself. Raises his cup to his lips but cannot
drink. Sets it back down and stares at it.* MARSHA
continues to watch. Dim to darkness.)

[END OF SCENE]

Scene Six

That same night. After hours at the restaurant. CHIYO *and*
CURLEY *with microphones singing a song like "Sukiyaki" to
the accompaniment of the Karaoke machine.* CURLEY *begins
to do the hula.* KIYOKO *laughing and clapping along. They're
all having a good time.* NOBU *enters. He wasn't expecting this
and is not sure what to do. As* CHIYO *continues to sing,*
CURLEY *notices him.*

CURLEY *(calling)*: Nobu! Nobu!
*(*KIYOKO *goes up to* NOBU, *who is turning to leave.)*
KIYOKO *(catching him and trying to make him enter)*: Nobu,
come in, come in—Chiyo and Curley set up the machine
and we're all singing . . . *(*NOBU *doesn't budge.* KIYOKO
notices that he is upset about something. Gently) Nobu? Sit
down. Come in for a while. Sit, sit. I'll get you a beer.
*(*KIYOKO *leads the reluctant* NOBU *to his seat as* CHIYO
and CURLEY *continue to sing.* KIYOKO *clears the table
and goes back up to the counter for his beer.* CHIYO *and*
CURLEY *have just finished their song and are now teasing*
NOBU *to also join in.)*
CURLEY: Come on, your turn, Nobu.

CHIYO: Sing, sing.
CURLEY: It's Karaoke night at Hasegawa's!
CHIYO: Ojiisan, dozo!*
CHIYO and CURLEY *(chanting)*: Nobu, Nobu, Nobu . . .
KIYOKO *(returning with his beer)*: Chiyo, Curley, leave him
alone, leave him alone . . .
(They stop, move back to the Karaoke machine.)
CURLEY *(muttering)*: What a bugga.
KIYOKO *(to* NOBU*)*: Tsukemono?**
*(*NOBU *nods and* KIYOKO *exits.* NOBU *is left alone. Then
he begins to sing, first softly, then growing in volume.)*
NOBU: Nen, nen kororiyo okororiyo,
Bōya wa yoi ko da nen ne shina.
Bōya yo mari wa doko e itta?
Ano yama koete sato e itta.†
CURLEY: What's he singing?
CHIYO: I don't know.
KIYOKO *(reentering)*: It's a lullaby.
*(*CHIYO *and* CURLEY *start to laugh at* NOBU *singing a
baby's song.)*
KIYOKO: Shh! Shh!
(Hearing them, NOBU *stops.* KIYOKO *walks to* NOBU*'s
table.* KIYOKO *starts to sing to help* NOBU *out.* NOBU
joins back in. NOBU*'s voice is not pretty. But it is earnest
and straightforward, filling the traditional song with a
gutsy soulfulness.* KIYOKO *and* NOBU *finish the song
together.)*
NOBU *(quietly)*: My papa used to sing it to me.
(Dim to darkness.)

[END OF SCENE]

* Old man, please!
** Japanese pickled vegetable.
† Sleep, sleep, hushabye, / Little boy, good boy, go to sleep now. / Little boy, where
has your ball gone? / Way over the mountains to the distant fields.

Scene Seven

The

MASI's place, three weeks later. Afternoon. MASI *at*
clothesline. JUDY *visiting with* TIMOTHY.

Wash

JUDY: I don't see how you had two of us, Mom. I need sleep.
    Large doses of it. Jimmy's so lazy sometimes. I even kick
    him "accidentally" when Timothy starts crying. Think he
    gets up to feed the baby?
MASI: Daddy used to.
JUDY: Used to what?
MASI: Get up at night and feed you kids.
JUDY: Dad? You're kidding.
MASI: He used to sing to you. No wonder you kids would
    cry.
    (They laugh.)
JUDY: I saw your new phone-answering machine.
MASI *(proud)*: Yeah. For messages.
JUDY *(kidding)*: What? You got a new boyfriend?
MASI: Judy.
JUDY: Well, why not, Mom? You moved out. It's about time
    you started meeting new people. Once you get a divorce
    you're going to have to do that any . . .
MASI *(interrupts)*: I'm not getting a divorce.
JUDY: What are you going to do? You live here, Dad's over
    there . . . *(No response)* You can't do that forever.
MASI: I just do his wash. That's all I do. Just his wash. *(Pause.*
    MASI *hanging clothes)* I think you should call Dad.
JUDY: Mom, what can I say to him? I can't talk about my
    husband, I can't talk about my baby.
MASI: Judy, you know how Dad is.

JUDY: All he can talk about is how he can't show his face at
Tak's barbershop because I married a kurochan.* *black*
MASI: He's not going to call you.
JUDY: Of course not—we'd have to talk.
  (Silence. JUDY *goes back to the baby.* MASI *watches her.)*
MASI: Judy.
JUDY: What?
MASI: He needs you.
JUDY: Why can't he accept it? Why can't he just say, "It's
  okay, it's okay, Judy"? I just need him to say that much.
MASI: He can't. Papa can't.
JUDY: Why? Why the hell not?
  *(*MASI *and* JUDY *look at each other. Dim to darkness.)*

[END OF SCENE]

Scene Eight

KIYOKO's *restaurant, that same evening. We hear the rhythmic
pounding of fists on flesh. As lights come up,* NOBU *and*
KIYOKO *are lit in a pool of light.* KIYOKO *is standing in back
of* NOBU *pounding his back with fists in a punching manner.
She is massaging* NOBU. *This is a supreme joy for him.*
KIYOKO *likes doing it for him.*

KIYOKO *(not stopping)*: Enough?
NOBU *(voice vibrating from the steady blows)*: Nooo . . .
  (They continue in silence, both enjoying the activity.)
KIYOKO: Enough?
NOBU: Noo . . . *(*KIYOKO *'s arms are just too tired.)*

*A black.

160

KIYOKO *(stopping)*: Ahh . . .

NOBU *(stretching)*: Oisho!* Masi used to do it. Sometimes Marsha does it now.

KIYOKO *(pouring tea)*: You're lucky you have children, Nobu. Especially daughters. Harry and I wanted children. They're good, neh.

> *(Awkward silence.* NOBU *abruptly pulls out a small gift-wrapped box and holds it out to* KIYOKO.*)*

NOBU: Here.

> *(*KIYOKO*'s too surprised to take it. From here, spoken in Japanese, except where otherwise indicated.)*

NOBU: Anata no birthday present. Hayo akenesai.**

KIYOKO *(taking it)*: Ara! Nobu . . . *(Opens it and holds up the earrings)* Nobu-chan.

NOBU: Earrings. Inamasu Jewelry Store no mae o totara me ni tsuitanda ne.†

KIYOKO: Mah, kirei, Nobu-chan. Tsukete miru.‡

> *(*KIYOKO *exits.* NOBU *lit in pool of light.)*

MEMORY SEQUENCE. MASI *lit in pool of light.*

MASI: Why don't you want me anymore? *(No response)* We don't sleep . . . You know what I mean and don't give me that kind of look. Is it me? The way my body . . . I've seen those magazines you keep in the back closet with your fishing and hunting gear. I mean, it's all right. I'm just trying to know about us. What happened.

NOBU: Nothing. Nothing happened. What's the matter with you?

MASI: Then why don't you . . . sleep with me?

NOBU: By the time I get home from work I'm tired. Shig all day long, ordering me around, do this, do that. I even had

---

*Ahh!
** Your birthday present. Hurry, open it.
†I was walking by Inamasu's store when I spotted them.
‡They're pretty, Nobu. Let me try them on.

The

Wash

to get up at five o'clock this morning to pick up the produce 'cause his damn son-in-law is a lazy son of a bitch. I'm
tired, I'm tired, Masi.

MASI: What about those magazines?

NOBU: I'll throw 'em out, okay? First thing tomorrow I'll
throw 'em in the trash and burn 'em. That make you feel
better?

(MASI *is hurt by his angry response.*)

NOBU: Masi? *(No response)* Masi. You're pretty. You are.

(Memory ends. MASI *withdraws into shadows.)*

KIYOKO *returns to* NOBU *with the earrings on. Lights come
up.*

KIYOKO *(posing)*: Nobu-chan?

NOBU: Suteki da nah.*

(KIYOKO *attempts to embrace* NOBU. *It's too
uncomfortable for* NOBU *and he gently pushes her away.*
KIYOKO *is quite embarrassed. From now on they speak
in English again.)*

KIYOKO: How come you do that to me? *(No response)* Don't
you like it?

NOBU: I like it. But I don't like it, too.

(Dim to darkness.)

[END OF SCENE]

Scene Nine

$\wedge$

MASI's *apartment, four or five days later. Couch has rumpled
blanket on it. Morning.* SADAO *is standing holding the door*

*Looks beautiful.

open for a surprised MARSHA. SADAO *is dressed only in pants and an undershirt.* MARSHA *is holding a box of manju (Japanese pastry). They have never met.*

SADAO: Good morning.

MARSHA: Is my mother . . . Is Mrs. Matsumoto here?

MASI *(off)*: Who is it?

SADAO: Come on in, please come in.

*(*MASI *enters in a bathrobe with her hair tied up in a towel as if just washed.)*

MASI *(momentarily caught off guard)*: Oh, hi, Marsha. Come in.

MARSHA *(entering hesitantly)*: Hello, Mom.

MASI: This is Sadao Nakasato. *(To* SADAO*)* My eldest one, Marsha.

SADAO: Hello, Marsha.

MARSHA: Hello. *(Awkward pause.* MARSHA *remembers her package.)* Oh, I just thought I'd bring some manju by. *(Handing it to* MASI*)* I didn't think it was that early. Next time I guess I'll call first.

SADAO: Hmm, love manju. Some of my favorites. Especially the ones with the kinako on top. The brown powdery stuff?

MARSHA: I meant to drop it off last night but I called and no one was here.

MASI: Oh, we got in late from fishing.

SADAO: We caught the limit.

MASI *(looking at phone-answering machine)*: I have to remember to turn this machine on.

SADAO: In fact, Masi caught more than me.

MASI: Teamwork. I catch them and Sadao takes them off the hook. Sit down and have breakfast with us. Sit, sit.

MARSHA: That's okay, Mom.

MASI: It was so late last night I told Sadao to sleep on the

emphasize (handwritten annotation)

couch. So he did. He said he would cook breakfast for me in the morning. Right over there on the couch.
(MASI *and* SADAO *are nodding to each other in agreement.* MARSHA *doesn't move.*)

SADAO: Waffles.

MASI: You sure you know how?

old / *poor* / *woman* (handwritten annotation)

SADAO: I can make them, good ones. From scratch.

MASI: Sit down, sit down.

MARSHA: No, no, Mom. I really should be going. I'm going to stop over at the house. To see Dad, too.

MASI: No, wait, wait . . . I have some fish for you.
(MASI *is wrapping up two packages of fish with newspaper.* MARSHA *notices.*)

MARSHA: Mom, I don't want any fish.

MASI *(handing her a package)*: Then give it to Brad.

MARSHA: Mom, I'm not seeing him anymore.

MASI: Oh. Then give it to Dad.

MARSHA: What do I tell him?

MASI *(momentary pause)*: Just give it to him. No use wasting it. He can eat fish morning, noon, and night.
(MASI *hustles* MARSHA *towards the door.*)

SADAO: No waffles? They're low cholesterol.

MARSHA: Uh, no thanks. Nice to meet you, Mr. Nakasato.
(MARSHA *pauses at door. They exchange glances.*) Bye, Mom. (MARSHA *exits.*)

He doesn't know how to wash his own clothes. Still depends on his wife. (handwritten annotation)

MASI *(calling after)*: Tell Daddy I'll bring his clothes by, that I've been busy. And tell him to put his old clothes in a pile where I can see it. Last time I couldn't find one of his underwear and he got mad at me. *(Closes door)* It was under the icebox.
(*As* SADAO *rambles on,* MASI *seems lost in her thoughts.*)

SADAO *(caught up in his cooking)*: Everything's low cholesterol. Except for the Cool Whip. But that doesn't count because that's optional. Where's the MSG? That's my secret. My daughter gets so mad at me. "Dad, you're a

pharmacist, you should know better than to use MSG."
She's a health food nut . . .   The
*(SADAO is bending down to look in a lower cabinet for
the MSG. As he disappears, MASI moves into a pool of*   Wash
light.)

MEMORY SEQUENCE. NOBU *lit in pool of light.*

NOBU: No, Masi, I said size eight, size eight hooks.
MASI: You told me to buy size six, not size eight. That's not
what you told me.
NOBU: I get home from the store I expect you to . . . Jesus
Christ . . . *(Starting to pace)*
MASI: Nobu, Nobu, you didn't tell me to get size eight
hooks. You told me size . . .
NOBU *(interrupts)*: I said size eight. I said size eight hooks.
(Pause) This is my house. Masi? After I come home from
that damn store—here . . . This is *my* house.
(Silence.)
MASI *(quietly)*: I'm sorry. I'm wrong. You said size eight
hooks.
(NOBU withdraws. Lights up. End of memory.)

SADAO *gets up from behind the cabinet with the MSG.*

SADAO: You don't mind, do you? Masi? The ajinomoto, the
MSG. Is it OK with you?
MASI: Yes, yes, it's fine.
(SADAO is aware of MASI's pensiveness.)
SADAO: Sometimes I add prune juice, but then you have to
go easy on the MSG. The prune juice really does add a nice
hint of flavor to the waffles if you don't overdo it.
*(NOBU lit in half-light looking at his unfinished kite
frame.)*
SADAO: Everything in moderation. I think these people got

a little carried away with this MSG thing. Of course, I'm not running a Chinese restaurant, either. I'm just talking about a tiny pinch of the stuff . . .

(As lights go to half on SADAO *and* MASI, NOBU *is lit in a pool of light. He lifts the kite above his head and begins to move it as if it were flying. For a moment* NOBU *seems to be a child making believe that his kite is soaring high above in the clouds.* NOBU *goes to half-light.)*

[END OF SCENE]

Scene Ten

Neighborhood streets. KIYOKO *and* CHIYO *enter, checking the addresses on houses.*

CHIYO:: Kiyoko, what's the address? What's the number?
KIYOKO *(looking at a piece of paper)*: 2158 A Street.
CHIYO *(looking)*: 2152, 2154 . . . There it is.
  *(*JUDY *hurries in, wiping her hands.)*
JUDY: Just a minute, I'm coming! *(*JUDY *stops when she sees the two strangers at her door.)* Yes?
KIYOKO: I am a friend of your father. My name is Kiyoko Hasegawa.
CHIYO: Chiyo Froelich.
JUDY: Hi.
KIYOKO: I run a restaurant. Hasegawa's?
CHIYO: Chiyo's Hair Salon, right next door.
JUDY: Oh . . . Yeah, yeah.
KIYOKO: We are having a small get-together at my place for your father.

CHIYO: A birthday party.
(They hear the baby crying.)
KIYOKO: Oh, that must be Timothy.
CHIYO: Nobu should see him.
(Awkward pause.)
JUDY *(starting to withdraw)*: I really should . . . Excuse
me . . .
CHIYO *(to KIYOKO)*: Show Judy your earrings. Kiyoko,
show her.
KIYOKO: Chiyo.
CHIYO: He gave them to her. Your father. For her birthday.
KIYOKO: For my birthday. He comes to my restaurant
almost every day. He likes my cooking. That's how come I
know him so good.
CHIYO *(kidding)*: He's so mendokusai.* I don't like cucum-
ber pickle, I like eggplant. Monku, monku all the time.
KIYOKO: Oh, it's no trouble at all. I like to do things like
that. I like to cook for Nobu. *(TIMOTHY starts to cry in the
back.)*
JUDY *(starting to leave)*: I really need to get back to the
baby . . .
KIYOKO: So can you come?
CHIYO: To the birthday?
JUDY *(exiting)*: I'm not sure. I'm really busy these days. Nice
meeting you.
(Dim to darkness.)

[END OF SCENE]

*Troublesome.

Scene Eleven

The

Wash

Lights up on NOBU *with his kite.* MASI *in half-light moves away from* SADAO. *She's holding the fishing pole.* NOBU *puts down the kite frame. Thinking. Picks up the phone and dials* MASI'*s place.*

    MASI'*s place in half-light.* SADAO *at the counter making waffles. He hears the phone machine click on but does not answer it.* MASI *is off to the side studying her rod and reel.*

NOBU: Masi? You got any . . . Masi?
> (MASI'*s phone machine kicks in.* NOBU *doesn't know how to deal with it.*)

MASI'S RECORDED VOICE: Hello. This is Masi Matsumoto. I'm not in right now, so please wait for the tone and leave your name, your number, and a short message. Thank you. Bye-bye.
> (NOBU *listens to the message end. The beep sounds. He's panicked, not quite sure what to do.*)

NOBU: I am Nobu Matsumoto. My telephone number is 751 . . . damn. *(Checks the number)* 751-8263. *(Not sure if he has said his name)* I am Nobu Matsumoto.
> (NOBU *hangs up. Picks up his kite and stares at it.* MASI *lit in pool of light. Casting. She is working on perfecting her technique, putting together all the little things that* SADAO *has taught her. She goes through one complete cycle without a hitch. Very smooth. Having done the whole thing without a mistake gives her great satisfaction. She smiles to herself. It feels good. She begins again. Dim to darkness on* MASI *and* NOBU.)

[END OF ACT ONE]

KIYOKO's *restaurant, four weeks later. Surprise birthday party
for* NOBU. JUDY *stands by herself out front, picking
at the food.* CURLEY *and* MARSHA *are in the kitchen and*
KIYOKO *and* CHIYO *scurry about with last-minute
preparations. Over the restaurant speakers we hear
a forties tune like "String of Pearls."*

KIYOKO *(calling)*: Curley! Hurry up with the chicken teri!
(Checking the food items) Ara! I forgot the dip. Chiyo, go
talk, go talk.
　　*(*KIYOKO *pushes* CHIYO *towards* JUDY, *then hurries
　　back into the kitchen as* CURLEY *and* MARSHA *enter,
　　carrying more food.* MARSHA *is holding her nose.)*
CHIYO *(to* JUDY, *in passing)*: Nobu's favorite song. *(Stops
momentarily, touching* JUDY's *hair)* You come see me, I
know what to do with it.
　　*(*CHIYO *heads back to the kitchen as* MARSHA *and*
　　CURLEY *are setting their dishes down.)*
CURLEY: If you think this stink, wait 'til you try my famous
homyu.
MARSHA *(attempting to be polite)*: No, really, it wasn't that
bad.
CURLEY: All orientals gotta have stink food. It's part of
our culture. Chinese, Japanese, Koreans, Filipinos—we all
got one dish that is so stink. Filipinos got fish-gut paste,
bagaoong. Koreans, kim chee. Whew! Chinese got this
thing called hamha, shrimp paste. My mudda used to cook
with it. Whew! Stink like something went die.
　　*(*CHIYO *enters.)*

CHIYO *(admonishing)*: Curley.

CURLEY *(ignoring* CHIYO*)*: And us Buddhaheads eat takuan, the pickled horseradish. When you open up the bottle, the neighbors call to see if your toilet went explode!

CHIYO *(poking head into the kitchen)*: Kiyoko! He's at it again!

CURLEY: Next time you come I make you my homyu.

JUDY: Homyu? *(To* MARSHA*)* You know homyu?

MARSHA: It's some kind of vegetable dish or something? . . .

CURLEY: No, no, no . . . What's a matta? You guys live on Mars? You never heard of homyu? Homyu. Steamed pork hash. It's my specialty. Gotta have the stinky fish on top. That's the secret. Lotsa pake places don't use that fish anymore. Know why? Too stink! Chase all the haole customers away. Take pork butt, chop it into small pieces. Little pig snout, huh? Throw it in. Tastes so ono.* Four water chestnuts, chopped. Teaspoon of cornstarch . . .

*(*KIYOKO *enters with dip,* CHIYO *trailing.)*

KIYOKO *(interrupts)*: Curley! Curley! Go do the cake!

MARSHA *(to* CURLEY*)*: I'll help you.

CHIYO: Kiyoko, when is he coming?

KIYOKO *(to* CHIYO*)*: He should be on his way . . . *(To* MARSHA*)* You shouldn't help anymore. Eat, eat. Talk to Chiyo. *(Continues.)*

MARSHA *(overlapping)*: We met already . . .

KIYOKO *(continues. To* CURLEY*)* Go, go, put the candles on the cake. No beer, either.

CURLEY *(exiting, calling back to* MARSHA *while scratching his butt)*: Stinky fish. Don't forget the stinky fish . . .

KIYOKO *(following him out)*: Don't scratch your . . .

*(*KIYOKO *remembers the guests. As they exit,* CHIYO *approaches* JUDY *and* MARSHA*.)*

CHIYO: I've never seen her like this. She's acting like a kid

*Pake, "Chinese"; haole, "white"; ono, "tasty."

back there. *(Catching her breath and looking the two daughters over)* You're Judy, neh, the fifth grade teacher?

JUDY: I am the fifth-grade teacher.

CHIYO: And you're the dental . . . *(Continues.)*

MARSHA *(overlapping)*: . . . Hygienist, I told you earlier . . .

CHIYO *(continues)*: . . . hygienist—yeah, yeah, you told me before. *(Quietly laughs about her mistake. Calms down.)* So. What do you think of the both of them? Nobu and Kiyoko? *(Awkward pause.)*

MARSHA: I think it's . . . good. I think it's good.

(CHIYO looks to JUDY, who is silent.)

CHIYO *(touching her hair gently)*: You come see me. I know what to do with it.

(CHIYO turns and walks back towards the kitchen.)

MARSHA: Judy.

JUDY: This is stupid—what am I doing here?

MARSHA: We're doing this for Dad.

JUDY: You really think he's going to want us here?

MARSHA: Judy . . .

JUDY: Do you?

(KIYOKO hurries in, followed by CHIYO.)

KIYOKO: Curley called—Nobu's not home, so he's coming. *(To MARSHA, feigning enthusiasm)* I'm so glad you could make it. Judy said you weren't sure whether you could all come or not.

MARSHA: Oh no, no. We wouldn't have missed it.

KIYOKO: Nobu-chan will be so happy you are here.

MARSHA: It was very kind of you to invite us.

KIYOKO: Oh no, no, no. I wanted all of you here.

CHIYO: Yeah, yeah, we wanted all of you here.

KIYOKO *(to JUDY)*: Where is the baby?

JUDY: Jimmy's home baby-sitting him.

CHIYO: Next time you bring him. We got plenty of room here.

KIYOKO: Yes, please, please. Next time you bring the baby

and Jimmy, too. I want to get to know all of Nobu-chan's family.

(CURLEY *rushes in with his ukelele.*)

CURLEY: HAYO! HAYO!* THE BUGGA'S COMING! THE BUGGA'S COMING!

CHIYO: I'll get the cake. Hide! Hide!

CURLEY: I got the lights.

KIYOKO (*to* MARSHA *and* JUDY): In here, in here . . .

(*Darkness.* NOBU *enters cautiously.*)

NOBU: Kiyoko! Kiyoko!

(*The lights come up abruptly, then begin a slow fade through the rest of the scene.*)

ALL: SURPRISE!

(NOBU *is first happy. Then he sees* JUDY *and* MARSHA. *He is in shock.* CHIYO *and* CURLEY *lead everyone in a rousing, celebratory birthday song as* KIYOKO *enters with a birthday cake decorated with burning candles.* NOBU *is attempting to appear happy, but he is becoming more and more upset that his daughters are there. Lights continue their slow fade through the song, which is beginning to fall apart.* KIYOKO *is now standing next to* NOBU *holding the cake out in front of him. She senses something is wrong. The song ends with* CURLEY *and* KIYOKO *mumbling the last few lyrics. Silence.* NOBU's *face is illuminated by the glowing candles.* NOBU *makes no move to blow out the candles. The moment is now uncomfortable.* KIYOKO *is very upset.*)

KIYOKO: Nobu-chan, please.

JUDY (*irritated*): Dad.

(NOBU *still refuses to blow out the candles. Moment is now extremely awkward. No one knows what to do.*)

*Hurry! hurry!

MARSHA *(gently)*: Daddy.

(Slowly NOBU *leans forward and with a forceful breath* The

extinguishes the candles.)

[END OF SCENE] *Wash*

Scene Two

MASI's *place, the same night.* SADAO *and* MASI *on couch. Both are propped up,* SADAO *intently watching TV and* MASI *peering at the TV over the magazine she holds in front of her.* SADAO *keeps switching the channel with his remote control. Each time* MASI *starts to settle into a program,* SADAO *switches the channel, causing her to jerk her head from the shock.*

MASI: Sadao? *(*SADAO *is busy switching channels.)*

MASI: Sadao?

SADAO: Hmm?

MASI: Could you please keep it on one?

SADAO *(realizing what he's been doing)*: Oh. I'm sorry. *(Starts switching channels again)* Which one? This one? How's this?

MASI: Fine, fine. That's fine.

(They settle into watching TV.)

MASI: Sadao?

SADAO: Hmm?

MASI: I don't feel good. *(Pause)* I think something's wrong with me.

SADAO: What, what? Want me to call Doc Takei?

MASI: No, no . . .

SADAO: You have a fever? Headache? What's wrong?

The   MASI: No, no, nothing like that. *(Pause. Thinking.)* I'm too happy.

Wash   SADAO: What?

MASI: I feel . . . too happy.

(SADAO stares at her, uncomprehending.)

MASI: I used to feel like this as a kid, I think. But it was . . . different.

(Pause.)

SADAO: You feel too happy?

MASI: When you're a kid you get ice cream and 'member how you used to feel? Happy, right? But then you eat it all up and it's gone, or you eat too much of it and you throw up. But this just goes on and on.

SADAO: You mean us?

(MASI nods.)

SADAO: Yeah, but this is a little different from ice cream, don't you . . .

MASI *(interrupts)*: Of course, of course, Sadao.

SADAO: What about with Nobu? Didn't you go through this with him?

(MASI shakes her head.)

SADAO: I mean in the beginning when you first met? When you got married?

MASI: No, it wasn't like that. *(Pause)* I think something's wrong with me. You know how they say there's no such thing as an accident? That you really wanted it to happen and so it did? I don't think I ever really cared for Nobu. Not the way he cared for me. There was someone else who liked me in camp. I liked him, too. I married Nobu. Something's wrong with me, huh? Now you make me feel too happy. I don't like it. It makes me . . . unhappy.

(They both laugh. Sadao reaches out and places his hand on top of hers.)

MASI: Was she in a lot of pain?

(SADAO *doesn't follow her comment.*)

MASI: Your wife. Towards the end. In the hospital.

SADAO (*realizes she's talking about his first wife, Mary*): She just slept all the time. No, not too much. After about two weeks she went into a coma and that was it. You can't tell. Cancer's like that. Mary was pretty lucky, I guess. (*Pause. Thinking.*) There's nothing wrong with you. Really, there isn't. (*Pause. Trying to decide whether to say something or not.*) You scare me. You know that? Sometimes you scare me half to death. I don't want to go through that again. I told myself, "Never, ever again." Dead is better than feeling that kind of pain. But this . . . this is . . . I don't know . . . To get a second chance . . . (*Pause*) There's nothing good about growing old. You spend most of your time taking medicine and going to the doctor so you won't die. The rest of the time you spend going to the funerals of your friends who did die, and they were taking the same medicine and seeing the same doctors, so what's the use, anyway? Huh? (*Sarcastically*) The golden years . . . Look at us. Here we are. At our age. Not even married. Can you imagine what the kids are thinking?

MASI: We're not doing anything wrong.

SADAO: Of course, I know, I know.

MASI: We're not doing anything wrong, Sadao. We're not.

SADAO: I know. But when I really think about what we're doing . . . it embarrasses the hell out of me!

(*They look at each other, then suddenly burst out laughing. They gradually calm down.*)

MASI: I scare you half to death. And you . . . you make me feel so good I feel awful.

(*They look at each other for a moment, then slowly reach out and embrace. Dim to darkness.*)

[END OF SCENE]

The

Wash   KIYOKO's *restaurant, one week later.* NOBU *is sitting at counter sipping sake and eating eggplant pickles.* CURLEY *is watching him from the service window. He comes out, sipping on a beer.*

CURLEY *(takes a big gulp)*: Know why I like to drink beer? Know why? *(As* NOBU *looks up,* CURLEY *answers his own question with a loud, satisfying burp.)* Ahh. I like to let things out. Makes me feel good. Don't like to keep things bottled up inside. Not good for you. Give you an ulcer. Cancer. Maybe you just blow up and disappear altogether, huh. *(Laughs at his own joke. Notices* NOBU *isn't laughing.)* That's the problem with you kotonks. You buggas from the mainland all the time too serious.
     *(*NOBU *glances back towards the door.)*
CURLEY: No worry, no worry. Kiyoko going be back soon. Chiyo's place—yak, yak, yak. Hey, you had lots of girl friends when you was small kid time?
     *(*NOBU *shrugs.)*
CURLEY: Strong silent type, huh? Me? Lotsa wahinis. All the time like to play with Curley. *(Mimicking the girls)* "Curley, darling, you're so cute . . . you're so funny" . . . But I not all the time cute. I not all the time funny. How come you all the time come around here and you still got one wife?
NOBU: We're separated.
CURLEY: So when you gonna get the divorce?
NOBU: No.
     *(*CURLEY *doesn't understand.)*
NOBU: *No.*
CURLEY: What about Kiyoko?
     (No response. NOBU *keeps drinking.)*
CURLEY: I don't like you. I like you. I don't like you 'cause

176

you make Kiyoko feel lousy. I like you 'cause you make her
happy. Hey, she's my boss—who you think catch hell if she
not feeling good? Hey, I don't like catching hell for what
you do . . .
NOBU (interrupts): It's none of your business—Kiyoko and
me.
CURLEY: None of my business? Hey, brudda, Kiyoko may be
feeding your face but I'm the guy who's cooking the meals.
(NOBU stares down at his pickles.)
CURLEY: Nobu?
NOBU: What?
CURLEY: You like Kiyoko? (No response) Well, do you?
NOBU (under his breath): Yeah, I guess so.
CURLEY: "Yeah, I guess so" what?
NOBU (mumbling): I like Kiyoko.
CURLEY: Jesus. Talking to you kotonks is like pulling teeth.
NOBU: I LIKE KIYOKO! (Pause) I like Kiyoko.
(CURLEY leans forward towards NOBU and burps loudly.)
CURLEY: Feels good, huh?
(NOBU is disgusted. CURLEY smiles. Dim to darkness.)

[END OF SCENE]

Scene Four

NOBU's place, one week later. MASI enters, carrying the wash
in a brown paper bag. She unpacks the clothes and stacks them
neatly on the kitchen table. She picks up the old clothes off the
floor, folds them, and puts them in the bag. As she looks up,
one gets the sense that she is trying to decide whether to say
hello to NOBU or just leave. She looks for a moment towards

The

the hallway, then decides otherwise. Just as she turns and starts to make her way towards the door with the bag, NOBU *enters from the hallway.*

Wash

NOBU: Masi, is that you?
*(*NOBU *realizes that she's leaving without bothering to say hello.* MASI *senses this and feels guilty.)*

MASI: I was going. I'm a little late. I was just going to leave the clothes and go. *(As she speaks, she notices the dirty dishes on the coffee table. She puts down the bag and proceeds to clean up the mess as she continues to talk.)* I didn't know you were in the back . . . (MASI *points to the dishes in the sink, while* NOBU *just watches.)* Nobu, why don't you wash the dishes once in a while? Clean up.

NOBU: Place is a dump anyway.
*(*MASI *stops and looks at him.* NOBU *presses the point.)*

NOBU: Place is a dump, Mama. Neighborhood's no good. Full of colored people. Mexicans . . .

MASI *(putting dishes in sink):* Well, move then. Move to the north side like me. I kept saying that all along. For the kids—better schools, better neighborhood . . . Think you listen to me? *(Mimicking* NOBU*)* "I don't like hakujin— white people make me nervous." So you don't like white people, you don't like black people, you don't like Mexicans . . . So who do you like? Huh? Monku, monku, monku.

NOBU *(muttering):* I don't mind Mexicans. *(Pause)* I told Shig you can't keep stocking all that Japanese things when the Nihonjins* are moving out of the neighborhood. You gotta sell to the Mexicans and not all that cheap crap too, 'cause they can tell. Think Shig listens to me? He's the big store owner. The big man. If I was running the store it woulda been different. Different. *(Pause)* And your old man said he'd get me that store.

*Japanese.

MASI: It wasn't his fault. He didn't plan on the war, Nobu.

NOBU: He promised he could set me . . . *(Continues.)* **The**

MASI *(overlapping)*: It wasn't his fault.

NOBU *(continuing)*: . . . up in business or anything else I **Wash**
wanted to do.

MASI: IT WASN'T HIS FAULT! *(Silence)* Who wanted to
be in the relocation camps? Did you? Do you think he
wanted to be in there? It broke Papa's heart. He spent his
entire life building up that farm. Papa was a proud man. A
very proud man. It broke his heart when he lost it. And
how come you didn't go to the bank like I told you? I told
you to go to the bank and ask for . . .

NOBU: I'm just saying I'd run the business different. Shig is a
baka, a fool. That's all I'm saying.

MASI: You're retired. Shig passed away eight years ago. The
store's not even . . . *(Continues.)*

NOBU *(overlapping)*: If all the Japanese move out you can't
keep selling all those Japanese things, you can't. That's all
I'm saying.

MASI *(continuing)*: . . . there any more. It's a cleaner's.
(Silence. MASI *picks up the paper bag of old clothes and
starts to move towards the door. She's had enough.)*

NOBU: Masi?

MASI *(stops)*: What?

NOBU: Mr. Rossi give you any more fish?

MASI *(uncomfortable lying)*: No. Not lately.
(Pause.)

NOBU: Mama?

MASI: Is your back bothering you, Nobu? *(No response)*
Want me to momo* it for you?
*(*NOBU *nods. As* MASI *moves to put the bag down,* NOBU
*removes his undershirt so he is bare chested. He seats
himself.* MASI *begins to massage his shoulders from*

*Massage.

behind. They continue in silence. NOBU *is enjoying the moment. He begins to laugh quietly to himself.)*

MASI: What?

NOBU: When I started work at your papa's farm, he wanted to put me in the packing shed. I said, "No, I want to work in the fields." It was so hot, 110 degrees out there. He thought I was nuts. But I knew every day at eight in the morning and twelve noon you and your sister would bring the water out to us.

MASI *(laughing as she recalls)*: Nobu.

NOBU: I wanted to watch you.

MASI: You would just stand there with your cup, staring at me.

NOBU: Hell, I didn't know what to say.

MASI: You drank so much water, Lila and I thought maybe you had rabies. We used to call you "Nobu, the Mad Dog." *(Both laughing)* Papa liked you.

NOBU: Boy, he was a tough son of a bitch.

MASI: I didn't think anyone could keep up with Papa. But you could work like a horse. You and Papa. Proud. Stubborn.

(MASI massages NOBU in silence.)

NOBU: Masi? Why don't you cook me breakfast?

MASI: What?

NOBU: Cook me breakfast. I miss my hot rice and raw egg in the morning.

MASI: It's late, Nobu. You have your wash. I'm not going to come all the way back over here just to cook you . . .

NOBU *(interrupts)*: Just breakfast. Then in the morning when we get up you can go back to your place.

(MASI stops, realizing he is asking her to spend the night. MASI does not move. NOBU stares ahead. More silence.

*Then, tentatively, she moves her hands forward and begins
to massage him. A faint smile appears on* NOBU's *face.*   The
Dim to darkness.)

[END OF SCENE]   *He misses her*   Wash

Scene Five

KIYOKO's *restaurant, one week later.* CURLEY, *after hours,
seated in semidarkness. Feet up on table, accompanying
himself on the ukelele and singing a sad Hawaiian folk song,
like "Manuela Boy."*

As he sings, MASI's *place lit in pool of light.* SADAO *stands
before the door* MASI *has just opened. In* SADAO's *right hand
he holds a suitcase and in his left several fishing poles. On his
head sits a fishing hat.* SADAO *has come to move in with*
MASI. *For a moment they look at each other in silence.
Then* MASI *invites him in.* SADAO *enters. Dim to darkness.
Dim to darkness on* CURLEY *as he finishes the song.*

[END OF SCENE]

Scene Six

NOBU's *place, three days later. Late afternoon.* JUDY *has
stopped by with* TIMOTHY. JUDY *sets the baby down on the
kitchen table upstage of* NOBU. NOBU *turns to look at* JUDY,
then returns to working on the kite and watching TV. This is

181

the first time JUDY *has visited* NOBU *since their breakup over her marriage. He has never seen* TIMOTHY.

JUDY *(moving down towards* NOBU*)*: I was just driving by and I thought I'd stop in. *(No response)* You doing okay, Dad? *(Silence)* You know, Mom? I just wanted to say . . .

NOBU *(interrupts)*: Did he come?

JUDY: *(exasperated)*: No, he did not.

NOBU: He can come to the house now.

JUDY: "He can come to the house now"? Jesus Christ. Dad, he isn't one of your children. He doesn't need your permission. He's a . . . *(Continues.)*

NOBU *(overlapping)*: This is my house. He needs my permission.

JUDY *(continues)*: . . . grown man. I don't want to fight. I didn't come here to fight with you, Dad.

NOBU: I *said* he can come . . .

JUDY *(interrupts)*: He won't come, he doesn't like you! *(Silence.)*

NOBU: Damn kurochan . . .

JUDY: He's black, not kurochan. It's "African American." *(Pause)* Everybody marries out, okay? Sanseis don't like Sanseis.

NOBU: Tak's son married a Nihonjin, Shig's daughter did, your cousin Patsy . . . *(Continues.)*

JUDY *(overlapping)*: Okay, okay, I didn't, I didn't, all right.

NOBU *(continues)*: . . . did, Marsha's going to. *(Pause. Looks back to* TIMOTHY.*)*

JUDY: But is that any reason not to see my baby? He's a part of you, too.

NOBU: No, no. Japanese marry other Japanese, their kids are Yonsei—not these damn ainoko.*
(Silence.)

* Yonsei, "fourth-generation Japanese American"; ainoko, "biracial person."

JUDY: You're gonna die out, you know that. You're gonna
be extinct and nobody's gonna give a goddamn.   The
*(TIMOTHY has begun to cry softly. She goes over and
picks the baby up, trying to soothe him.* JUDY, *compos-*   Wash
*ing herself, decides to try one last time to say what she
came to tell her father.* JUDY *walks back to* NOBU, *this
time carrying* TIMOTHY *with her.)*
JUDY: Dad? *(No response)* Dad, you know Mom's moving
out of the house? I didn't put her up to it. Honest. *(Silence.*
NOBU *stares straight ahead.* JUDY *begins to cry.)* If I did . . .
I'm sorry.
NOBU: Judy . . .
(More silence from NOBU. JUDY *gives up trying to talk to
this man. As she turns to leave, she notices* NOBU. *He is
looking towards her, at* TIMOTHY. *Something in his
expression makes* JUDY *bring the baby over to* NOBU.*)
JUDY *(holding the baby out)*: Timothy. Your grandson.
*(For a moment there is hesitation. We are not sure whether
NOBU is going to take the baby. Then, NOBU reaches out
and takes TIMOTHY. JUDY watches as NOBU awkwardly
holds his grandson for the first time. As JUDY begins to
withdraw from the scene upstage into a pool of light,
MARSHA is also lit upstage in her own separate pool
of light. NOBU remains lit holding TIMOTHY. He begins
to hum the traditional Japanese lullaby "Donguri."
MARSHA and JUDY watch NOBU and TIMOTHY as
they speak.)*
MARSHA: You didn't tell Dad, did you?
JUDY: No. I just brought the baby by.
MARSHA: It's going to kill him when he finds out.
JUDY: He's got that other woman.
MARSHA: Judy. *(Pause)* Maybe he already knows about
Mom and Mr. Nakasato.
JUDY: I don't think so. I really don't think so.
(They continue to watch as NOBU *begins to sing the
"Donguri" song to* TIMOTHY.*)*

NOBU *(singing)*:

Donguri koro koro, donguri ko
Oike ni hamatte, saa taihen
Dojō ga dette kite, "konnichiwa"
Timothy isshoni, asobimashō . . .*
(Repeat.)
(MARSHA *and* JUDY *dim to darkness first.* NOBU *is left
alone in a pool of light singing to* TIMOTHY. *As he dims
to darkness, we hear the whir of a coffee grinder.)*

[END OF SCENE]

Scene Seven

MASI's *place, two days later.* MASI *has asked* JUDY *and*
MARSHA *over for a talk. She has just told them she is going
over to see* NOBU. *She is going to tell him that she wants to
divorce him and to marry again.*

The two daughters sit uneasily while MASI *is at the counter
preparing coffee.* MASI *is trying to get the Braun grinder to
work. She's getting the feel of it by pushing the button. We hear
the whir of the spinning rotor blade.*

*She's ready. Takes the plastic top off and pours the beans in.
Then, presses the start button. Just as the grinder picks up top
speed* MASI *accidentally pulls the plastic top off. Beans go
flying every which way! Pelting her face, bouncing off the
cabinets. Quiet.* MASI *peeks from behind her hands. A couple*

*Acorn, acorn, rolling along
Fell into a pond, what will we do?
Up comes a loache fish, says, "Good afternoon."
Timothy, let's go play together.

of beans embedded in her hair fall to the counter. MASI *is upset. The daughters are embarrassed. Normally, this would be a funny situation for them.*
    MARSHA *starts to pick up the beans scattered on the floor.* JUDY *starts to giggle—it's all too ridiculous.*

The
Wash

JUDY *(trying to suppress her laughter)*: I'm sorry, I'm sorry . . .
MARSHA: I'll clean it up.
    (MASI *begins to laugh.*)
JUDY: God, what a mess.
MASI *(to* MARSHA*)*: Let it go, don't bother. I'll take care of it later.
    (JUDY *finds a man's sock.*)
JUDY *(teasing)*: What's this? This belong to Mr. Nakasato?
MASI *(grabbing it)*: Judy.
MARSHA: Why didn't you just leave sooner? You didn't have to stick around for us.
MASI: I didn't. I was . . . I was scared.
MARSHA: Of Dad?
MASI: I don't know. Everything.
JUDY: Was it 'cause I kept harping on you to move out on him all those years? Is that why you left?
MARSHA: What's the difference now?
JUDY: Marsha.
    (*Pause.*)
MASI: There are things you kids don't know. I didn't want to talk about them to you but . . . Daddy and I, we didn't sleep . . . *(Continues.)*
JUDY *(overlapping)*: That's okay, Mom. Really, it's okay . . .
MASI *(continues)*: . . . together. Every time I wanted to, he would push me away. Ten, fifteen years he didn't want me. *(Pause)* We were having one of our arguments, just like always. And he was going on and on about how it was my fault this and my fault that. And I was trying to explain my

**The
Wash**

side of it, when he turned on me, "Shut up, Mama. You
don't know anything. You're stupid." Stupid. After forty-
two years of letting him be right he called me that. And I
understood. He didn't even need me to make him be right
anymore. He just needed me to be stupid. I was tired. I
couldn't fight him anymore. He won. He finally made me
feel like shit. *(Shocking* JUDY *and* MARSHA *with her strong
language)* That was the night I left him and came over to
your place. *(Nodding towards* JUDY*)* I like Sadao. *(Turns to*
MARSHA*)* I like Sadao very much.
   (MARSHA *turns away, then gets up and exits.* MASI *sends*
JUDY *after* MARSHA *to comfort her. Dim to darkness.)*

[END OF SCENE]

Scene Eight

NOBU's *place, the same day. "String of Pearls" can be heard
playing faintly in the background. He's fixing himself in front
of a small wall mirror. He adjusts the collar of his shirt and
tugs at his sweater until it looks right.* NOBU *checks his watch.
As he begins to pick up some of the scattered clothes on the
floor,* MASI *enters. Music cue ends.*
   NOBU *quickly gets up and moves to the sofa.* MASI *goes
over to the kitchen area and takes clothes out of the bag,
setting them neatly on the table. She picks up the dirty clothes
off the floor, folds them, and puts them into the bag. As she's
doing this,* NOBU *gets up, shuffles over to the stove, and turns
on the flame to heat some water. Stands there and watches the
water heat up.*

MASI *(sits down on sofa)*: I want to talk, Nobu.
(*No response.* NOBU *gets the tea out and pours some into*   **The**
the pot.)
MASI: I have something I want to tell you.   **Wash**
NOBU *(moving back to couch)*: Want some tea?
(*As* NOBU *sits,* MASI *gets up and moves towards the sink
area. She gets a sponge and wipes off the tea leaves he has
spilled on the counter.* NOBU *turns on the TV and stares
at it.*)
MASI: You know Dorothy and Henry's son, George?
NOBU: The pharmacist or something?
MASI: No, the lawyer one. He's the lawyer one. I went to see
him. I went to see about a divorce. About getting one. *(No
response)* I want to get married again. So I went to George
to see about a divorce. I wanted to tell you first so you'd
know. I didn't want you to hear from someone else. I know
how you hate that kind of thing. Thinking something's
going on behind your back.
NOBU: Wait, wait, wait a second. You want to get . . . What?
What's all this?
MASI: It's the best thing, Nobu. We've been separated how
long now? How long have we been living different places?
NOBU: I don't know. I never thought about it. Not too long.
MASI: Thirteen months. over a yr
NOBU: Thirteen months, who cares? I never thought about
it.
MASI: It's the same as being divorced, isn't it?
NOBU: It doesn't seem that long. You moved out of this
house. It wasn't my idea. It was your idea. I never liked it.
MASI: It doesn't matter whose idea it was. It's been over a
year since we . . .
NOBU *(interrupts)*: You want to get married? Yeah, I know
it's been over a year but I always thought . . . You know,
that we'd . . .
MASI *(interrupts)*: It's been over a year, Nobu.

NOBU: I know! I said I know.

(Pause.)

MASI: I've been seeing someone. It wasn't planned or anything. It just happened.

NOBU: What do you mean, "seeing someone"? What do you mean?

MASI: He's very nice. A widower. He takes me fishing. He has a nice vegetable garden that he . . .

NOBU *(interrupts)*: Who is he? Do I know him? Is it someone I know?

MASI: His name is Sadao Nakasato. His wife died about two years ago. He's related to Dorothy and Henry. Nobu, it's the best thing for both of us.

NOBU: You keep saying it's the best thing, the best thing. *(Pause)* Masi, why did you sleep with me that night? *(Silence.)*

MASI: Aren't you seeing somebody?

NOBU: No. Not like that.

MASI: But the kids said she's very nice. That she invited . . .

NOBU *(interrupts)*: It's totally different! I'm not seeing anyone! *(Pause)* How long have you been seeing this guy? How long?

MASI: Please, Nobu. You always get what *you* want. I always let you have your way. For once just let . . .

NOBU *(interrupts)*: HOW LONG!

MASI: About five months.

NOBU: FIVE MONTHS! How come you never told me? Do the girls know, too? The girls know! Everybody knows? Five months. FIVE GODDAMN MONTHS AND I DON'T KNOW!!

(NOBU breaks the kite.)

MASI: I asked them not to tell you.

NOBU: Why? Why the hell not? Don't I have a right to know?

MASI: Because I knew you'd react this way. Just like this. Yelling and screaming just like you always do.

NOBU: Everybody in this whole goddamn town knows except me! How could you do this to me! Masi! HOW COULD YOU DO THIS TO ME?? *The Wash*
(NOBU *has her by the shoulders and is shaking her violently.*)
MASI: Are you going to hit me?
(*Pause.* NOBU *slowly composes himself and lets her go.*)
MASI: Because I want to be happy, Nobu. I want to be happy.
(MASI *exits.* NOBU *left standing alone. Dim to darkness.*)

[END OF SCENE]

She wasn't happy with him

Scene Nine

KIYOKO's *restaurant, evening of the same day.* CHIYO *and* KIYOKO *seated at table, lit in pool of light.*

KIYOKO: Nine years. That's how long it has been. Nine years since Harry passed away. He never treated me like this. I call, I go over there. Harry never treated me like this.
CHIYO: Kiyoko. Maybe you have to stop thinking about Nobu. Hmm? Maybe . . . maybe you should give him up. (*Silence*) Kiyoko. Lots more fish in the ocean. Lots more. Go out with us. Come on.
KIYOKO: I don't do those kinds of things.
CHIYO: I'll introduce you to some new guys. Remember Ray—you met him? I've been telling him about . . .
KIYOKO (*interrupts*): I don't do those kinds of things. (*Pause*) It's not easy for me, Chiyo. (*Silence*) When Harry died, right after? I started taking the bus to work. I had a car, I could drive. It was easier to drive. I took the bus. For

twenty-five years you go to sleep with him, wake up next to him, he shaves while you shower, comes in from the yard all sweaty. Then he's gone. No more Harry in bed. No more smell of aftershave in the towel you're drying off with. No more sweaty Harry coming up and hugging me. I had a car. I took the bus. I missed men's smells. I missed the smell of men. Every morning I would get up and walk to the corner to take the bus. It would be full of all these men going to work. And it would be full of all these men coming home from work. I would sit there pretending to read my magazine . . . *(Inhales. Discovering the different smells.)* Soap . . . just washed skin . . . aftershave lotion . . . sweat . . .

(Lights come up to half in the restaurant. CURLEY *bursts through the kitchen doors holding a plate of his famous homyu. Brings it over and sets it down on the table, which is now lit in a full pool of light.)*

CURLEY: Homyu! Homyu!

CHIYO: Curley, kusai yo!

CURLEY: I know stink, but stink GOOD!

KIYOKO: Curley!

CURLEY *(motioning)*: Hayo, hayo—all dis good food back dere going to waste. Gonna need a gas mask for all da stinky stuff back dere. Come on, come on. I been cooking all day. Hayo, hayo, Kau Kau time.*

(As lights dim, CURLEY *ushers* KIYOKO *and* CHIYO *offstage into the kitchen.)*

[END OF SCENE]

*Time to eat.

Scene Ten

The

Wash

NOBU's *place, two days later. Knock at the door, and* MARSHA *enters carrying a brown paper bag.* NOBU *is watching TV.*

MARSHA: Mom asked me to drop these by and to pick up the dirty clothes.
> (*No response.* MARSHA *unpacks the newly washed clothes.*)

MARSHA: Kiyoko's been calling me. She's worried about you. She says you won't see anybody. Why don't you just talk to her, Dad?

NOBU: How come you didn't tell me? All the time you come here and you never mention it once. You. I feel so goddamn ashamed. All the time right under my nose. Everyone laughing at me behind my . . .

MARSHA (*interrupts*): Dad, Dad, it's not like that at all. I just didn't think it was all that important to tell . . .

NOBU (*interrupts*): Oh, come on! Mom told you not to tell me so she could go sneaking 'round with that son of a bitch!

MARSHA: All right, all right, but it's not like that at all. No one's trying to hide anything from you and no one's laughing at you.

NOBU (*moving her towards the couch and pushing her down while speaking*): Sit down, sit down over here. Who is he? What does he do? Tell me 'bout him! Tell me!

MARSHA (*seated*): What do you want me to say? Huh, Dad? They're happy. He's a nice man.

NOBU (*repeating*): "He's a nice man." What the hell's that supposed to mean?

MARSHA: He treats her like a very special person.

NOBU: Well, everyone does that in the beginning. In the beginning it's so easy to be . . .

MARSHA *(interrupts)*: She laughs. All the time she's laughing. They're like two little kids. They hold hands. Did you ever do that? I'm embarrassed to be around them. He takes her fishing. He has a little camper and they drive up to Lake Berryessa and camp overnight . . . *(Continues right through)*

NOBU: All right, all right . . .

MARSHA *(continues)*: . . . He teaches her how to bait the hook and cast it out.

NOBU *(overlapping)*: She doesn't like fishing.

MARSHA *(continues)*: I mean you never even took her fishing.

NOBU: I tried to take her lots of times. She wouldn't go.

MARSHA *(continues)*: They even dig up worms in his garden at his house. I saw them. Side by side . . . *(Continues.)*

NOBU: All right, I said.

MARSHA *(continues)*: . . . sitting on the ground digging up worms and . . . *(Continues.)*

NOBU *(overlapping)*: ALL RIGHT! ALL RIGHT!

MARSHA *(continues)*: . . . putting them in a coffee can! I MEAN DID YOU EVER DO THAT FOR MOM!! *(Pause. Quieter.)* Did you? *(Getting worked up again)* You're so . . . so stupid. You are. You're stupid. All you had to say was "Come back. Please come back." You didn't even have to say, "I'm sorry." *(Continues.)*

NOBU *(overlapping)*: I'm your father . . .

MARSHA *(continues)*: . . . Mom would've come back. She would've. That's all you had to say. Three lousy words: "Please come back." *(Continues.)*

NOBU *(overlapping)*: I'm your father . . .

MARSHA *(continues)*: . . . You ruined everything. It's all too late! YOU WRECKED EVERYTHING! *(Pause. Composing herself.)* I'm so mixed up. When I look at Mom I'm

happy for her. When I think about you . . . I don't know.
You have Kiyoko.

NOBU: That's not the same. I'm talking about your Mama.

MARSHA: Dad, Kiyoko cares a great deal about you. She's
been calling Judy and me day and night.

NOBU: She knocks on the door but I don't let her in. She's not
Mama.

MARSHA: Dad. What do you want me to say? That's the way
it is. I used to keep thinking you two would get back
together. I couldn't imagine life any other way. But slowly
I just got used to it. Mom over there, and you here. Then
all this happened. I mean, sometimes I can't recognize
Mom anymore. What do you want me to say? You'll get
used to it.

NOBU *(Pause, upset, then stubbornly)*: No.
   (MARSHA looks at her father sadly.)

MARSHA: You'll get used to it.
   (Dim to darkness on MARSHA and NOBU.)

[END OF SCENE]

Scene Eleven

MASI *and* JUDY *at the clothesline.* JUDY *holds* TIMOTHY
while MASI *hangs clothes. An agitated* NOBU *enters and
begins to pull* MASI *home.*

JUDY: Dad . . .

MASI: Nobu . . .

NOBU: I won't yell, Mama, I won't yell at you anymore. I
won't monku about . . . *(Continues.)*

193

▲

The

Wash

MASI *(overlapping)*: Nobu? Nobu, what are you . . .
(Continues.)

JUDY *(overlapping)*: Dad, Dad . . .

MASI: *(continuing)*: . . . doing? Let go, Nobu . . .

NOBU *(continuing)*: . . . the store or about your papa—I won't monku, I won't do any of that stuff . . .

MASI: Let go of my arm!
(Silence.)

NOBU: I tried, I tried, Masi. After the war, after we got out of camp? After . . . *(Continues.)*

MASI *(overlapping)*: Nobu, camp? What are you . . .

NOBU *(continuing)*: . . . we got out I went to the bank like you told me. So your papa can't give me money, that's all right . . . *(Continues.)*

MASI *(overlapping)*: Nobu, what's this—you never told me . . .

NOBU *(continuing)*: . . . I'll do it on my own. I got there and ask the man how do I sign up to get money. He says, "Sit there and wait." I wait, I wait, I wait five whole goddamn hours. I go up, "How come nobody sees me?" He says, "Sorry, but the person to see you is sick, come back tomorrow." I get so pissed off I throw the magazines all over the place. Everyone is looking. I don't give a damn, I'm shaking I'm so pissed off. And then, and then . . . I'm filled with shame. Shame. Because I threw their magazines all over. After what they did to me, *I'm* ashamed, me, *me*. When I get home I feel something getting so tight inside of me. In my guts, tighter and tighter, getting all balled up. How come I feel like this? Huh? How come I feel like this? I'm scared, Masi. I'm scared. Please. I need . . . *(Continues.)*

MASI *(overlapping)*: You don't understand, you don't . . .

NOBU *(continuing)*: . . . you. I need you. You. You know. You understand how it is now. Please, please, you come home, you come . . . *(Continues.* NOBU *begins to pull* MASI *home.)*

MASI *(overlapping)*: Nobu, Nobu, I can't, I . . .

NOBU *(continuing)*: . . . home now, Mama. Just like always. You come home . . . *(Continues.)*

MASI *(overlapping)*: . . . can't, Nobu.

NOBU: . . . just like always . . .

MASI: I can't.

> *(NOBU begins to break down, letting go of MASI. Begins to plead.)*

NOBU: I'm sorry, I'm sorry, Masi. It's no good, it's no good, Masi. Please come home. Please come home. Please . . .

> *(JUDY pulls MASI away and they withdraw from the scene. NOBU is left alone in a pool of light. Slowly he pulls himself upright, staring into the darkness. He turns and crosses back to his room. He reaches behind his chair and pulls out a long, narrow object wrapped in cloth. As he unwraps it, we see what it is, a shotgun. We hear the mournful wail of a shakuhachi flute. NOBU sits down on the chair with the gun across his lap. Dim to darkness on NOBU.)*

[END OF SCENE]

Scene Twelve

KIYOKO's *restaurant.* CHIYO *at the phone dialing* NOBU's *number. A concerned* CURLEY *stands guard next to her.* KIYOKO *has told them not to bother with him anymore.* KIYOKO *appears and watches them. She makes no attempt to stop them.* CHIYO *lets the phone ring.*

NOBU, *seated in his chair, stares at the phone ringing next to him. He gets up, still holding the gun, and exits.*

No one is answering. CHIYO *and* CURLEY *exchange disappointed looks. Only then does* KIYOKO *burst in on them.*

KIYOKO: How come you keep doing that? Huh? Don't phone him anymore. I told you, didn't I?
(KIYOKO *exits.*)
CURLEY (*to* CHIYO): Hey, maybe it's none of our business.
(*Dim to darkness on the restaurant.*)

[END OF SCENE]

Scene Thirteen

MASI's *place, one week later.* NOBU *standing inside with a shotgun.* SADAO *asleep offstage in the bedroom.*

NOBU: Where is he?
(MASI *stares at the gun.*)
MASI: He went to buy the newspaper.
NOBU (*notices* MASI *watching him cautiously*): It's not loaded. (*Beat*) I thought about it all week, all week. Coming over here, shooting the son of a bitch. I coulda. I coulda done it. (*Pause*) I just wanted to show you. Both of you. That's why I brought it. Don't worry. It's not loaded. (NOBU *cracks the gun and shows her that it is not loaded.*) I just wanted to show both of you how it was, how I was feeling. But it's all right. You two. It's all right now. (NOBU *sets the gun against the wall.* MASI *watches him, trying to decide if it is indeed safe.*)
MASI: Nobu.
NOBU: Yeah?

196

MASI: He's taking a nap. In the bedroom. He likes to do that
after dinner.

The

NOBU: What is he? An old man or something?

MASI: He just likes to take naps. You do, too.

Wash

NOBU: In front of the TV. But I don't go into the bedroom
and lie down. Well, where is he? Bring him out. Don't I get
to meet him?

MASI: You sure? (MASI *looks at him for a long while. She
believes him. She turns to go wake* SADAO *up, then stops.*)
Chester Yoshikawa? That night in the camps when I didn't
show up for the dance? Chester Yoshikawa? We just
talked. That's all.

> (MASI *leaves for the bedroom to awaken* SADAO. NOBU
> *looks slowly around the apartment. It's* MASI *and yet it
> isn't.* NOBU *suddenly has no desire to meet* SADAO.
> *He doesn't want to see them together in this apartment.*
> NOBU *exits abruptly.* MASI *appears cautiously leading
> out a yawning* SADAO. *They look around. No* NOBU.
> *All they see is his shotgun leaning against the wall.*
>
> *As* MASI *and* SADAO *dim to darkness,* MARSHA *and*
> JUDY *are lit in a pool of light extreme downstage.*
> MARSHA *is holding a small kite and slowly moving it
> above* TIMOTHY *who is held by* JUDY. *They sit in silence
> as* MARSHA *moves the kite.*)

JUDY: I can't believe he gave the kite to Timothy. He gets so
mad if you even touch them. And he never flies them.
(Pause.)

MARSHA *(moving the kite)*: No. He never flies them.
*(They dim to half. They turn to watch the action taking
place center stage.)*

[END OF SCENE]

Scene Fourteen

The

Wash

Darkness. Two days later. Onstage, the TV light comes on.
NOBU's *face lit by the screen's light. Lights come up and* NOBU
*is now lit in a pool of light, seated at sofa watching TV. No kite
on the coffee table. The rest of the place is in darkness.* MASI *is
lit in a pool of light. She stands, staring pensively downstage
into space. In her arms she is holding the brown paper bag of
newly washed clothes. She turns and moves towards* NOBU's
place.
As she enters the lights come up full on the house.
   NOBU *is still sitting on the sofa watching TV.* MASI *goes
over to the kitchen table and takes out the newly washed
clothes, stacking them in neat piles on the table. She then
proceeds to pick up the clothes scattered on the floor and to put
them in the bag. She is ready to leave.* MASI *takes the bag of
dirty clothes and moves towards the door, then stops. She
makes up her mind about something she has been struggling
with for a while. Masi returns to the kitchen and leaves the bag
of* NOBU's *dirty clothes on the table. As she opens the door to
leave,* MASI *looks back at* NOBU *and watches him for a brief
moment.*
   During this whole time, NOBU *has never turned around to
look at* MASI *though he is very aware of what is going on.*
MASI *sadly turns and exits through the door. Lights dim with*
NOBU *silently watching TV. Briefly,* NOBU's *face is lit by the
dancing light of the television screen. At the same instant, the
brown paper bag of wash on the table is illuminated by a shaft
of light. His phone begins to ring.* NOBU *turns to look at it.
Blackout on* NOBU. *The wash fades into darkness. The phone
continues to ring for a few moments. Then, silence.*

[END OF PLAY]

▲

A Song

For A

Nisei

Fisherman

A Song For A Nisei Fisherman had a workshop production at Stanford
University in 1980 by the Asian American Theatre Project.

DIRECTOR. David Henry Hwang

ITSUTA MATSUMOTO played by David Pating

The play was first produced at the Asian American Theater Company in 1981.

DIRECTOR. David Henry Hwang
PRODUCER. Wilbur Obata
LIGHTING DESIGN. Linda Obata
COSTUME DESIGN. Lydia Tanji
SOUND DESIGN. Christopher Moore
STAGE MANAGER. Stan Wong

Cast

ITSUTA MATSUMOTO. Marc Hayashi
MICHIKO MATSUMOTO. Judi Nihei
TOCHAN. James Hirabayashi
KACHAN. Suzi Okazaki
MOSAN. Lane Nishikawa
ROBERT. Kent Horii
JEFFREY. Ken Narasaki
KATS. John Nishio
TAXI DANCERS. Taylor Gilbert and Peggy Ford
MILITARY PERSON. William Ellis Hammond
SINGER. Mitzi Abe
MUSICIAN. Lane Hirabayashi

The second production was with the Mark Taper Forum as part of the New Theatre for Now Festival in 1982. Gordon Davidson was artistic director.

DIRECTORS. Mako and Shizuko Hoshi
SET AND LIGHTING DESIGN. Fred Chuang
COSTUME DESIGN. Terence Tam Soon
MUSIC COMPOSITION AND PERFORMANCE. Kazu Matsui and
  Jeffrey Takiguchi
STAGE MANAGER. Dianne Lewis Hall

Cast

ITSUTA MATSUMOTO. Mako
MICHIKO MATSUMOTO. Dian Kobayashi
TOCHAN. Ernest Harada
KACHAN. Josie Pepito
MOSAN. Keone Young
ROBERT. Leigh Kim
JEFFREY. Nelson Mashita
KATS. Jim Ishida
TAXI DANCERS. Diane Civita and Sarah Ballantine
MILITARY PERSON. Charles Tachovsky
SHAKUHACHI. Kazu Matsui
BASS. Jeffrey Takiguchi

Author's thanks to David Hwang, Mako, and Eric Hayashi

Characters

ITSUTA "ICHAN" MATSUMOTO, the Nisei (second generation
   Japanese American) FISHERMAN
MICHIKO, Wife. Nisei woman
TOCHAN, FISHERMAN's father. Émigré from Hiroshima, Japan,
   living in the Hawaiian Islands
KACHAN, FISHERMAN's mother
MOSAN, FISHERMAN's older brother. In his twenties
ROBERT, FISHERMAN's older son. Doctor. Late twenties
JEFFREY,* FISHERMAN's younger son. Law school dropout. Late
   twenties
KATS, Nisei. FISHERMAN's longtime fishing buddy from Stockton,
   California. Produce man
JOSEPHINE, taxi dancer. Caucasian female, around thirty
CORA, taxi dancer. Caucasian female, around thirty
MILITARY PERSON/RACETRACK ANNOUNCER, Caucasian male,
   around thirty-five
MUSICIANS, a *shakuhachi* (Japanese flute) and an acoustic double
   bass

*If the songs are used in the production, then JEFFREY is also the SINGER.

Place
Stockton, California.

Time
1981.

Settings

Scene 1. Catching fish.
Scene 2. Cleaning fish.
Scene 3. Cooking fish.
Scene 4. Eating fish.
Scene 5. Catching fish.

Rough Timetable

ITSUTA MATSUMOTO: Born around 1913 in the Hawaiian Islands.
TOCHAN *scene (eleven years old):* 1924 in Kauai.
KACHAN *scene (seventeen years old):* 1930 in Kauai.
UCLA (eighteen to twenty-one years old): 1931–35 in Los Angeles.
University of Arkansas (twenty-one to twenty-five years old): 1935–39
   in Arkansas.
Taxi dance hall scene: 1938 in San Francisco.
Buddhist Church bazaar scene with MICHIKO: 1940 in Stockton,
   California.
Internment camp scene: 1942 in Rohwer, Arkansas.
Swan and the baby scene: 1947 in Stockton.
KATS *and the boat scene:* 1970 in Stockton.
FISHERMAN, MICHIKO, *and* ROBERT *scene:* 1973 in Stockton.
MICHIKO's *diary scene:* 1974 in Stockton.
FISHERMAN *and* JEFFREY *scene:* 1976 in Stockton.
MICHIKO *passes away:* 1978.
FISHERMAN *dies:* 1981 (sixty-eight years old).

Notes

SET. The set should be as simple as possible. Several low risers
accommodate the needs of various scenes. Along the upstage area
there is a riser with a scrim in front of it. It should be a large enough
area to hold the bass player, the *shakuhachi* player, and the
SINGER.

PROPS. All props, such as fishing pole, creel, or frying pan, are to be
mimed except where otherwise noted.

MUSIC. A *shakuhachi* (Japanese flute) player who, ideally, can play
other percussive instruments such as *taiko* (Japanese drum).
An acoustic double bass player. If songs are used, then these
instruments provide accompaniment. Otherwise, musicians
should attend rehearsals and compose music.

Preset

A pool of light center stage.
  Darkness. Musicians lit behind scrim on upstage riser.

SINGER:
  Shadows wash the room, linger in the air,
  Fall upon the man, sleeping in the chair.
    It's a photograph in black and white
    The characters are grey.
    Caught precisely in a tragic pose
    Of strange decay.
  Your rich embroidered memories . . .
    The feast after the hunt;
    Those fine college days;
    The wife, the home, the children;
    Your song it plays and plays.
  The rich American dream is here to stay, is here to
    stay . . .
  (MUSICIANS *dim to darkness.)*

Scene One

Catching Fish

Lights up onstage. A tree motif gobo is lit against the upstage backdrop. The FISHERMAN *enters looking for a spot to fish. He moves quite easily, though appearing to be in his mid-sixties. The* FISHERMAN *wears baggy khaki pants with a faded red flannel shirt. On his feet, a pair of dark brown work shoes and on his head, a hat. Over his shirt he wears a worn tan fishing vest. He mimes carrying a spool and creel.*

FISHERMAN: Now that looks like a good spot. It's deep but with a bit of swirl on the top so that you know there's some current there, not stagnant. And see all those overhanging cypresses? They provide a little cool shade. Not too much, but just enough so the fish can rest and hide away for a while. And you know what's in all those leaves and branches? Mushi,* bugs. Lots and lots of bugs. And when they fall in the water, oh, the fish gobble them up. *(Sees a fish jump)* Ara!** *(Lowering voice)* See the big one jump. Right near the swirl. What'd I tell you. *(Setting down the creel and preparing to fish)* Now me, I use about a two- to four-pound-test line. Usually I prefer four pound 'cause if you catch a big one they'll snap your line. And around a size eight hook. I don't like the pretied ones. Like to tie my own.
　　(Ties hook onto line while talking. Cuts excess line off with his teeth, spitting it out. Pulls hook while gripping line to make sure it holds.)
　　And two or three small BB shots for weight.
　　(Clamps lead weights onto line with his teeth again instead of using pliers)

*Mushi, "insects."
**Ara, "oh."

207

Mako in A Song For A Nisei Fisherman,
Aquarius Theatre, Hollywood
Photo by Craig Schwartz,
courtesy Nancy Hereford/MTF Press

Now the bait. Oh, first I get out a small marshmallow.
That's right. Now don't laugh. This old Buddhahead's not
crazy. *(Playfully, looks around secretively)* That's my secret.
Now watch. I get the marshmallow. Okii no wa dame.*
Gotta be small size. Push the marshmallow through the
hook and slide it all the way up the line to where the BB
shots are. Then put some salmon eggs, oh, two or three, on
the hook. Gotta be Pautzke's Balls O'Fire salmon eggs.
Only problem is, this stuff is so damn expensive. *(Holds
bottle up)* Two dollars and twenty-five cents, and that's on
sale. Stuff's like caviar. And the bottle's half the size it used
to be. Hell, I ought to put this stuff on rice, eat it like sushi.
Now I want to put the line right near the swirl where the
fish jumped. *(As he casts forward, he tangles his line in some
overhanging branches. Embarrassed.)* Must have grown
down since I was here last. *(Casts the line)* Yosh!** *(Admiring cast. Sets pole down.)* Now, as the BB shots sink the line,
the bait comes to rest on the bottom. And a lotta times
there's moss and snags down there, especially in a cool
shady spot like this, so the eggs are hidden away in all that
and the fish can't see it. But, the marshmallow floats. And
because it floats, as it melts, the marshmallow slides up the
line from the BB shots toward the bait, causing the bait to
slowly rise. It's no longer hidden in the moss or snags.
Instead, the salmon eggs are proudly floating there, looking so tasty.
　　*(Reaches into his creel and furtively pulls something out,
　　looking around to see if anyone's watching. Then he
　　quickly starts throwing stuff in the water, all the while
　　looking around to see if he's being watched.)*
　　What am I doing? Shhh! I'm chumming. Is it illegal?
(Innocently) I don't know. *(Back to normal self)* Besides, it
attracts the fish. Hell, they love cottage cheese. Oh, you can

*Big ones are no good.
**Got it!

use lots of stuff to chum. Corn, they love corn, except that it always attracts the carp. Carp, they eat anything. Once I even tried some old nuka, the stinky paste Michiko puts the vegetables in to make pickles. Whew! Kusai yo!* Could smell the stuff for miles. Had the whole place to myself. Just me . . . and the carp. And if the carp are big enough they snap your line. And if they're just small fry and you catch 'em, you can't even eat the damn carp. Meat tastes funny, chotto kusai.** But back in the islands— Kauai, that's where I grew up—it was different. We had fish just like the carp, a trash fish, and we used to feed 'em to our hunting dogs. Fillet 'em real quick and just toss 'em to the dogs raw.

(Reflecting. Reaches down to check his line.)

You know, there was one dog, what was his name . . . Tengu. Yeah, that's what I called him, Tengu. He was my dog. Well, he wasn't really mine. One of the family's hunting dogs, but I sort of unofficially adopted him. It was a secret just between me and Tengu. That was a long time ago, I was a kid, but I can still remember him. Boy, was Tengu a tough son of a bitch. Wasn't that big, almost on the small size, but tough, a real scrapper. Wouldn't take any crap from any of the other dogs . . . and wouldn't let anybody touch him. It's like he wanted to get petted but there was always something inside that just wouldn't let go, and he'd end up growling and barking at you.

Anyway, in Kauai, we lived in the inaka, out in the sticks, and we used Tengu and the other dogs for boar hunting. One day Mosan—he's one of my brothers, boy, he's a crazy one—he and I decided to go hunt boar, so we packed everything and headed out with the dogs.

(Turns and transforms into a young man. Acts out the following.)

*Stinky!
**Slightly smelly.

Right off Tengu and the dogs caught the scent of something and took off running after it. When we caught up the
pigs were already cornered. A female and two small pig-
lets, backed against some rocks. Mosan and I were just
bringing our guns up when suddenly something jumped
right past us. It was a huge male boar. One of the biggest
I'd ever seen. It was an ugly, mean sucker with two big
tusks. Slammed right into Tengu's side and then all hell
broke loose. Pigs squealing, dogs barking, Mosan cursing,
"Goddamn son of a bitch, you goddamn son of a bitch!"
He was kicking and punching, trying to clear out the dogs
so he could get a clear shot. And then, suddenly . . . it was
all quiet. Everybody was gone. Taken off running every
which way, except for Tengu. He was lying on the ground.
His side had been ripped open and he was making these
funny gurgling sounds in his throat.

I knelt down beside him and examined the wound.
About a five-inch tear with part of the intestine bulging
out. Using some old rags, I wrapped them around his body
so the wound was at least covered. It didn't look too hope-
ful, but it was the best I could do. I poured some water into
my cupped hand and offered it to Tengu but at first he
wouldn't drink. "Drink, Tengu, just a little. Come on, boy.
That's good. That will make you feel better." *(Getting up
to leave)* "Take care, Tengu. I'll be back in a little while."
*(Stops, turning back to Tengu. Puts hands together in Bud-
dhist prayer.)* "Namu Amida Butsu."

I turned and left to catch up with Mosan and the dogs.
Later, when we returned, Tengu's body was gone. Except
for the blood spilled where he had fallen, nothing. We
returned home. Days passed and the incident was slowly
forgotten.

About three weeks later, the family was sitting down to
dinner when the dogs began barking wildly. We all ran outside to see what it was. I couldn't believe my eyes. There,

limping slowly into the yard, was Tengu. He looked horrible, all skin and bone. But he was alive. *(Runs up and puts arm around the imaginary dog, hugging and petting him)* "Tengu! Hey, he's still alive! Tengu! Tengu! Hey, he's letting me pet him." *(Tengu starts to growl at the others and has to be restrained.)* "Watch out, stay back! Only me." *(For a moment he quietly pets Tengu. Then slowly rises, becoming the old fisherman.)*

Well, Tengu lived for about six months after that. He wasn't too good for anything. He would just lie on the porch, napping in the sun. He'd yawn occasionally, growl now and then at the world to let it know Tengu was still there. And as the sun moved across the porch, he'd get up from the shadows, move into the sunlight, and plop down again, yawn and fall asleep. But one day Tengu wouldn't eat. He'd never done this before and he seemed restless. That night I woke up. *(Sound cue of a dog barking)* I could hear Tengu barking like hell. As if something was out there. None of the other dogs were barking, only Tengu. And it was an unusually loud bark for Tengu, like his old bark when he was healthy. But it was a short burst and then it was quiet, so I went back to sleep.

The next morning when I got up, Tengu was gone. I kept wondering if maybe he caught the scent of some big boar and was off chasing it down. And that one day he'd come limping back home just like last time, good old Tengu. But this time, this time Tengu didn't come home . . .

(Composing himself, he notices a nibble. Carefully picks up the pole, waiting, waiting . . . snags for a moment, thinks he has it. Then, realizes he's missed it. Reels up slack line, slightly embarrassed. Sits down on the edge of the riser as if it were a shoreline holding the fishing pole.)

I remember once—this is back in Kauai—oh, I was 'bout eleven years old, Tochan* and I had taken a load of

*Papa.

fish in the wagon to sell in town. Usually Kachan* and I
took the fish to town to sell but Kachan was very pregnant
. . . again. Anyway, it was the end of the day. We'd sold
everything and we were starting to return home. Tochan
let me hold the reins to Taro, that was our one and only
horse. Boy, that bugger was old . . .

TRANSITION. *Fishing pole that is still being held in*
FISHERMAN's *hands gradually becomes the reins to the*
wagon. FISHERMAN *is now eleven years old.* TOCHAN *enters*
counting money he has made from the day's fish sale. Sits
down beside FISHERMAN *and motions for him to get the*
wagon moving. FISHERMAN *speaks with a slight Hawaiian*
pidgin nuance.

FISHERMAN *(holding reins)*: Come on, Taro. Come on, boy.
Let's go . . .
TOCHAN *(interrupts. Sees his drinking buddy, Isamu)*: Itsu,
matte, matte.** OI! ISAMU! YO! ISAMU!
(TOCHAN *listens to Isamu's response. Isamu is unseen*
and unheard by audience. ITSUTA *doesn't like this man.)*
TOCHAN: Ore? Sold all our sakana. Business been going real
good. Making good money, lotsa money. Nomu? Drink?
Yosh!†
FISHERMAN: Tochan, mo' better we go home . . .
TOCHAN *(interrupts)*: One drink, Itsu, one drink, that's all.
FISHERMAN: We told Kachan we be home early, she's going
to be plenty angry yo. 'Member what happen last time?
TOCHAN: Ano nah, Itsu. I haven't seen Isamu in a long time.
We talk business. Right, Isamu? We going talk business.
FISHERMAN: But getting dark and we told Kachan we
be . . .

*Mama.
**Itsu, "wait, wait."
†Ore, "me"; sakana, "fish"; yosh, "alright."

TOCHAN *(interrupts)*: Yakamashi! *(Giving* FISHERMAN *some money)* Here's the money. Go pake,* Chinaman's store and pick up Kachan's medicine. Come right back with the leftover money. I'll meet you here by the wagon. Read your book. Yosh, Isamu.

*(*TOCHAN *walks over to the riser stage right with Isamu. They enter a small cafe/bar. At the same time, the* FISHERMAN *goes stage left to complete the transaction at the store. He returns and seats himself in the wagon reading his book.)*

TOCHAN *(bowing and greeting other people)*: Dōka, dōka.** The mango? No worry, no worry. The new mango I going make going to be the biggest, tastiest—no spots, too. I get your money back. You get two times your money back. Oh, Isamu, don't pour so much. *(Gulps down the sake. Holds out his glass while Isamu pours.)*

You already know why I put my family out in inaka. How many times I gotta tell you? 'Cause of the big fish pond. Like one private fish stock. Got all we need to live on. What we don't need, sell to people in town. Extra money, Isamu. Even you buy the fish. And the kids work on old man Knapper plantation. Bumbye with the Matsumoto Mango, the fish, kids working, going come rich, Isamu. Oh, domo, domo.†

(Accepting drink. FISHERMAN *has become impatient waiting for* TOCHAN *at the wagon. Enters tavern, bows to people shyly, and tugs at* TOCHAN's *sleeve.)*

FISHERMAN: Tochan. We go home.

TOCHAN *(notices son)*: Eh? How come you're in here? Tochan told you to wait outside. Go. Study your book.

*(*FISHERMAN *exits tavern but waits right outside door.)*

* Yakamashi, "quiet"; go pake, Hawaiian for "Chinese."
** How are you?
†Inaka, "the sticks"; bumbye, pidgin for "by-and-by"; domo, "thanks."

TOCHAN: He's a good student, yeah. Can read American like
haole.* Best student in class. Not like Mosan.
*(Feeling his sake. Starts to clap hands, singing a lively
Japanese drinking song. Gets up and drunkenly begins
to dance around. Stops, laughing loudly and wiping
perspiration from his brow. Accepting another drink
from Isamu.* FISHERMAN *enters.)*

TOCHAN: Domo. Easy, if you use atama** like me. Good
business sense. Gonna be big important man, Isamu.
When I go back Japan they going meet me at the train sta-
tion like one boss man. *(Standing)* BANZAI! BANZAI!
BANZAI MATSUMOTO-SENSEI!
(Unnoticed by TOCHAN, FISHERMAN *is watching.*
TOCHAN *notices Isamu and others laughing at his boasts.*
TOCHAN *is upset.)*

TOCHAN: Yeah, that's it. Go ahead and laugh. All the time
laugh at Matsumoto, neh. Big joke, nah. Horafuki,† nah.
You wait and see. My new mango going make me rich.

FISHERMAN: Tochan, let's go. Kachan's gonna worry yo.
And you drink too much already.

TOCHAN *(irritated by son's admonition)*: Too much drink?
Itsu, men never drink too much. Never. Men can always
drink more sake. Maybe cannot talk haole good. Maybe
cannot read those books of yours. But men can always
drink. Oi! Arakawa-san! More sake for me and Isamu.
(As TOCHAN *is bringing a cup to his mouth to drink,*
FISHERMAN *reaches in and tugs on his sleeve.)*

FISHERMAN: Tochan, come on. We go home.
(Sake spills all over.)

TOCHAN: Ah kuso!‡

FISHERMAN: They're poking fun at you.

*Caucasian.
**Head.
†Big liar.
‡Shit!

TOCHAN *(angered by his comment)*: Nanda? Gaki!* *(Slaps* FISHERMAN *on the back of his head. Realizes what he's done. Composes himself.)* Itsu, we're talking business. Nah, Isamu. And men drink when they talk business. *(Offers money to* FISHERMAN*)* Buy some candy or something.

FISHERMAN *(refusing to take money)*: Store went closed already.

TOCHAN: Go. Tochan finish soon.

*(*FISHERMAN *turns to leave.)*

TOCHAN: Itsu.

*(*FISHERMAN *turns to look at* TOCHAN. TOCHAN *seems on the verge of saying something but changes his mind. Motions for his son to leave. As the* FISHERMAN *returns to the wagon,* TOCHAN *begins to drink again while singing a sad melody. Slowly falls asleep.*

FISHERMAN, *who has fallen in the wagon, is suddenly awakened by Isamu.)*

FISHERMAN: Tochan pilikia?** Again? *(*FISHERMAN *goes into the tavern and helps his father back to the wagon.)* Tochan, we go home.

TOCHAN *(drunkenly)*: Banzai, banzai Matsumoto-sensei . . . *(*FISHERMAN *helps* TOCHAN *sit in the back of the wagon. He grabs the reins, glances back at* TOCHAN, *then forward again.)*

FISHERMAN: Come on, Taro. Come on, boy . . . *(Continues.)*

TRANSITION. *Holding reins to handling a fishing pole, as* TOCHAN *exits from the scene.*

FISHERMAN *(continuing)*: . . . Come on. Come on, fish. Just a little nibble. Ah, that's it. A little bit more. *(Snags and hooks fish)* Gotcha! *(Talks while playing fish)* It's a shoreline so don't need my net . . . *(Points to net strapped around his*

*What? Brat!
**Hawaiian for "in trouble."

shoulder) . . . to land the fish. In the islands we used throw nets to catch fish. Illegal here, though. Can't catch 'em with a net. Big fine.

(Just as he pulls it up on the shore, the fish wiggles off the hook. Gets on knees and scrambles around after the flapping fish but it's slippery. It falls into the water and he lunges in, cornering it against the shoreline. Pulls out his net looking around to see if anyone is watching.)

FISHERMAN *(to the audience):* Shhh! *(Scoops up fish triumphantly)* Yosh!

(Blackout on FISHERMAN. MUSICIANS *lit behind scrim.)*

Scene Two

Cleaning Fish

Lights come up on FISHERMAN *cleaning fish.*

FISHERMAN: See the kinda brownish color on this trout?
That's because it's newly planted. The native ones don't
have that. Like this one over here. See, no brown color, just
beautiful rainbow. It doesn't affect the meat, still good eating, just doesn't look good.

Trout you really don't have to scale much. Not like
striped bass. They got lotta scales. Good eating though,
good sashimi if it's fresh. Not as soft as maguro, tuna, but
I think it has more taste. Besides, I like my sashimi kinda
chewy. Maguro just melts in your mouth, too soft.

See, now you grab the fish from the back with your
thumb and middle finger in the gills, get a good grip that
way. And the belly facing up towards you. And you cut
from the gills to the anal opening. Then you just reach in
and grab from the gills and pull out and down. See the gills
come out with all the intestines attached.

*(Stands and walks towards audience to give them a better
view.)*

Let's see what we have here. This is the peritoneum, the
smooth membrane covering, and this is like the main aor-
tic vessel in the human body. And that's . . .

TRANSITION. KACHAN *enters carrying a load of fish for*
FISHERMAN *to clean. Notices he isn't cleaning.* FISHERMAN
is around seventeen years old.

KACHAN *(irritated)*: Ichan. Nan shitoru?*

*What are you doing?

FISHERMAN: Kachan, more fish?

KACHAN: What look like? Now clean, clean. Plenty more to go yet.

FISHERMAN: Kachan, I've been working since I got back from school. I still got plenty of homework to do . . .

KACHAN: Hayo, clean. Tochan get mad, yo.* He wants these all salt-packed for later on. You know who catches hell if it's no done when he gets back. Work first, then school. Chichan, abunai yo! yo! Get down from that tree. Yachiyo, you suppose to watch your sister.

> (KACHAN *dumps a load of fish while* FISHERMAN *sits down behind table and starts to clean. She takes the fish cleaned by* FISHERMAN, *places it in a barrel, and sprinkles it with salt.*)

FISHERMAN *(cleaning)*: Kachan, are we samurai?

KACHAN: Samurai? Who told you that?

FISHERMAN: Mosan. That's what he telling people at school. He's telling them that we come from a great line of samurai. And that it's their duty as good Japanese to show him their homework, or they get one broken head. *(Imitates hitting someone with a sword.)*

KACHAN: Aho! Idiot! That brother of yours. My back, Ichan. That comes from working the rice fields. Farmers from Hiroshima. That's what we are. Plenty of families around here big talk being samurai. All liars, Ichan. Anyone who left Japan had nothing but big dreams and empty pocket. Work, work. *(Under breath)* Wait till Tochan hears about that brother of yours . . . Samurai . . .

> *(Both working.)*

FISHERMAN: Know what else happened at school?

KACHAN: Mata fight?** Mosan get you into . . .

FISHERMAN: No, no.

KACHAN: Mosan flunk class?

*Hurry, Tochan will get mad.
**Fighting again?

(Margin text:) A Song For A Nisei Fisherman

FISHERMAN *(interrupts)*: No, no Kachan, nothing like that.

(KACHAN notices FISHERMAN has stopped cleaning.)

KACHAN: Holo, holo then.*

FISHERMAN: I went transferred to a new class. I'm taking homemaking, a homemaking class.

KACHAN: Homemaking? What for? That's just for girls. Your sister maybe, but you one boy.

FISHERMAN: Mr. Marshall, the principal . . . remember Mr. Marshall? Mr. Marshall and Mrs. Thompson, the teacher, said can.

KACHAN: You're gonna shame Tochan. Between you and Mosan . . .

FISHERMAN: I went talk to them and they both said it was all right. Told them I like learn how to cook.

KACHAN: You no like my cooking?

FISHERMAN: No, I mean . . . it's just we no more money so I figured that . . .

KACHAN *(interrupts)*: I know that, Ichan, but we always get plenty to eat. You like people think we no more shame or what? I always think you liked Kachan's cooking.

FISHERMAN: I do, I do. But I like go to college. Like Knapper-san's kids. I like study to be . . .

KACHAN *(interrupts)*: College? Sure, sure, Ichan. That's nice but no can; something like that takes . . .

FISHERMAN *(interrupts)*: I want to be a doctor.

KACHAN: Doctor? Ichan, Ichan. Sure we get enough to eat. And enough for clothes, maybe. But no extra. You know that. College, doctor's school, where we going to get the money? All that's for rich white people. Ah, nani guzzu, guzzu shitoru no!** Hayo, clean. Ichan, what's that got to do with homemaking? You giving Kachan a headache.

FISHERMAN: That's why I'm taking the class. See, that's my

*Hawaiian for "Hurry, hurry."
**Oh, why are you so slow?

plan. If I can cook, I figure I can work my way through
school. Here, I like show you something.

(Pulls KACHAN *away from her work so he can show her
the college catalogue)*

KACHAN: What you doing? *(Notices Yachiyo)* Yachiyo, you
supposed to watch your sister.

FISHERMAN: I already discussed it with Mr. Marshall and
he says he can get me a job as a cook at his friend's house
on the mainland side.

KACHAN: Mainland?

FISHERMAN: He's a professor at the University of California. Here, try look the pictures . . .

KACHAN *(uncomfortable)*: No can, no can. It cost so much,
too far. What you gonna do over there? And you know
what Tochan think about spending so . . .

FISHERMAN *(interrupts. Getting excited about the classes)*:
Try look. These are all the classes they offer there. I can
take physics and organic chemistry . . . *(Continues.)*

KACHAN *(overlapping)*: You go? What about all this work?

FISHERMAN *(continuing)*: . . . that is if my grades are good
enough to get me in there, and Mr. Marshall says no
problem.

KACHAN: Yeah, but Ichan . . .

FISHERMAN: What do you think?

(Awkward pause. FISHERMAN *anxiously awaits*
KACHAN's *reply.)*

KACHAN: Go, go if you like, go. Go drown in the ocean!
(Moving back to work) Hayo!* Clean, clean. No more
waste time thinking. So many things to do before Tochan
gets home. Holo, holo. Way behind. *(Notices that the* FISH-
ERMAN *is disappointed)* Itsu.

(No response) Ichan. *(Pause)* Why you wanna go so far
away, Ichan?

*Hurry up.

(FISHERMAN doesn't respond. Goes back to work cleaning fish. KACHAN starts to leave to get another load of fish. Stops.)

KACHAN: When Tochan come back we talk to him, yah? I no promise nothing, but we see. Now finish clean the fish.

(KACHAN exits. FISHERMAN excitedly begins cleaning fish again.)

TRANSITION. *Back to present.* FISHERMAN *cuts finger.*

FISHERMAN: Ouch! . . . Gotta watch out for spines while you're cleaning. Trout usually aren't so bad at all. Usually, anyway. Catfish are the worst. Really spiny and they stay alive out of water a long time. So at the end of the day when you reach down to clean them, they jerk around and you end up with a spine right through your finger. They're a son of a bitch to clean. *(Notices something and picks it up)* Dime. Eat anything. Once found a cigarette butt in the stomach. I've even found marshmallows in there. *(Washes dime off and looks at it. Remembering.)* Fifty dollars is all I had. *(Pockets the dime)* Fifty dollars and a one-way boat ticket to California, and I threw up the whole way. Actually I was headed for Los Angeles. Didn't know anybody there. Just fifty dollars, the ticket, oh, and a letter of introduction to a professor at UCLA, where I was to go for the next four years.

I worked my butt off. Get up at five o'clock in the morning, study for an hour, cook breakfast for Professor and Mrs. Jameson. Nice people, both grey-haired ojiichan and obaachan* type. Then go to classes till four o'clock, come home, prepare and cook dinner. That took until seven-thirty with dishes. Then back to the books till twelve o'clock. Sleep, get up at five o'clock and start again.

*Grandfather and grandmother.

So for the next four years I worked, I studied and studied. At the end of my third year, I sent off my applications to med school. I applied to four. I had to get a full scholarship or I wouldn't be able to go.

TRANSITION. *During college;* FISHERMAN *is about twenty-one years old.*

FISHERMAN *(standing. Mimes reaching out and receives a letter)*: The first letter came back. *(Opening and reading it)* "We are happy to inform you that you have been accepted . . . However, you were not selected as a scholarship recipient. . . We hope this does not inconvenience you. . . look forward to seeing you in the coming year." Well, at least I'm getting accepted.

(Reaches out and receives letter) Second letter. *(Opens it quickly)* "We regret to inform you that we do not have space for you in our first-year class . . ."

(Reaches out and receives letter) Third letter.

(Opens more apprehensively) "We regret to inform you . . ." *(Reaches out and receives letter. Stares at it, looks at audience.)* My only out-of-state school. University of Arkansas. Home of the Razorbacks. Only one that offered a full scholarship to out-of-state residents. *(Slowly opens it up)* "We are happy to inform you that you have been accepted . . . and that you have been awarded a full scholarship!" Hey, I got in! Professor Jameson . . .

TRANSITION. *From excitement over being accepted to satisfaction about passing first-year medical school exams and talking to his roommate. Runs upstage shouting to Professor Jameson that he got in, and then turns and moves downstage talking to Sam, his roommate.* FISHERMAN *is around twenty-two years old.*

FISHERMAN: I passed my exams! My first-year exams! Even got an A in Anatomy and Biochem. Come on, Sam, this calls for a celebration. We both passed first-year exams and we deserve a drink. Let's go down to the Razorback Inn. Come on, let's . . . What? *(Listening)* Sam, how many times do I have to tell you? They aren't looking at us funny. You're imagining it, they like us here. Some of the other guys from the class will be there, James and . . . *(Listening and becoming upset)* Jap and the Jew, Jap and the Jew, you're always talking about that. Look, I . . . *(Listening)* Who knows why they put us together? We get along as roommates, don't we? Maybe they figured the only Japanese and Jew in the class would have something in common. And we do. We both work harder than anybody else here, and we get the best grades—well, most of the time.

Sam, I don't notice any prejudice. I don't have to use the colored facilities. In fact, when I first got here I used them and got bawled out by some coloreds. They said to use the white ones. I've been treated real good. Most don't even know what I am. They've never even seen a Japanese before. They think I'm an Eskimo. If you're so goddamn sensitive about what you are, tell 'em you're an Eskimo. They'll treat you real good. I think you're just too sensitive. Wanna go or not, 'cause I'm going.

TRANSITION. *From talking to Sam into a dancing sequence in a taxi-dance hall in San Francisco. Sound cue of a late thirties dance.* MOSAN *and taxi dancer,* CORA, *enter dancing. The other taxi dancer,* JOSEPHINE, *approaches* FISHERMAN.

JOSEPHINE: Where your tickets?
    (FISHERMAN *holds them out and she takes all of them.)*
CORA *(while dancing with* MOSAN, *hollers to* JOSEPHINE): I don't care what he says, I'm not going back. Hell no, not this time.

JOSEPHINE *(ignoring* CORA*)*: First time taxi dancing, huh? You can hold but no touching. Got that? No touching.

CORA *(shouting to* JOSEPHINE*)*: He lays a hand on my kid again, I'll kill him.

JOSEPHINE *(to* CORA*)*: You can stay at my place. And the kid, too.

CORA: I swear it this time, Josephine, I swear it.

MOSAN *(to* CORA*)*: Hey, darling, you dancing with me or what?

JOSEPHINE: Where are you from anyway? What you do?

FISHERMAN: Arkansas. Going to medical school out there.

JOSEPHINE *(incredulous)*: A Chinaman doctor from Arkansas?

*(*FISHERMAN *ignores her response, keeps dancing. She realizes he's not kidding.)*

JOSEPHINE *(sarcastically)*: God, America—that's what I love 'bout this country. Opportunity. One minute you're in some rice paddy in China, and the next you're a Chinaman doctor in Arkansas.

(Dance for a moment in silence. FISHERMAN *feeling very uncomfortable.)*

JOSEPHINE: So why you come out here to San Francisco, doctor?

FISHERMAN: I came out here to see about some . . .

JOSEPHINE *(interrupts. Stops dancing)*: Is that all you have?

FISHERMAN: What?

JOSEPHINE: Tickets, tickets. Come on, doctor from Arkansas, you can afford it.

FISHERMAN: How many did I give you? *(Checking pockets)* I gave you the whole bunch when we . . .

JOSEPHINE *(interrupts)*: One ticket, that's all you gave me. One ticket. You musta . . . *(Continues.)*

*(*MOSAN *notices* FISHERMAN's *dilemma and comes to his rescue.)*

JOSEPHINE: . . . dropped 'em on the floor. You have to get some more if you wanna dance.

MOSAN: Don't be so nervous, Itsu. Here, take some of mine. *(As he hands the tickets to the* FISHERMAN, JOSEPHINE *reaches in and takes them.)*

MOSAN *(to* FISHERMAN*)*: Got lots more so don't be shy. *(To* JOSEPHINE*)* Take good care of my brother.

*(*MOSAN *playfully slaps the* FISHERMAN *on the back and returns to* CORA. *At this point, the* FISHERMAN *and* JOSEPHINE *dance out of the way up right while* MOSAN *and* CORA *move down center and do about a twenty-second choreographed dance routine.* MOSAN *loves to show off his dancing moves and* CORA *has to hang on to keep up with his enthusiasm. At the end of their dance routine,* FISHERMAN *and* JOSEPHINE *start up conversation and the focus shifts back to them.)*

JOSEPHINE: Don't see too many of you in here. Lotta sailors. Lotta them Filipinos from the valley—they stink like whores with all their perfume. Not too many Chinamen, though.

(This is too much for the FISHERMAN. *Stops dancing.)*

FISHERMAN: Excuse me. *(Hurries over to* MOSAN*)* Mosan.

MOSAN *(dancing)*: Nothing like this in the islands, huh. Place is crazy, huh.

FISHERMAN *(trying to pull* MOSAN *off to side)*: Mosan, come over here. I want to talk to you. Come on.

MOSAN *(to* CORA*)*: Little brother like to talk to me. *(To a sailor)* Hey, Mac, I'm dancing with her. *(To* CORA*)* Don't go away. I'll be right back.

(They move downstage while JOSEPHINE *and* CORA *chat upstage.)*

MOSAN: What's up, anyway? Huh?

FISHERMAN: Mosan, let's get outta here. I like go.

MOSAN: What? We just got here. You must be joking.

FISHERMAN: Place's dirty, it stinks. Smells like shiko.*
Come on, let's go someplace else.
MOSAN: This place is good for you. You got too much book
learning.
FISHERMAN: I don't like it here. Let's go bowling.
MOSAN: Bowling? Is that what they teach you in Arkansas?
Jesus! *(Continues.)*
(JOSEPHINE starts to walk over to them.)
MOSAN: . . . Tonight big brother is giving you one real edu-
cation. *(Sees JOSEPHINE approaching)* Oh-oh, here comes
your sensei.**
*(MOSAN pushes FISHERMAN into JOSEPHINE's arms.
They start dancing once again.)*
CORA *(to JOSEPHINE)*: What if he tries to call?
JOSEPHINE *(to CORA)*: Don't worry, I'll handle him.
MOSAN *(grabbing CORA)*: You dancing with her or me?
JOSEPHINE: You can hold but . . . *(Continues.)*
FISHERMAN *(overlapping)*: "No touching." I remember.
JOSEPHINE *(continuing)*: . . . no touching.
(They dance. The FISHERMAN is stiff as a board.)
JOSEPHINE: Come on, loosen up. This is supposed to be
fun. Ya know fun?
FISHERMAN: Yeah, I'm having a good time.
JOSEPHINE: So why you here? In San Francisco?
FISHERMAN: I might move to Stockton.
JOSEPHINE: That's where all them Flips come from.
FISHERMAN: A lot of Japanese there, too. All the farming.
JOSEPHINE *(studying him)*: You a Jap boy, huh?
FISHERMAN: Might set up my practice there.
JOSEPHINE: Come on, loosen up. You're stepping all over
me.
FISHERMAN: Too many Japanese doctors in Los Angeles.
San Francisco's the same.

*Urine.
**Teacher.

A Song

For A

Nisei

Fisherman

227

(FISHERMAN *keeps stepping on* JOSEPHINE'*s feet.*
She's getting disgusted with his dancing.)

JOSEPHINE: How come you're in here?

FISHERMAN *(nodding towards* MOSAN*)*: Brother brought
me.

JOSEPHINE: Thought he was one of those horny little Filipinos.

(MOSAN *and* CORA *have stopped dancing and are*
involved in an argument. Focus shifts to them.)

CORA: Who gives a damn?

MOSAN: But you already took the tickets.

CORA: My feet are tired, my back hurts. I want to go to the
toilet.

(CORA *turns to leave.* MOSAN *grabs her.*)

MOSAN: All right, all right. You dance with me when you get
back.

(CORA *shakes his hand off.*)

CORA: Buzz off.

(*As she starts to leave,* MOSAN *grabs her again.*)

MOSAN: You dance with me when you get back. I already
gave you the tickets.

CORA *(trying to knock his hand loose)*: Who cares 'bout your
damn tickets.

MOSAN: Then give me back my tickets! You not gonna steal
my . . .

(FISHERMAN *has come over in an attempt to calm*
MOSAN *down.*)

FISHERMAN *(interrupts)*: Mosan, take it easy.

MOSAN: Just want my tickets back.

CORA: Let go, let go of my arm, you bastard!

JOSEPHINE *(to* FISHERMAN*)*: Calm your brother down or
get him out of . . .

FISHERMAN *(interrupts)*: Mosan, Mosan. Take it easy.
Mosan.

MOSAN *(struggling with* CORA*)*: I want my tickets. She stole . . .
(CORA *pulls out a knife and shoves it threateningly in* MOSAN's *face. He immediately lets go.)*

CORA: You want a cut-up face, is that what you want? Is that . . . *(Continues.)*

JOSEPHINE *(overlapping)*: Put it away, Cora! Put it away! *(Calling for the bouncer)* Jimmy! Jimmy, get over here!

CORA *(continuing)*: . . . what you want? Huh? You want me to cut you? Is that what you want?

MOSAN: You're not gonna make one fool outta me!

FISHERMAN *(holding* MOSAN *back)*: Mosan! Mosan!

MOSAN: Give me my goddamn tickets! You give me my tickets!

JOSEPHINE: Get your brother outta here! Get him out!

FISHERMAN: Mosan! Come on . . .
(FISHERMAN *pulls* MOSAN *out of the dance hall.* JOSEPHINE *and* CORA *exit. Nighttime. Outside of the dance hall.)*

FISHERMAN *(upset)*: Mosan, you almost got us killed in there! What's gotten into you? Ever since you come to the mainland. Drinking, gambling, fooling around with haole wahini.*

MOSAN: What about you? You been acting like one stupid kotonk.**

FISHERMAN: What are you trying to do? Huh? What are you trying to do?

MOSAN: Nothing already.

FISHERMAN: What do you mean "nothing"?

MOSAN *(getting angry)*: I said nothing.

FISHERMAN: You nearly got us killed just . . .

MOSAN *(interrupts)*: You don't know nothing about nothing, Itsu!

*White women.
**Mainland-born Japanese American.

FISHERMAN: Spend good money buying a damn race horse, and the damn horse can't even . . .

MOSAN *(interrupts)*: You shut up! As long as me and the family giving you money for go to school, you keep your mouth shut about how I spend my money. Besides, the horse can run.

FISHERMAN: If it is your money.

MOSAN: Where I get my money is none of your goddamn business.

FISHERMAN: What, you went stole the money?

(MOSAN shoves the FISHERMAN.)

MOSAN: You shut up, asshole!

FISHERMAN *(pushing MOSAN back)*: You the asshole!
(They rush towards each other as if to fight. Standing face to face, they both raise their right hands as if to trade blows. Freeze. Lights come up. The next day. Instead of swinging at each other, they both bring their hands down in a lively game of jan ken po *[Japanese hand game]. They're at the racetrack.)*

FISHERMAN, MOSAN *(together)*: Jan ken po! Ai kanna sho!

FISHERMAN *(laughing)*: You lose, Mosan! You go place the bets.

MOSAN *(moving towards the betting window)*: All right, all right.

FISHERMAN *(watching MOSAN placing the bet)*: Win?

MOSAN: Hell yes, everything on win.

FISHERMAN: That much money?

MOSAN *(leading FISHERMAN to the viewing stands)*: My horse no can lose. I feel it in my bones. No worry, no worry. Sit, sit.
(They seat themselves on one of the risers to watch the race. As the race is called their faces move in unison as they watch the horses circle the track, all the while hollering encouragement. RACE TRACK ANNOUNCER appears holding an old-fashioned microphone. Sound cue of a bell ringing.)

RACE TRACK ANNOUNCER: And they're off! As they go
away from the gate, it's Lady Luck moving out ahead, fol- *A Song*
lowed by Baby's Dream, Velvet Girl, Mr. Dancer, and
bringing up the rear of the pack . . . Buddha Buggy. Into *For A*
the far turn, it's Lady Luck opening up a lead of two
lengths, followed by Velvet Girl moving into second, and *Nisei*
. . . Oh-oh, here comes Buddha Buggy, challenges Mr.
Dancer and moves ahead into fourth . . . Passing Baby's *Fisherman*
Dream into third . . . Passing Lady Luck into second . . .
Down the home stretch now it's Velvet Girl and Buddha
Buggy neck to neck. It's Buddha Buggy . . . It's . . . BUD-
DHA BUGGY!
   (FISHERMAN and MOSAN jump around excitedly.)
MOSAN: What'd I tell you! Buddha Buggy's number one!
Number one!
FISHERMAN: Hey, that's my brother's horse! Buddha Bud-
dy's number one!
   *(They calm down as they move across stage. Lighting
   change. Later that day. MOSAN is singing a Hawaiian
   tune and doing the hula. Both have been celebrating all
   day.)*
FISHERMAN: Mosan?
MOSAN: Yeah?
FISHERMAN: Sorry about some of the things I said last
night.
MOSAN: Sorry? Hey, I'm the one that hit you.
FISHERMAN: Yeah, but I knocked you down.
MOSAN: You a damn good fighter, that's why. Hey, who
taught you everything you know?
FISHERMAN: She's a good horse, she really is. Buddha Bug-
gy's number one horse.
MOSAN: Hey, forget it. Pau* already. *(MOSAN pulls out a wad
of money from the race track earnings.)* Here.

*Hawaiian for "okay," "all right."

A Song   FISHERMAN: No, no. Cannot, cannot.

MOSAN *(putting money in* FISHERMAN*'s pocket)*: Here.

(FISHERMAN *finally accepts the money.)*

For A   MOSAN: No shame, no enryo. Enough for tuition, books, and maybe even some taxi dancing.

Nisei   FISHERMAN *(laughing)*: Next time we go bowling! *(Calming down)* We go to Chinatown, have some noodles?

Fisherman MOSAN: No, I gotta go now. Some people like talk to me.

FISHERMAN: You're not in trouble again?

MOSAN: No, nothing like that.

FISHERMAN: You sure.

MOSAN: Yeah, yeah. I gotta go. *(*MOSAN *turns to leave. Stops.)* Hey, Itsu?

FISHERMAN: Yeah?

MOSAN: Good luck.

(MOSAN *turns and leaves.)*

FISHERMAN *(watching him leave)*: Hope your luck holds out, Mosan. I'll pay you back every penny. I promise . . .

TRANSITION. *He turns and faces audience and begins to recite the Hippocratic Oath. Medical school graduation. Slow fade as he recites.*

FISHERMAN: . . . by Apollo, the physician, and Aesculapius . . . and all the gods and goddesses, that according to my ability and judgement, I will keep this oath . . . according to the law of medicine.

(FISHERMAN *dims to darkness.* MUSICIANS *lit.)*

[END OF SCENE]

Scene Three

Cooking Fish

FISHERMAN: Trout you just flour like this and fry till golden brown. Gotta be careful on a warm day 'cause the fish get kusateru, rotten. If you catch them early in the day, keep them covered with leaves in the creel, otherwise they go bad. You can tell if the meat is spoiled by looking on the inside of the fish, the rib bones start to peel away from the flesh. See, these are fresh trout—good color, firm meat, the bones still attached to the meat, see.

Now, I like frying fish but my favorite is kasuzuke. Most of you non-Nihonjin* don't know what that is, huh. "Kasu" are the dregs, the leftover stuff when making sake. What you do is get the fish—oh, I use striped bass—cut it in chunks and put it into the kasu and let it set for a couple of days. Then take it out, wash it off, and fry it. Ummm, oishii yo!**

TRANSITION. *To Buddhist church bazaar in Stockton.*
MICHIKO *appears as a young woman of twenty-five.*
FISHERMAN *and* KATS *are around thirty in this scene. We hear loud laughter. Lights up on* MICHIKO *and* KATS. KATS *is teasing with suggestive jokes.*

MICHIKO *(calling for help while laughing)*: ICHAN! *(To* KATS*)* Yarashii!†
KATS: You wanna see a one-eared elephant?
    *(*KATS *pulls one of his pockets inside out so it sticks out like a white elephant ear. Then, with* MICHIKO *watching*

*Non-Japanese.
**Tasty.
†Nasty.

curiously, KATS *mischievously reaches for the buttons on his fly and starts to undo them.* MICHIKO *catches on to the joke and screams in shocked amusement.)*

MICHIKO *(laughing)*: You're awful, Kats!

(The FISHERMAN *enters the scene and observes them.)*

MICHIKO: Hi, Ichan.

KATS *(uncomfortable)*: Hi, Doc.

FISHERMAN: Hi, Kats.

(Awkward moment between KATS *and* FISHERMAN. FISHERMAN *notices* KATS's *pocket sticking out.)*

FISHERMAN: What's wrong with your pocket?

KATS *(embarrassed. Hurriedly pushes pocket back in while he exits)*: See you at the poker game.

*(*MICHIKO *is working inside one of the food booths. As* KATS *exits,* FISHERMAN *reaches down to sample some of the food. He's about to put it into his mouth when* MICHIKO *notices and snatches it away.)*

FISHERMAN: Hey, what are you doing?

MICHIKO: Ichan, if you want to eat, you have to pay. See the sign?

FISHERMAN: Yeah, but I helped you make all this last night, Michiko.

MICHIKO: That was last night. Tonight is the church bazaar and everyone has to pay. And that includes you. Come on, come on. You can afford it.

(While FISHERMAN *reaches into his pocket for change,* MICHIKO *grabs the piece of food out of his hand, and pops it into her mouth.)*

FISHERMAN: Hey!

MICHIKO *(taking the money out of his hand)*: It's all right, I work here.

FISHERMAN: Michiko, you've been here all day. Why don't we go for a walk?

MICHIKO: Who's going to watch the booth?

FISHERMAN: Someone else will take care of it. Come on, it's too noisy here.

MICHIKO: But I like church bazaars. All the food and dancing . . . oh, look, there's Sumiko. She looks good in   *A Song*
kimono, neh? She's nice and light. Mama always says my
complexion's too dark. She's always telling me to stay out   *For A*
of the sun.

FISHERMAN: You are kind of dark.   *Nisei*

MICHIKO: She's pretty fast, ya know.

FISHERMAN: Who? Sumiko? With her daikon* legs?   *Fisherman*
Who'd go out with her?

KATS'S VOICE *(off)*: Hey, Sumiko! Wanna see a one-eared
elephant?

MICHIKO: Kats said so.

FISHERMAN: He did? What'd he say?

MICHIKO: Said she go out on a date the first time you ask
her. She's just asking for it.

FISHERMAN: First time you ask her, huh? How many times
did I have to ask you? Once?

MICHIKO *(quickly)*: Twice.

FISHERMAN: Twice? Whoo, this girl is loose.

MICHIKO *(defensive)*: I am not. Papa introduced us so it was
all right. Only had to refuse you once. Besides, Mama likes
doctors and she was afraid you might give up.

FISHERMAN: Mama likes me, huh?

MICHIKO: No. Likes doctors, that's all. *(Sees someone and
bows)* Konbanwa. Ikaga desu ka?**

FISHERMAN *(bowing)*: Konbanwa. Yes, Tuesday, two-thirty.
(Repeats loudly as the person is hard of hearing) Tuesday,
2:30. Come on, Michiko, let's go for a walk.

MICHIKO: Where do you want to go?

FISHERMAN: Where there aren't so many people. We never
get to be alone.

MICHIKO: What kind of Buddhist are you, anyway? We're

*Japanese horseradish.
**Good evening. How are you?

supposed to like people. *(Teasing)* Neh, Ichan. What do you have in mind?

FISHERMAN: Come on and find out.

MICHIKO *(calling to* KATS): Kats! Can you watch the booth?

KATS *(off)*: All right! Sumiko, you busy . . .

(They stroll across the stage. FISHERMAN *dusts off a spot and offers her a seat. He seats himself beside her on the riser.)*

FISHERMAN: How old are you?

MICHIKO: You know.

FISHERMAN: I want you to tell me.

MICHIKO: What for?

FISHERMAN: Come on, how old are you?

MICHIKO *(slightly uncomfortable, lowers voice)*: Twenty-five.

FISHERMAN *(acting surprised)*: Twenty-five? You're twenty-five?

MICHIKO *(irritated)*: You know that.

FISHERMAN *(voice getting louder)*: Twenty-five? You're practically an old lady, an obaachan.*

MICHIKO: I am not.

FISHERMAN *(loudly, as if announcing to the world)*: Twenty-five! She's twenty-five years old and not even married yet! . . .

MICHIKO *(interrupting, trying to quiet him down)*: Shhh! Ichan, shhh! People are looking.

FISHERMAN *(same loud voice)*: . . . And she thinks she's young!

MICHIKO *(embarrassed)*: Shhh! Not so loud.

FISHERMAN *(calms down. Back to normal voice)*: Your body's already past the prime age for childbearing.

MICHIKO: My body's none of your business, buster.

FISHERMAN: Take it easy. I'm a doctor. Bodies are my business.

*Grandmother.

MICHIKO: You sound just like Mama. And I'm still young. I'm only twenty-five years old.

FISHERMAN: That's a quarter of a century. And you still think you can make healthy babies, huh?

MICHIKO: Stop talking nasty. (Lowers voice so no one can hear) And I can too make babies.

FISHERMAN: Sure, little funny ones like Tanaka-san's little kid . . .

MICHIKO (interrupts, irritated): I can make babies, healthy ones too.

(FISHERMAN notices, then MICHIKO notices, that the imaginary Reverend Taniguchi has walked up and is listening.)

FISHERMAN (bowing): Konbanwa, Reverend Taniguchi.

MICHIKO (surprised, bowing nervously): Oh, konbanwa, Sensei.

(Both FISHERMAN and MICHIKO laugh nervously, worried that Reverend Taniguchi may have overheard some of their conversation.)

FISHERMAN: We were just talking about . . . about Buddha . . .

MICHIKO: When he was a baby . . . Sumimasen, Sensei.*

FISHERMAN (bowing, then breaking into laughter after he's gone): Boy, gonna hear about this in church. He's such a stuffed shirt anyway.

(They calm down.)

MICHIKO: You know Mrs. Kanemoto? The old woman who works at Papa's drugstore? She couldn't have any children.

FISHERMAN: Sometimes that happens. Can't be helped.

MICHIKO: I'd hate to be like Mrs. Kanemoto.

FISHERMAN: I got a big mouth, Michiko. I was just teasing.

MICHIKO: What if I can't have children?

FISHERMAN: Don't worry, Michiko. You're healthy as a horse.

*Sorry to have troubled you, Reverend.

MICHIKO: Just forget it.

FISHERMAN: Well, what do you recommend we do to find out? *(Mischievously)* We could practice. *(Both laugh.)* Well, practice does make perfect.

MICHIKO: Perfect babies?

FISHERMAN: No, a perfect marriage.

(They embrace. Transition into marriage ceremony. FISHERMAN and MICHIKO turn so they both face upstage. MOSAN enters stage right, and KATS stage left, as if part of the wedding ceremony. As they position themselves, FISHERMAN and MICHIKO march up the aisle. They turn and face each other.)

MILITARY PERSON *(as Reverend's voice, off)*: I now pronounce you . . . *(MILITARY PERSON walks in.)* . . . Next!

TRANSITION. MILITARY PERSON *carries a folder and makes the voice of the Reverend change to that of the* MILITARY PERSON. *Transition from wedding ceremony to relocation camp loyalty oath scene.* FISHERMAN *and* MICHIKO *hug and she joins* MOSAN *stage right on platform.* KATS *is on stage left platform.*

MILITARY PERSON *(checking his watch and looking at schedule. Obviously impatient: it's been a long day)*: Could you please hurry it up with the questionnaire, Mr. Matsumoto, we're running behind schedule here.

FISHERMAN: I want to ask about questions 27 and 28. There's been a lot of talk in the camps about why we have to . . .

MILITARY PERSON *(interrupts)*: Look, everyone in all the relocation camps seventeen and older has to fill them out, okay? I just administer the thing. That's all I do.

FISHERMAN: Questions 27 and 28, though. I don't understand why we have to . . .

MILITARY PERSON *(interrupts)*: You're having trouble with that, too. Here, let me read it to you. Question 27: "Are you willing to serve in the armed forces of the United States on combat duty wherever ordered?" Okay? Question 28: "Will you swear unqualified allegiance to the United States from any attack by foreign or domestic forces, and forswear any form of allegiance or obedience to the Japanese emperor, to any other foreign government, power, or organization?" Now, I haven't got all day. How are we going to sign? Yes, yes, or no, no?

(In the following sequence, MOSAN, KATS, *and* MICHIKO *are figments in* FISHERMAN's *mind, and are not acknowledged in the physical by* FISHERMAN *or* MILITARY PERSON. MOSAN's *initial "No, no" overlaps with* MILITARY PERSON's *"No, no.")*

MOSAN: No, no. You gotta sign that thing no, no, Itsu. Look what they doing to the Issei. Michiko's parents. They sign that thing, they lose their Japanese citizenship. They can never go home. That would kill 'em. You know that, Itsu. No, no.

KATS *(his initial "No" overlaps with* MOSAN's *"No, no")*: No. They think we're not loyal American citizens, Itsu. That's why they put us here in the first place. We gotta prove to the rest of the country that we are loyal citizens. And if that means joining up and fighting . . .

MOSAN *(interrupts)*: And dying?

KITS: And dying, then we gotta do it. *(To* FISHERMAN*)* Yes, yes.

MOSAN *(to* FISHERMAN*)*: For what? We shouldn't have to prove nothing to nobody. They take away all our land. We're sitting behind barbed wire. They ask us to be loyal after they put us in here. For what? No, no, Itsu.

MICHIKO *(her initial "Itsu" overlaps with* MOSAN's *"Itsu")*: Itsu. I don't like what's happening but I'm not Japanese. Ichan, I'm an American. We're Americans. This is our home. I hear rumors the no-no boys may go to prison.

There's even rumors they might get sent back to Japan.
Yes, yes.

MILITARY PERSON: Come on, come on. We're running
behind. Now how we gonna sign?

*(MICHIKO, MOSAN, and KATS begin to chant "Yes, yes"
and "No, no" respective to their positions. They start
softly and crescendo until FISHERMAN cuts them off.
Each says his or her chant differently, either in tempo or
style of pronunciation. The FISHERMAN can't make up
his mind.)*

MILITARY PERSON: Listen, we don't have all day.

*(The chanting gets louder. The FISHERMAN is still
undecided.)*

MILITARY PERSON: I'll read the question again. Question
27 . . .

*(He starts to read questions 27 and 28. The chanting gets
louder and louder.)*

FISHERMAN: All right!

(Silence.)

MILITARY PERSON: Next . . .

*(MILITARY PERSON, MICHIKO, MOSAN, and KATS
exit.)*

TRANSITION. FISHERMAN *returns to cooking his fish.*

FISHERMAN: The camps weren't so bad. I don't think about
it too much, happened all so long ago . . .

*(Pause. He starts to remember the pleasant stuff, then
slowly the unpleasant stuff. Catches himself just as he
starts to remember the unpleasant things.)*

FISHERMAN: Good fishing, though. In Arkansas they have
good perch fishing, blue gills. Really tasty. *(Laughs to himself)* I go to Arkansas to study to be a doctor and all the
time I want to be fishing. Then when I get out and want to
be a doctor, they send me back to Arkansas and make me
fish.

I don't think about the camps much. They're getting a
lot of attention now. The redress hearings. The Nisei are
finally starting to speak out like the young people.
*(The following speech gradually builds up in intensity of
feeling, passion, and anger, but it is always controlled.)*
FISHERMAN: I mean it wasn't fair what they did. Shoganai
nah,* but it wasn't right. I mean most of us were American
citizens. Why didn't they pick on the Italians or the Ger-
mans? That's what really pisses me off. No, they just pick
on us. And they were just waiting to move right in and take
over our businesses. Not just hakujin yo, Shin-sans** too.
Oh, they were the worst. Wore signs saying they were
Chinese. Can you believe that? So just like we're supposed
to get up and move. What am I supposed to do with the
house, my practice? Michiko's mother's too sick to be
moved. Put tags on us, gave us numbers, made us live in
horse stalls and then we get shipped all the way to Arkansas . . . *(Tempo winds down as he regains composure)* . . .
Rohwer, Arkansas . . . *(Reflective pause)* Boots. You had to
wear thick boots, otherwise it wasn't safe. 'Cause to get to
the lake you had to walk through thick grass, and there
were a lot of poisonous snakes. But the fishing was good,
lotta perch. Played some baseball in the camps, too. I was
the camp doctor. It wasn't so bad. I haven't thought about
it for years, so I don't remember too much about it. Fishing
was good, but no hunting of course. Wouldn't let us have
any guns . . .
*(Transition into hunting sequence. He holds an imaginary
shotgun, watching the skies for a bird. Gradually makes
out something in the distance coming towards him.)*
FISHERMAN *(talking to himself)*: That bird is huge. Talk
about beginner's luck. That is the biggest, whitest snow
goose I have ever seen . . . (FISHERMAN's *body follows the*

*It could not be helped.
**Hakujin, "Caucasians"; Shin-sans, "Chinese."

*goose's flight movements as it circles in closer. He raises gun
and shoots.)* Got it! Got it!
*(Runs upstage and exits and immediately runs back
downstage left. Winded, stands over the fallen goose.
Sets down gun and looks at bird.)*
FISHERMAN: Wait till I show this bird to Kats. *(Mimicking
his friend* KATS*)* I can hear him: "Shoot a goose? You don't
even know what Canadian snow goose look like."
*(He picks up bird and slings it over his shoulder. Then
looks up and notices a local game warden.)*
FISHERMAN: Oh, hello. Look at the size of this thing. I just
shot it. What? My hunting license? Sure, just a second.
*(Puts down bird, gets wallet out, and shows warden the
license)* Big bird, huh. My driver's license? *(Getting it out)*
I'm from Hawaii originally, but I have a California license.
Isn't this snow goose huge? *(Listening)* It's not a goose?
(Listening in disbelief) It's a swan?

TRANSITION. MICHIKO *enters up right carrying their newly
born first child.*

MICHIKO: Not a swan, a son. Ichan, look. Your son.
*(*FISHERMAN *looks across upstage. Dim to darkness.
Lights up on* MUSICIANS.*)*

Eating Fish

FISHERMAN: Two ways to eat this kind of fish. Michiko likes to pick the meat off the fish bone. She gradually works, or eats her way, till one half is bare, just bone. Pick, pick, pick. Then she turns it over and starts the whole damn thing over again. Now me, I like to make an incision along the dorsal spine, like this. All the way from the head to the tail. You poke fairly deep. Then slowly, by pulling on the head, all the fish meat in one chunk pulls away from the fish bone. There, then the job's easy. Just flip it over, pull the bone away from the other half. See how easy and cleanly you can do it. Then you can just concentrate on eating the fish. Big hunks. Not little pieces like Michiko's way, that's frustrating. You can take big bites of fish and not worry about any bones. A little shoyu . . . *(Eats contentedly. Then finds a fish bone and pulls it out. Embarrassed.)* Now, if you eat sashimi, don't have to worry about this stuff. You fillet the fish, so no bones. Hmm, love sashimi, but gotta be fresh. Some people like to let the meat sit for one day to age it, say it tastes better. I say, baloney. The fresher the better. In fact, one time I went striped bass fishing with my friend Kats out on his boat . . .

TRANSITION. *Into boat-fishing sequence with* KATS. *They are fishing in a boat with their profiles to the audience and their backs to each other. They sit for a while just holding poles and fishing.* KATS *is whistling.*

FISHERMAN: Hey, Sinatra. Shut up. Scare all the fish away. *(Teasing)* Catch any carp?

KATS: Shoots any swans lately? *(Notices something in the distance)* Doc, look.

FISHERMAN: Damn skiers. Scare all the fish away.
(Back to fishing)

KATS *(notices)*: Hey, they're getting close . . .

FISHERMAN: Don't worry.

KATS: No, look.

FISHERMAN *(notices that the water skiers are cutting close to their lines. Yells at them)*: Hey! Watch out for the lines! You're too close!

KATS *(yelling at skiers)*: Get outta here! We're fishing!
(The boat passes by.)

FISHERMAN: Damn yogore.* Scare all the fish away.
(They start to settle back to fishing when suddenly the boat begins to rock as the waves caused by the skiers' boat hit. FISHERMAN *and* KATS *rock back and forth.)*

FISHERMAN: Why don't you get a bigger boat instead of this goddamn dinghy? Every time a boat passes, we nearly tip over.

KATS: Why don't you buy a boat, you cheap bastard? You're a doctor.

FISHERMAN: All those doctors with their Cadillacs—got their noses up in the air.
(Boat settles down. FISHERMAN *gets a bite, snags, and hooks into fish.)*

KATS: Another one?

FISHERMAN: My day, Kats. Get the net.

KATS: Do it yourself. Too small. *(Back to his pole)*

FISHERMAN: Let's measure it.
(The fish flops around in his hand.)

KATS: You're wasting your time, Doc. Too small.
*(FISHERMAN *measures the fish with his hand span. Legal size for striped bass is sixteen inches or about two of* FISHERMAN's *hand spans.)*

*Punks.

FISHERMAN: Just by an inch, though.

KATS: Mottai nai, nah?* Small striped bass like that make   *A Song*
good sashimi.

FISHERMAN: Make good sashimi, nah.   *For A*
(*They both laugh.*)

KATS: Can't get much fresher.   *Nisei*

FISHERMAN: Right, can't get much fresher.

(*The fish flops in his hand. Laughing dies down as the two*   *Fisherman*
start to take the idea more seriously.)

FISHERMAN: Good eating . . .

KATS: Good eating . . .

FISHERMAN: Got rice balls and shoyu . . .

KATS: And hot tea in the thermos . . .
(*Both look at each other, then look around to see if*
anyone is watching. Slowly a sly grin appears on both
of their faces.)

FISHERMAN: Yosh! Fresh sashimi! Give me the knife!
(*Hits the fish to kill it.*)

TRANSITION. KATS *withdraws. Back to eating.*

FISHERMAN: And so right then and there we gutted it, fil-
leted it, and ate it. Even had some wasabi in the boat, that's
the hot mustard. Oh, it was good. The best way to eat it.
The meat still quivers on your tongue. Oishikata.**

TRANSITION. FISHERMAN *settles left.* MICHIKO *enters.*
ROBERT, *his eldest son, enters.*

MICHIKO: Robert is here.

ROBERT: Did I get any mail?

MICHIKO: Just a couple of things. I'll give them to you when
you leave.

*Waste, isn't it?
**Tasty.

FISHERMAN: Sit down, Robert.

(ROBERT *and* MICHIKO *seat themselves.* FISHERMAN *nods for* MICHIKO *to go ahead and speak.*)

MICHIKO: Robert, we called you last night.

ROBERT: I'm at the hospital most of the time. You have to call pretty late at night or you just can't get ahold of me.

FISHERMAN: We did call late.

ROBERT: Well, I get tied up down there a lot with late-night rounds and everything. Sorry no one answered the phone.

FISHERMAN: Someone did. *(Pause)* A girl, Robert.

MICHIKO *(awkward pause)*: Robert, are you seeing somebody?

(ROBERT, *about to answer, hesitates.*)

FISHERMAN: Are you living with a girl?

ROBERT: No.

FISHERMAN *(sternly)*: Robert.

ROBERT: Not exactly.

(FISHERMAN *is upset.*)

ROBERT: Don't worry, Dad. It doesn't interfere with my studies or anything. I'm not going to flunk out of medical school or anything like that.

FISHERMAN: You better not. After all the money Mom and I put into your education.

MICHIKO: Robert, does she come from a good family?

ROBERT: Of course, Mom.

MICHIKO: Well, what's her name?

ROBERT: Marilyn.

FISHERMAN: Marilyn what?

ROBERT *(uncomfortable)*: Marilyn Wong.

FISHERMAN: A Chinese? My son's going around with a damn Shin-san! Jesus Christ, Robert, you know better than that! Going around with Shin-san!

MICHIKO: Ichan. Take it easy. *(To* ROBERT*)* You know how Dad gets upset if you don't go out with a Japanese girl.

ROBERT: Look, we're just good friends, nothing serious.

FISHERMAN: You call shacking up with somebody "nothing serious"? What kind of sons have I raised? You talk to him, Michiko. *(Gets up and turns on TV down center)*

MICHIKO *(aside to* ROBERT*)*: If you have to, just don't tell him.

ROBERT: Mom, he asked me what her name was. What was I supposed to say . . . Marilyn Wongamoto?

FISHERMAN *(reseating himself)*: Don't get smart with your mother!

ROBERT: I'm not getting smart.

FISHERMAN: And I don't want any of my sons marrying a Shin-san.

ROBERT: Who said anything about marriage?

MICHIKO: You know how Dad is.

ROBERT: What's he talking about anyway? He had a Chinese girl friend himself.

FISHERMAN *(to* MICHIKO*)*: I did not.

MICHIKO *(to* ROBERT*)*: He did not.

ROBERT *(to* MICHIKO*)*: Yes, he did.

FISHERMAN *(to* MICHIKO*)*: I did not.

MICHIKO *(to* ROBERT*)*: He did not.

ROBERT: That's what he told me. During college. Mabel Chang.

(Pause. MICHIKO *looks at* FISHERMAN.*)*

FISHERMAN: She was just a friend.

MICHIKO: Who's Mabel Chang?

FISHERMAN *(flustered)*: There were a couple of us orientals in premed. We used to do things together.

ROBERT: Look, Mom, Marilyn and I are just friends. Okay? No big deal.

MICHIKO *(to* FISHERMAN*)*: You told me you studied all the time in college. Study, study, study.

FISHERMAN: Well, I had a little time here and there.

MICHIKO *(to* ROBERT*)*: What else did he say?

A Song

For A

Nisei

Fisherman

ROBERT: What time is it? I gotta be going back to the hospital. I'm late already.

MICHIKO: Robert, why don't you bring her over for dinner?

ROBERT *(nodding towards* FISHERMAN*)*: What about . . . ?

MICHIKO: Be good for him. Bring back some old exciting memories of Mabel Chang.

FISHERMAN: Michiko, I don't want any Shin-san in this house.

ROBERT: It's okay, Mom. Really, it's no big deal . . .

MICHIKO: And we'll have Dad's favorite—steamed bass in black bean sauce . . . Chinese style.

ROBERT: Okay, Mom. Just tell Dad he doesn't have anything to worry about.

*(*MICHIKO *helps Robert with his coat.)*

FISHERMAN: You damn right I don't have to worry about nothing. We'll talk about this later, Michiko.

*(*ROBERT *and* MICHIKO *exit.)*

FISHERMAN *(calling after her)*: Michiko? Michiko? . . .

TRANSITION. FISHERMAN *finds* MICHIKO's *diary. He opens it and begins to read aloud from it. At first we just hear* FISHERMAN's *voice. Then gradually we hear* MICHIKO's *voice overlapping the* FISHERMAN's *as she is brought up in a pool of light.* FISHERMAN's *voice fades out and* MICHIKO *continues alone.*

FISHERMAN *(reading* MICHIKO's *diary)*: Ichan. I've been your wife for twenty-eight years. *(Continues.)*

MICHIKO *(enters, gradually overlapping)*: Sometimes I'm amazed I even stuck it out. *(Continues.)*

FISHERMAN *(fading out)*: Sometimes I'm amazed I even stuck it out.

MICHIKO: And don't think I wasn't tempted to leave at times. Remember when we first got married and how you used to stumble in from Mosan's poker games three, four o'clock in the morning and pass out dead drunk on the living room floor. I know, I know, "It's Mosan's fault, it's Mosan's fault." Who cares whose fault it was? I was the one who had to take off your clothes and somehow haul you into the bed.

And I was the one who had to clean up all the vomit when you threw up. Ahh, the romantic years. Some of those times I just wanted to pack up and go back to Mama and Papa, but I knew how much it would hurt them. Oh, things weren't always that bad and I admit I wasn't always the best wife. Remember the time I got so mad at you, 'cause you were always going fishing and leaving me with the kids and never helping out around the house, that I broke your best fishing pole . . . I'm sorry. You know that's the only time you ever came close to hitting me.

(Pause.)

Twenty-eight years. I've been your wife for twenty-eight years. Cooked your meals, washed your clothes, bore your children. Right there by your side through all the rough times. You had things you wanted to do with your life, you had dreams. You cried when they seemed too far away and I comforted you. You yelled when you felt cheated from them and I took it all. And when you finally reached your dreams, I was so happy for you, though you never really thanked me.

I gave you two sons. They have things they want to do with their lives. Mommy do this, Mother do that. They have dreams. But what about my dreams, Itsu? What if, what if I could have anything I want? What if I could do anything I want? What would I want just for me?

TRANSITION. *Younger son enters scene.* MICHIKO *turns her attention to* JEFFREY *and* FISHERMAN.

JEFFREY: Mom, let Dad tell me himself what's bothering him.

FISHERMAN *(standing up)*: Sit down, Jeffrey.

JEFFREY: Why don't you sit down, you're the one with arthritis.

FISHERMAN: I don't want to sit down. Besides, I'm doing the talking.

JEFFREY: I don't want to.

FISHERMAN *(upset)*: Then stand for God's sake, stand there like an idiot, I don't care.

(FISHERMAN *sits down in a huff.)*

JEFFREY *(sitting down disgustedly)*: Why can't we for once just have a civil . . .

FISHERMAN *(interrupts, standing up)*: That's what I mean. That's what I mean. Every time I tell you to do something you always do the opposite. Now stay put.

JEFFREY *(standing up)*: I do not.

FISHERMAN: Oh, sit down, will you.

JEFFREY: I don't want to. You sit down.

MICHIKO *(can't take any more)*: Why don't you both sit down!

(Both are rather shocked at her outburst. They both slowly seat themselves. MICHIKO exits.)

FISHERMAN: How come you quit?

JEFFREY: Dad.

FISHERMAN: Jeffrey, when you gonna grow up? Huh? You're thirty years old.

JEFFREY: I'm twenty-nine.

FISHERMAN: Twenty-nine, thirty, what's the difference? You're a grown man. What you gonna do with your life? You're no kid anymore. Mom and I aren't going to be around much longer to support you.

JEFFREY: I'm not asking for support.

FISHERMAN *(mimicking son sarcastically)*: "Mom, please send me some money, I ran out." I know you're broke half the time. She tries to hide it from me, but I know. Go back to law school. Finish it off. Get your law degree and start practicing like your older brother—he's a doctor. Then you can do whatever you want in your spare time.

JEFFREY: Dad, I'm not Robert and I don't like law.

FISHERMAN: Who cares whether you like it or not? That's not the way life is. That's your problem. Any time anything gets a little too hard you quit, no guts. No gaman.* *(Mimicking son)* "I don't like it. It's not right for me." Well, what the hell do you want to do?

JEFFREY: Write. I want to write.

FISHERMAN: Write? Before, it was playing music—you can't even feed your face, keep a steady job, support yourself. How . . . *(Continues.)*

JEFFREY *(overlapping)*: Forget it, just forget it . . .

FISHERMAN *(continuing)*: . . . you gonna write? What you even gonna write about?

JEFFREY: You, it's a piece about you. *(Decides it's no use)* Forget it, Dad . . . *(Tries again)* It's just some of the stories you told me as a kid, remember when I was little? Like that hunting dog of yours that got gored and lived . . . Tengu. And how Uncle Mosan used to race that horse of his. Remember when you told me about the time the two of you got in a fight and . . .

FISHERMAN *(interrupts)*: Who cares about that stuff? Huh? How you gonna live, support yourself? How about when you get married, have a baby? What you gonna do then?

JEFFREY: That's not the point, Dad. You're missing the whole . . .

FISHERMAN *(interrupts)*: That is the point! I know, I know, you know how to express yourself. You're good with words. You're like hakujin.

JEFFREY: Dad, come on.

*Perseverance.

FISHERMAN: But what you gonna do? Feed your wife and baby words? You shame me. And how do you think it looks to other people for me to have a grown son who's a regular bum!

JEFFREY *(pause. Quietly)*: Okay, I'm a bum. All right? That make you feel better, Dad? I'm a bum.

(JEFFREY exits.)

FISHERMAN: Jeffrey. Jeffrey, come back here! Jeffrey!

TRANSITION. MICHIKO *is lit in a pool of light upstage.* FISHERMAN *seats himself and watches TV.* FISHERMAN *is recalling her death.*

MICHIKO: Please not so loud, Itsu. I'm not feeling too well, so don't shout around the house. I've been getting these headaches lately. Feels like it's right here, on the left side of my head.

(Pause. Musical punctuation. Lights dim.)

Don't you think I should go see a specialist, Ichan? It's been hurting a long time. Neh? I'm calling your friend, Dr. Scott, okay? Ichan?

(Pause. Musical punctuation. Lights dim. More discomfort.)

He took x-rays, Ichan. They found a tumor. I'm worried. Should I see another doctor? Ichan?

(Pause. Musical punctuation. Lights dim. Now she appears very ill but no longer worried, almost tranquil.)

Do you remember the day you asked me to marry you? It was a church bazaar. You had on brown baggy pants and a shirt that was full of bright yellow flowers. You looked so funny in it I had to keep myself from laughing at you. The things you remember.

(Pause. Musical punctuation. Lights dim. Gravely ill, no longer tranquil.)

Itsu? Hold my hand. I'm feeling nauseous again. I feel so
sick. Itsu?

(Pause. MICHIKO *is barely visible in the shadows. She
becomes young again. She calls his name affectionately
and laughs.)*

Ichan?

(Dim to darkness. Musicians are lit. FISHERMAN *exits.)*

[END OF SCENE]

Scene Five

Catching Fish

FISHERMAN *enters as he did in Scene I, looking for a spot to
fish. He moves slowly. Though in age he appears the same as he
did in Scene I, one senses he feels much older. He seats himself
rather gingerly, as his back is bothering him just a little bit
more than usual, and prepares his pole and line to fish. He does
exactly what he did in Scene I except that all his movements
take on a ritualistic quality. All movements are distilled in
action and compressed in time so that the whole process is
done in far less time than it took previously. He pulls things out
of the air as if magically—his hook, the salmon eggs, etc. He
casts out and immediately hooks and reels up a fish. He pulls it
off, sets it aside. He casts out again and in the same motion
falls asleep.*

TRANSITION. *Visited by ghosts.* TOCHAN *appears upstage
right.* MUSICIANS *underscore the appearances.* FISHERMAN
awakens and peers downstage.

FISHERMAN: Tochan? Tochan?

TOCHAN *(looking at him from upstage)*: Yah, it's me, Itsu. It's
been a long, long time, nah. How you been?

FISHERMAN: I've been all right, Tochan. How about you?

TOCHAN: Good, good. *(Pause)* You know I been meaning to
talk to you.

FISHERMAN: There's something I wanted to ask you, too.

TOCHAN: Itsu, I know I wasn't best papa. But I was busy,
eleven kids and everything. But I did my best. I like drink
sake too much. And when I drink sake, I like to make
speech. My friends, they like when I make speech. They
give me a drink, they say, "Oi, Matsumoto-Sensei. Let's
hear your plan to make big money." *(Acts out as if in front*

of friends) Yosh, I work hard, make lots of money. *(Takes a drink)* When I go back Japan, they meet me at train station. Banzai! Banzai!...

(Abruptly stops in mid-cheer, slowly bringing his arms down. He looks sadly at FISHERMAN, *who is looking away uncomfortably.)*

Itsu. Itsu. I know they were laughing at me. Tochan's not stupid. Just like sake a little too much. But you, good boy. You one doctor. Make Tochan and Kachan so proud. Nah, Kachan.

*(*KACHAN *appears upstage right, wiping her hands on her apron.)*

KACHAN *(kidding)*: More fish to clean?

FISHERMAN *(smiling, holds up the trout he caught)*: Just one small lake trout.

KACHAN: No can feed eleven kids with just one small fish, Ichan. Need plenty more so we can dry 'em and salt-pack 'em for later. And if got time we make kasuzuke. You like that, huh, Ichan.

FISHERMAN: Kachan?

KACHAN: Yes, Ichan.

FISHERMAN: I'm worried.

KACHAN: About what?

FISHERMAN: I'm old. It's dying. I tried to ask Tochan about it but you know how he is.

KACHAN: Yeah, he's always busy, neh. Working and drink-ing—and you know Tochan and his sake. Me, I'm not smart like Tochan, but I no drink sake either. I work, work, like a horse. I can always work.

FISHERMAN: Yes, but what about . . .

KACHAN *(interrupts)*: What about what?

FISHERMAN: What about dying, Kachan?

KACHAN: What about living, Ichan? You're still alive.

FISHERMAN: I know, but it worries me. I can't stop thinking

about it. I want you to tell me about . . . about what it's like.

KACHAN: Ichan, I no can tell you nothing. Remember, I'm dead, yo.

(FISHERMAN *notices* MICHIKO, *who has appeared upstage left.* MICHIKO *never speaks. Only quietly observes him.*)

FISHERMAN: Michiko? Michiko? Can we talk some? It's not always easy to say what I'm feeling inside. Things just don't come out that easy, you know that. I haven't been able to sleep too well lately. No, it's not the coffee or anything like that. It's just I've been thinking about things lately. You know, just things. *(Pause)* Where'd they go? Mosan, Kats. What happened to them? Mosan was only thirty-eight when he had the accident. Kats was older but it's still difficult . . . Michiko, I meant to tell you before but never got the chance.

(Lights on Michiko begin to dim.)

There were so many people at the hospital and you looked so different lying there. Michiko . . . I love . . .
(FISHERMAN *looks up and sees that* MICHIKO *is gone. He's unable to complete his confession.)* Michiko? Michiko?
(Exhausted, he lowers his head and falls asleep. All three ghosts remain on stage lit at half. They silently observe him.)

TRANSITION. ROBERT *enters. Present time.* ROBERT *sees his father and smiles. He gently touches his father's shoulder to waken him.*

FISHERMAN *(waking)*: Michiko?

ROBERT: No, Dad. Mom passed away three years ago, remember? It's Robert.

FISHERMAN *(waking up)*: Oh. Yeah, yeah.

ROBERT: Just dropped by to check on you. You okay?

FISHERMAN: Fine, fine. Heard from Jeffrey?

ROBERT: I'm sure he's doing okay over there.

FISHERMAN: Still in Tokyo?

ROBERT: Hiroshima. He wanted to see where Grandma and Grandpa came from.

FISHERMAN: Still at it, huh? Wish he'd come home.

ROBERT: How's the fishing?

FISHERMAN (showing the fish): Small, neh. Not like the old times.

(They sit for a moment quietly looking out at the water.)

FISHERMAN: Robert?

ROBERT: Yes, Dad?

FISHERMAN: Why don't we go fishing sometime? Together. Just you and me. Like old times when you and Jeffrey were kids. We can go to Lake Berryessa, like we used to. Rent a boat . . .

ROBERT (interrupts. Sincere): Sure, Dad, but right now Kathryn and the kids are waiting in the car. We're going on a short vacation. When I get back we'll get together, I promise. I'll call you about it, okay? I have to go now. You take care, Dad.

(ROBERT exits. FISHERMAN watches him leave. Reels up line to check bait. He casts out again. As he settles back, holding his pole, he quietly smiles to himself. Gradually he falls asleep. Sound cue of a dog barking. FISHERMAN awakens with a start and stares out into the darkness.)

FISHERMAN: Who's there? Who's out there?

(The three ghosts silently observe him. No response so the FISHERMAN settles back down to his fishing. Slowly falls asleep. MUSICIANS are lit and the SINGER sings the final song. At this point, the FISHERMAN is seated in a pool of light with the three ghosts watching him quietly. As the song is performed, the lights begin a very slow fade on the FISHERMAN.)

MUSICIANS:

Walks into the room, shadows rise and fall;

A Song

For A

Nisei

Fisherman

	Ticking of the clock, echoes down the hall.
A Song	Standing at his favorite spot,
	He casts into the wind.
For A	Silently he reels up
	And casts out once again.
Nisei	Your rich embroidered memories . . .
	The feast after the hunt;
Fisherman	Those fine college days;
	The wife, the home, the children;
	Your song it plays and plays.

The rich American dream is here to stay, is here to stay . . .
(By the time the song has ended, the stage is dark and the ghosts and FISHERMAN *have exited. An empty pool of light appears center stage. Silence.)*

[END OF PLAY]